LAURENCE KING

Published in 2010 by
Laurence King Publishing Ltd
361–373 City Road
London EC1V 1LR
United Kingdom

telephone
020 7841 6900

fax
020 7841 6910

e-mail
enquiries@laurenceking.com

website
www.laurenceking.com

A catalogue for this
book is available from the
British Library.

ISBN
9781 85669 688 3

Design
Lucienne Roberts +

Fonts
Univers 55 Roman
Univers 57 Condensed
Univers 67 Bold Condensed
Univers 75 Black

Printed and bound in China

Thank you

A book like this is impossible
to produce without the support
of others. ¬

We would like to thank firstly
all the interviewees who gave
their time so generously and
patiently: Stefan Sagmeister,
Borries Schwesinger,
Homework, Meirion Pritchard,
Emmi Salonen, Dalton Maag,
Frauke Stegmann, Bond and
Coyne, Experimental Jetset,
Paula Scher and Airside. ¬

Thanks are also due to
Ralph Ammer, Nigel Robinson
and Daniel Weil and to
André Cruz, Joe Shouldice,
Tony Chambers, Sarah Douglas,
Lee Belcher, Dominic Bell,
Tony Howard, Richard de Jager,
Julio Etchart, Steve Mosley,
Kurt Koepfle, Lenny Naar and
Daniel Nelson. ¬

We would also like to gratefully
acknowledge the cooperation
of Casa da Música, Verlag
Hermann Schmidt Mainz,
Vivarto, »Wallpaper*«,
Transport Dubai, PWHOA, War
on Want, 104, Cargill and Vitsœ.
¬

Thank you to Jo Lightfoot
and Donald Dinwiddie
at Laurence King Publishing
whose support and patience
has been hugely appreciated. ¬

Thanks are also due to
Lorna Fray, Deirdre Murphy
and James West for their
diligence and keeping us on
track. A very special thank you
goes to John McGill for his
technical wizardry, calm
and worldly wisdom and to
Dave Shaw for his photography,
friendship and counsel. Thanks
too to Malcolm Southward for
his support and steady hands. ¬

Lucienne would like to
thank Ray and Putzi, whose
enthusiasm for graphic design
remains a constant inspiration
and whose love and friendship
could not have been bettered.
Much love and gratitude is
due to Damian and Katy, whose
smile makes even the worst
work crisis fade. Also Diane
Magee and Annette Pitura, who
might be pleased to have their
friend back, and to Erna who
is wonderful to have found. ¬

Rebecca would like to thank
Patrick, Judy, Alexander,
Emma and William Wright for
unending support, sustenance,
shelter and so very much
more. Also Rohan McCarty,
Jessica Taylor, Tim Tzouliadis
and the many friends who
have provided generous
encouragement throughout and
accepted excuses for absence
for so long. Thanks are also
due to colleagues at Kingston
University, most particularly
Bernadette Blair and Lawrence
Zeegen and to the students who
continue to show how much
more there is to learn. ¬

Laurence King Publishing

Contents

↑
Clients' country of origin ¬

Stefan Sagmeister	Austria	USA
Borries Schwesinger	Germany	Germany / UK / Switzerland
Homework	Poland	Poland
Meirion Pritchard	UK	UK
Emmi Salonen	Finland	UK
Dalton Maag	Switzerland / France / UK	UK / Brazil
Frauke Stegmann	Namibia	South Africa
Bond and Coyne	UK	UK
Experimental Jetset	The Netherlands	The Netherlands
Paula Scher	USA	USA
Airside	UK	UK

↑ Designers' country of origin ¬   ↑ Designers' base at time of project ¬

When Laurence King Publishing asked if we would put together a proposal for a book about the process of graphic design our collective hearts sank. Wrongly fearing that a grandiose, but necessarily reductive, form of »how to do it« book was required, we set about listing all the reasons we thought this a bad idea. We found, however, that in articulating our discomfort we were by default formulating an approach – and then of course we were hooked. Luckily LKP were too... ¬

Our approach ¬ Graphic design is an idiosyncratic business. The term seems currently at its most indefinable – readily applied to both a small, self-initiated niche project produced by a one-person practice and to the highly commercial work of a multinational and interdisciplinary agency. It encompasses the routine work of walk-in print shops as much as the experiments of highly focused and driven designers, for whom work is their raison d'être. So, from the outset we thought that this book had to make clear the breadth of activity that constitutes graphic design, and we were determined to communicate our conviction that one-size-fits-all formulas are not only hard to find but undesirable to apply. Instead there are personal, flexible and evolving methodologies and it was these that we were excited to explore. ¬ Our brief was that, amongst other things, the book should be educational. We took this partly to mean »revelatory« and set about developing a structure that would allow us to tell design stories in significant depth so that lessons could be learnt and conclusions could meaningfully be drawn. We identified that one of our objectives was not to focus on final pieces of work or on contributors as personalities – but to tell the individual story of several contrasting design projects. We started by identifying what types of venture these should be and which designers we would most like to approach. ¬ Alongside wanting to cover a variety of projects, we were determined that our contributors be varied in background and age. Seeing no merit in portraying the activity disingenuously, we wanted to encourage them to be as honest as possible and we looked forward to asking questions that would perhaps generally be prohibited! Overall our goal was that our contributors and their work should collectively be international in reach and relevance so that »Design Diaries«, as it quickly became known, would represent the diversity and richness of current graphic design. ¬ Of course this all sounds easier than it turned out to be! The paucity of older women graphic designers became all too obvious, for example, as did the rarity of practitioners whose work isn't orientated towards the West. But with the inclusion of projects as diverse as an identity for a fashion label in Cape Town, a font for the new transport system in Dubai and a book on the design of forms we hope that »Design Diaries« goes some way to disclosing what it means to produce graphic design today. We found it to be tortuous but magical, competitive but restorative, indulgent but valuable and utterly absorbing... ¬

Each case study occupies several spreads with the story told under the headings above. These headings are combined and omitted as necessary. We loosely followed this structure in our interviews too, asking contributors to bear these themes in mind as they gathered together visual material for us to show. We found, of course, that each project followed its own individual path, with some moving forward, back and forward again to further demonstrate that graphic design isn't always a linear process. ¬

We chose Univers as the »Design Diaries« font using these variations: 55 Roman, 75 Black, 57 Condensed and 67 Bold Condensed all in 7.75/9.6pt. Released in 1957 it was designed by Adrian Frutiger, one of the most prolific and illustrious type designers working today. Frutiger's concept was to develop a font family that included a vast variety of weights and styles that would be homogeneous when used together. We needed a font that would be suitable for continuous text over a fairly wide measure and also extended and short captions running to a narrow column width. Both were to have headings integrated with the text. Considering Univers to epitomize a rational and rigorous approach to design, we decided to put it to the test! Our grid is subdivided into 19 columns, each measuring 6mm with an intercolumn space of 4mm. Our baseline unit is 3.2pt, which informs all fields and further horizontal alignment points. ¬

»Design Diaries« is a paperback book, thread sewn and made up of 2 x 8-page and 14 x 16-page sections. It uses the three paper types most commonly available — matt coated, uncoated and gloss coated. The front-matter is printed on an 80gsm matt art. An uncoated stock, 140gsm Thai Woodfree, is used for the case studies and an 80gsm gloss art paper is used for the last 16-page section. Each stock has its own characteristics, not only do they all feel dissimilar, but they take colour differently too. The uncoated is the most absorbent, for example, so the colours on this stock are slightly darker and are the most subtle. ¬

Despite the faltering steps made during the design process it is a continuum, and one decision does generally inform the next. Bleeding off the right-hand edge of each spread of every case study is an image strip that gives a visual taster of what is to come. ¬

As befits a book called »Design Diaries« room is allocated on each spread for designers' contemporaneous diary entries. We asked that these be as honest and personal as possible to provide a real sense of what the project involved and to act as »scene-setters« to place the work within the broader context of the life of each contributor. ¬

Although graphic design practice is not only focused on print we wanted the production of this book to foreground its production. The front- and end-matter are each printed in one spot colour. The front in Pantone 021, the end in Pantone 354 — both are vibrant colours impossible to achieve out of cmyk. Each contributor's story is colour-coded using this corner device. The colours were chosen to incrementally demonstrate just some of the range achievable through the cmyk process. ¬

The case study colours breakdown as follows:
Stefan Sagmeister
80c/0m/100y/0k ¬
Borries Schwesinger
60c/0m/100y/0k ¬
Homework
40c/0m/100y/0k ¬
Meirion Pritchard
20c/0m/100y/0k ¬
Emmi Salonen
100c/0m/0y/0k ¬
Dalton Maag
50c/50m/0y/0k ¬
Frauke Stegmann
0c/100m/0y/0k ¬
Bond and Coyne /
0c/20m/100y/0k ¬
Experimental Jetset
0c/40m/100y/0k ¬
Paula Scher
0c/60m/100y/0k ¬
Airside
0c/80m/100y/0k ¬

25/01/10 ¬ Finalising front- and end-matter. It's late — Laurence King must be so fed up with us! ¬

Stefan Sagmeister (born 1962) is something
of a graphic design superstar and one of the
most closely watched graphic designers working
today. Famed initially for carving lettering into
his own body for the 1999 AIGA Detroit poster,
Stefan has continued to create arresting and
original graphic design solutions. His work shuns
convention in favour of conceptually appropriate
but frequently audacious ideas. We were curious
to find out whether his reputation affects the
creative freedom a client allows, and how
he balances commercial expectation with his
experimental approach. ¬ We were particularly
interested in following this project – the identity
for Casa da Música, a music centre in Porto,
Portugal – because Stefan's views on branding
are so unambiguous. On the homepage of his
website Stefan says, »Branding is overrated,
outdated crap! Nobody said that (but somebody
should have).« So, how does such a firmly held
view influence his approach when designing
a logo and identity system and what kind
of creative process does he employ? ¬ Casa da
Música is the home and performance space of the
Orquestra Nacional do Porto, Orquestra Barrocar
and Remix Ensemble. Intended as part of Porto's
cultural investment when it was European
Capital of Culture in 2001, the building was
designed by Dutch architect Rem Koolhaas with
the Office for Metropolitan Architecture (OMA)
and was completed in 2005. The innovative
structure, with its distinctive 17-faceted form,
has become an icon of the city. This poses another
interesting question for Stefan – how do you go
about designing an identity for something that
is already an iconic design? ¬

The benefits of absolute consistency when applying a design identity largely go unchallenged, but Stefan's starting point for this and many projects is to resist design »rules«. His approach to his work seems to epitomize the complex relationship between freedom and constraint with which most designers battle. But is this reflected in Stefan's influences or explicit in his design philosophy? As someone who is frequently cited as an inspiration by other designers, who or what inspires Stefan? ¬

Early starts in strange cities ¬ Early morning is Stefan's most productive »concept« time. This is especially true if he is travelling, when he starts as early as 5am, taking advantage of his disrupted sleep patterns. He finds the anonymity and atmosphere peculiar to hotel rooms particularly inspiring – and conducive to what he calls »dreaming freely«. As he explains, »It's easy to think there, specifically because you don't really have to think about the implementation. If the hotel room has a balcony, that's fantastic. If there is room service and coffee, even better.« ¬

Austria, America and abroad ¬ Born in Bregenz in the Austrian Alps, Stefan's early years were a far cry from Lower Manhattan, where he has lived and worked since 1993. After studying engineering, Stefan switched his focus to graphic design following his experience working at »Alphorn«, a left-wing Austrian magazine. On his second attempt, Stefan was accepted to study graphic design at the University of Applied Arts, Vienna and continued his studies in New York's Pratt Institute on a Fulbright scholarship. He had to return to Austria for military service but as a conscientious objector worked on community projects at a refugee centre. His work has taken him from an advertising agency in Hong Kong to a beach hut in Sri Lanka and he continues to travel widely for both work and inspiration. ¬

Tibor Kalman ¬ As a student Stefan's design hero was Tibor Kalman and his dream was to work at Tibor's renowned studio M&Co in New York. It took persistence – telephoning his office every week for six months – to get to meet Tibor, and a significant relationship grew from that first meeting. When Tibor later offered him a job Stefan turned it down, unable to give Tibor the requested guarantee that he would stay for two years. Three years later he finally joined M&Co but within six months Tibor closed the studio to relocate to Rome. This provided the spur for Stefan to start up on his own. Tibor died in 1999, but the influence of the man Stefan proudly calls his mentor has been far-reaching, not least in his advice to keep a studio small to maintain creative freedom: »The only difficult thing when running a design studio is not to grow, the rest is easy.« ¬

Designing for non-designers ¬ Stefan is famously outspoken about design. In a much-quoted interview with the American design writer Steven Heller, he expressed disappointment that the industry was full of »just so much fluff«, and outlined his own ambition to create design that can touch people's hearts. He knows that this is not an easy thing to do. »Can design touch someone's heart?« is a project Stefan sets students on the Designer as Author MFA he teaches at the School of Visual Arts in New York. Stefan's brief requires students to make work that touches – first, people they know; second, people they know of; and third, everybody else. He considers design for designers »sadly insular and consequently boring« and is interested by the possible reach of design as a language. He acknowledges that this calls for discrimination in »working out what it is you want to say« as designer and author. ¬

50/50 ¬ Stefan remembers fondly that Tibor Kalman loved to work on what he didn't know. Famed for the originality and bravery of his own work, we were interested in finding out if Stefan also enjoys exploring unfamiliar territory. He admits that he has a tendency to get bored repeating himself, but at the same time he also likes to know he is working from a solid foundation. He summarizes the perfect ratio within a job as: »50/50 – 50 per cent what I know and 50 per cent what I don't«. ¬

Out of the office ¬ Stefan's distinctive email sign-off, »100 greetings from lovely 14th Street« is testament to his affection for New York, but getting out of the studio is an important stimulus to his creative process. Unscheduled experimentation is easily crowded out by deadlines, so every seven years he sets aside what he calls an »experimental year, during which we don't design any jobs for clients but freely pursue new directions and avenues«. The first of these was in 2000, leading to the project and publication »Things I Have Learned In My Life So Far«. As we interviewed Stefan he was in the process of preparing for his 2008–09 sabbatical in Indonesia. Studio designer Joe Shouldice is in charge of the office while Stefan is away – however important it is to recharge his creative batteries, Stefan notes that, »It's good for clients to know there is still a presence.« ¬

Accounting of thoughts ¬ Stefan has kept written diaries since he was young, a weekly activity he describes as an »accounting of my thoughts«. He used to handwrite these in separate personal and business journals, but now Stefan types entries into a file on his laptop. He advocates keeping diaries as a means of personal development and refers back to them regularly, a reflective practice which bears fruit in his analytical and philosophical approach to design. Although Stefan makes a clear distinction between his diaries and his visual sketchbooks, the diaries formed the inspiration for »Things I Have Learned In My Life So Far«, in which some of his private thoughts are shown in the form of typographic installations in public places. ¬

Stefan met Guta Moura Guedes through ExperimentaDesign, a festival in Lisbon, which she was programming and directing. When Guta moved to Casa da Música as marketing director, she asked Stefan if he would pitch as one of three design companies submitting proposals for the centre's identity. »I thought this was crazy. Pitching is not the best way to get the best results and I advised her to look at companies she thought had done identities well in the past few years and choose one of them to approach.« He tells us he would have been just as happy if she'd gone with someone else – after his outspoken advice he was not expecting to be offered the job. ¬

As Casa da Música is part-funded by the Portuguese government, Guta had to ensure they were not bound by law to put the job out to tender. When she discovered that she was able to navigate round this process, she asked Stefan to take the job, without pitching: »It is always great to have a champion in the house who is the commissioner.« ¬

The initial briefing was by phone, and the only specifics mentioned were a list of deliverables: to create the brand marque; two sub-brands for the symphony orchestra and the orchestra of contemporary music; and five »branded programming points« which included systems for adverts and a monthly event guide. This provided Stefan with a concrete starting point but he felt that a three-day visit to Porto constituted the proper brief. He explored the area, experienced the building, shown above, and met with the director and house manager. ¬

Competition ¬ Although a clear and thorough brief is generally considered to be a critical part of any design project, there is no industry formula for how a brief should be delivered. Even the process of securing projects can vary wildly, depending on the job and the client. ¬ In the case of a project such as this – creating the identity for a celebrated arts institution – it is not uncommon that it be put out to competitive tender. In an attempt to ensure value for money and avoid cronyism, tendering for projects is mandatory in many publicly-funded bodies. Tenders often require designers to supply indications of approach and initial ideas, alongside budgets and proof of previous experience. Designers sometimes present (or »pitch«) this information at a meeting with the client. Tenders and pitches are usually unpaid, which often prohibits small teams from taking part. ¬ **Pitching** ¬ Like many designers, Stefan is unhappy with the process and philosophy of tendering and pitching. He talks of the lack of »open questions«, such as the identity of members of the judging panel and the hidden agendas they might hold. He expresses frustration that clients still labour under the false impression that pitches save money and time – that designers show up with their proposals and all they have to do is select the best. In his experience pitching rarely involves a proper briefing and so the winning work does not deliver what is really needed. Furthermore, Stefan notes that pitching is time-consuming and expensive for designers and can »create bad will in a project«. ¬

14/04 ¬ Three-day trip to Porto to visit Casa da Música and meet the musical director and manager. ¬ Events today at Casa da Música include an art exhibition in the morning, my design talk in the evening, an educational class for mentally impaired children, a chamber concert, a Russian concert and a midnight rave in the car park – all unbelievably well attended. ¬

Stefan's sketchbooks
show his early exploration
of Rem Koolhaas' iconic
Casa da Música building.
He first got to know its shape
by drawing it from a range
of angles, as if turning and
examining it in his hands.
Some images are annotated
thumbnails but others are
physical tests that are then
photographed. All helped him
to see quickly whether using
the structure as a starting
point for his design work
would be an avenue worth
exploring further. He used
colour to examine the spatial
configurations and composite
shapes of the form and
then took it apart to reveal
its component parts. ¬

This shows how 3D Stefan's
approach was, right from the
start. His initial ideas included
»Making the shape of the
building out of coloured glass
panels; semi-transparent
mono-colour glass; using
a strange colour and creating
a 3D glow.« There is also
mention of what becomes
a central concept of the
finished identity – the creation
of a software program that
renders the identity differently
every time. ¬

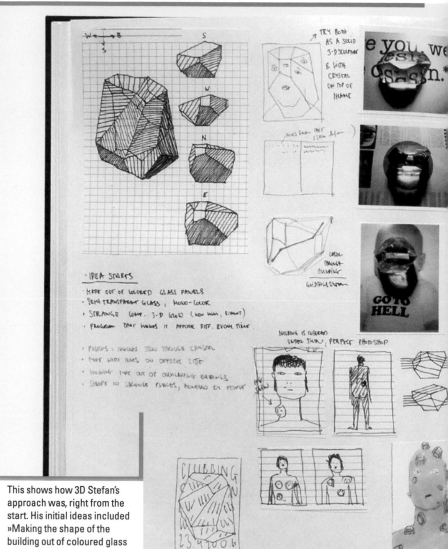

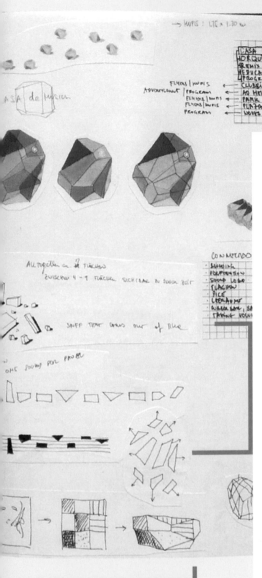

In organizing his thoughts on the page Stefan included a breakdown of Casa da Música into its constituent parts: »The Orquestra Nacional do Porto, Remix Ensemble, educational service, program, clubbing.« He also listed the platforms and spaces where the identity would need to work and the appropriate graphic format: »Advertising media, park, plaza, and inside the building itself; flyer or poster, advertisement or program listing.« Finding inspiration in a statement by the Casa da Música president, which suggested that each of the 17 faces of the building might be seen to represent a different facet of music, Stefan listed the associations this mental image conjured for him. This »connected stuff« included: »the building, dice, sound logo, faces« (planes). These sketches show him defining his conceptual approach to the brief while simultaneously exploring design possibilities. ¬

Generating ideas ¬ Even the most experienced graphic designer can find parts of the creative process uncomfortable. Stefan is refreshingly candid about this: »I find thinking very difficult«. To help overcome this he has evolved a strategy for what he calls his »concept time«. Rather than allow himself limitless time to think, Stefan finds he is more productive if he structures thinking time in a very disciplined way. He allocates himself clearly delineated short slots of time – two sessions of twenty minutes, or three sessions of ten minutes, for example. He confesses: »If I put aside three hours' thinking time, the chances of achieving nothing are pretty high.« ¬

Sketchbooks ¬ During the initial ideas stage Stefan makes notes and sketches. These are often in the back of his »daytimer«, a leather-bound personal organizer which he keeps with him at all times. He makes sketches during meetings, while waiting in airports or in the back of New York taxi cabs, the most salient of these eventually being transferred and collated into his sketchbooks where he explores and develops them further. These sketchbooks are always black and hardbound, measuring 9 by 12 inches. He has kept all of his sketchbooks from the last 15 years, as an ever-expanding library of thoughts and references. In addition, Stefan has always kept diaries, an activity that reveals further his comfort and familiarity with recording thoughts, analytical reflection and disciplined documentation. ¬

01/05 ¬ Working on billboards for Six Cities Design Festival in Scotland, UK. ¬

Designing identities ¬ Identity design uses the tools of graphic design to create and project the image of an individual or organization in a recognizable, clear and cohesive way across a range of media and items. The conventional view is that the authority of an identity is reinforced through consistent appearance and application. ¬ Stefan takes issue with this notion of »sameness« and is interested in questioning such an established view. He agrees that there are instances where sameness is appropriate, and uses the example of a ubiquitous multinational coffee chain: »The biggest achievement is to get the same quality and temperature of coffee anywhere in the world. The logo becomes a sign of this quality. If I were ever asked to redesign it, I would advise them not to change it.« What concerns him is that there are many other areas and companies »where this should be the last thing on their minds«, a view which runs counter to perceived wisdom. ¬ **Appropriateness** ¬ At the heart of this debate is the relationship between a visual identity and the place or product it represents. For Stefan this is a particular issue for institutions where the building or architecture is used within the visual brand or logo. He feels that too often such graphic identities reduce a spatial and emotional human experience to an unsatisfactory and static two-dimensional image. In this case he felt strongly that the breadth and variety of both the activities and audiences of Casa da Música needed to be reflected in the identity he designed and that pursuing »sameness« would be in direct opposition to this aim. ¬

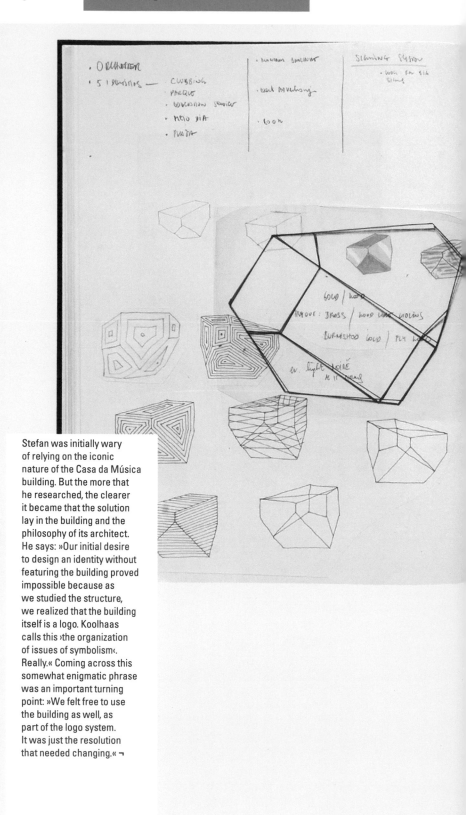

Stefan was initially wary of relying on the iconic nature of the Casa da Música building. But the more that he researched, the clearer it became that the solution lay in the building and the philosophy of its architect. He says: »Our initial desire to design an identity without featuring the building proved impossible because as we studied the structure, we realized that the building itself is a logo. Koolhaas calls this ›the organization of issues of symbolism‹. Really.« Coming across this somewhat enigmatic phrase was an important turning point: »We felt free to use the building as well, as part of the logo system. It was just the resolution that needed changing.« ¬

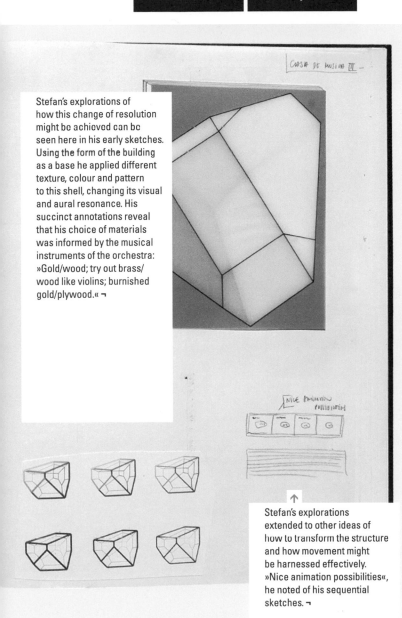

Stefan's explorations of how this change of resolution might be achieved can be seen here in his early sketches. Using the form of the building as a base he applied different texture, colour and pattern to this shell, changing its visual and aural resonance. His succinct annotations reveal that his choice of materials was informed by the musical instruments of the orchestra: »Gold/wood; try out brass/wood like violins; burnished gold/plywood.« ¬

Stefan's explorations extended to other ideas of how to transform the structure and how movement might be harnessed effectively. »Nice animation possibilities«, he noted of his sequential sketches. ¬

Keen to investigate other spatial interpretations, he involved Berlin-based designer and programmer Ralph Ammer to experiment with digital animations and renderings of the building. Alongside his own sketches, Stefan jotted »light moiré, as if moving«, a suggestion he asked Ralph to develop. The results are shown here. Drawn in Illustrator, the visual interference created by the overlapping patterns made each image dynamic, but Ralph adds that these experiments with moiré patterns were ultimately »a beautiful dead end«. ¬

24/06 ¬ Exhibition opening of »Things I Have Learned In My Life So Far« at Superspace Gallery in Belgrade. ¬

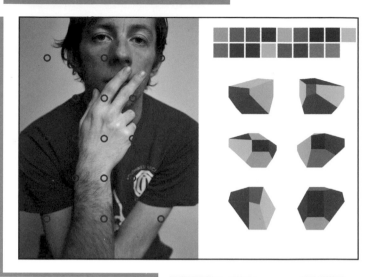

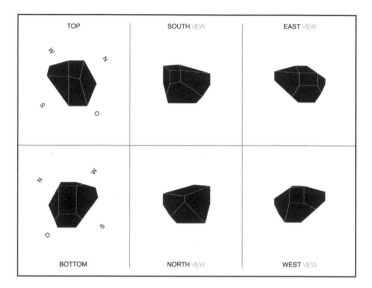

TOP   SOUTH VIEW   EAST VIEW

BOTTOM   NORTH VIEW   WEST VIEW

Ralph describes this logo generator as »a simple tool«. It allows the user to load their choice of image, from which it extracts colours to apply to each of the 17 facets of the building. This test uses an interactive 3D model of the building so that users can see how their choices of colour combinations look before they reach a final decision. When the user is happy with their colour selection they can export these images as vector-based graphics that can be used in any standard graphics software. ¬

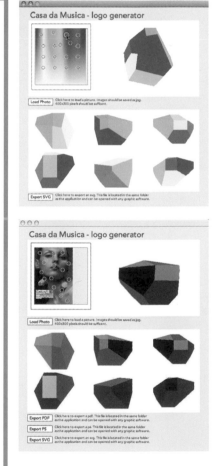

Ralph acknowledges that there was never really a specific brief from Stefan – instead the results emerged through »a kind of dialogue where we ping-ponged files and ideas across the Atlantic«. They worked on these individually, initially exploring the potential of using the form of the building, Stefan working on analogue experimentations and Ralph on digital versions. From these starting points Stefan identified the designs and concepts to pursue, and the idea for the logo generator evolved. ¬

Rather than developing a single visual identity or a series of interrelated identities to apply in various contexts (eg one version for stationery, another for advertising), Stefan and Ralph devised a system to create a mutable logo. Stefan saw an opportunity for individuals to create their own logo designs. It became clear to Ralph that this would require a custom software tool that every employee of Casa da Música would find easy to use. ¬

New technologies ¬ Many graphic designers explore new technologies and experiment with their potential to shape how and what we communicate. This involvement can extend to designing custom software and digital tools to meet specific briefs, for which designers often collaborate with specialist programmers, code writers or digital designers with complementary skills. Reflecting developments in communication technologies, successful identity design increasingly exploits the potential of the digital world and the possibilities of this multi-platform environment. ¬ **Digital design** ¬ Stefan met digital designer Ralph Ammer in 2004 while teaching at the Berlin University of the Arts, where Ralph is tutor in New Media. They worked together on an interactive typographic picture that used the aphorism »Being not truthful works against me.« for Stefan's series »Things I Have Learned In My Life So Far«, so each understood how the other worked. However, Ralph is based in Berlin and Stefan in New York and it surprised Ralph that their collaboration on the Casa da Música project ran so smoothly, particularly as they didn't meet in person for its whole duration. »I guess what makes work with people like Stefan so pleasant is his kind of professionalism combined with his joviality – as well as his extraordinary design skills and inventiveness.« As a designer and programmer Ralph is able to approach a project from both perspectives and swap roles as needed. His ability for flexible thinking informs his approach to interactive design. »I always try to distinguish between tasks that a machine can (and should) take over and the ones that can only be done by a human. Then I try to find a smooth interplay between both. And if things go well, these efforts culminate in results that are intuitive to understand and easy to use.« ¬

As he develops his ideas Ralph alternates between thinking as a designer and a programmer. »After thinking about what the software should do I work out the interactions and visual elements that are needed and plan the software on paper before typing the code. The production of the logo generator was relatively quick and took only about two days. It was so simple that I could do it in Processing, a readily available software development tool for designers, which I otherwise use mainly for sketching purposes.« This screenshot of the Processing environment shows a code snippet for the logo generator program. ¬

08/08 ¬ Speaking at FDG Expo 2007 in Jakarta, Indonesia. ¬
17/08 ¬ Speaking at Design Thinkers, RGD Ontario, Canada. ¬
01/09 ¬ Launch of Casa da Música identity this month. ¬ Pairing musicians with a 3D animator to create adverts for Casa da Música for 15-second slots on Portuguese TV. ¬
06/09 ¬ Speaking at Kyoorius Designyatra in Goa, India. ¬

The logo generator produces a bespoke logo each time it is used. It works with any image, whether a portrait of Beethoven or one of Casa da Música's president. Most identity systems use predetermined colour and typographic palettes. Here, although the colours change from logo to logo, the colour palette of the logo always relates to its context, from which they are taken. ¬

Stefan's ideas found resonance in the intentions and philosophy of Casa da Música architect Rem Koolhaas. Koolhaas had written of the building that it, »Reveals its contents to the city without being didactic; at the same time the city is exposed to the public inside in a way that has never happened before… Most cultural institutions serve only part of a population. A majority knows their exterior shape, only a minority knows what happens inside.« Koolhaas' intention was to create a space of positive encounter between the old and the new Porto »through both continuity and contrast«, themes that Stefan also explored. Casa da Música audiences are by and large local, but very different for each event. For example, the contemporary and symphonic audiences have, says Stefan, »Almost zero overlap. The logo therefore had to talk to a lot of different audiences so it was clear that they wanted – and needed – a system with adaptability.« ¬

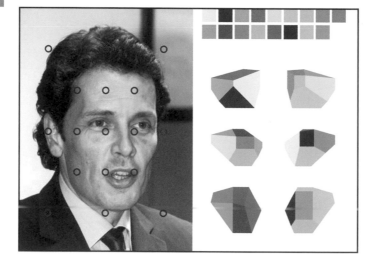

Nuno Azevedo
President

 casa da música

Stefan's logo had to work on its own, at small sizes and as part of a more complex visual system. Slightly redrawn logos are often supplied for use at large or small sizes but the flexibility of Stefan's system meant that this was unnecessary. Stefan chose Simple as the sole typeface for the logo. Set in lower-case, its angular geometric forms allude to digital patterns and quietly reinforce the contemporary character of the identity. ¬

 casa da música    casa da música

casa da música   casa da música

 casa da música    casa da música

Stefan's goal was that his identity would reflect the many different kinds of music performed in Casa da Música. The system he developed allows the logo to transform itself from application to application and from medium to medium. His logo changes character to reflect the performance, event or activity – whether club night, anniversary celebrations or education day. ¬

Message ¬ Identity design frequently involves the communication of complex messages. A successful identity projects the essential qualities of a product, person or organization and appeals to its target audience who, in some way, identify with it. It is important, therefore, for the designer to establish the core values and common ground between the client's need and the perception or expectation of the audience. ¬ **Audience** ⌐ In the case of many identity design projects the target audience or key demographic can to some extent be defined. For cultural institutions, attracting diverse audiences is an integral part of their mission and Casa da Música is no exception. Stefan found its tag line helpful in this regard. »My feeling is that, specifically for cultural institutions, if you have to say it, it normally isn't true and should be rendered obsolete. However I thought ›one house many musics‹ was pretty good.« ¬ **Application** ¬ Rigid visual systems are not always functional in a world of fast-moving communication technologies and increasingly interactive media. Most identities have to work across an array of media and in many different contexts. From print to web and physical to virtual, this means the designer must give careful consideration to how and where the identity might be seen and create a flexible system – for the range of applications and, in this case, the range of audiences too. ¬

27/09 Giving »Creative Genius: Things I Have Learned In My Life So Far« talk at PICNIC, Westergas, Amsterdam. ¬

The venue has so many design requirements and a constantly changing calendar of daily events, so it was impossible for Stefan to continue to design all the necessary publicity himself. The logo generator and design specifications were handed over to the two in-house designers at Casa da Música, André Cruz and Sara Westermann, who apply and interpret these as each new brief and event demands. ¬

remix ensemble

orquestra nacional
do porto

remix ensemble

orquestra nacional
do porto

The logos for Orquestra Nacional do Porto and Remix Ensemble were designed after Stefan's final concept presentation to Guta and Casa da Música's president and musical director. Although Stefan felt clear about the overall concept, which was well received, it took longer for him to see how these sub-brands might work. His solution was to return to his original ideas and early sketches (see pages 016–019). He applied the relevant textures of brass and wood to this early design for Orquestra Nacional do Porto (which ultimately became the logo for Orquestra Barroca) and treated the logo for Remix Ensemble as if it were a glass solid refracting the contemporary typography. In contrast to the bespoke solutions of the logo generator, the sub-brands are »locked-up«, so that their designs remain fixed and defined by Stefan. ¬

Coherent design ¬ From the first conversation between Guta and Stefan to the final presentation took nine weeks. The implementation of the logo took a further six months, which Stefan considers an average timescale for his studio to complete a project of this size. Following this, Stefan handed over his designs and specifications to the in-house design team at Casa da Música. Graphic designers put an extraordinary amount of time into ensuring that an identity remains coherent. This involves designing systems that determine how the identity should be applied. These rules and usage guidelines are commonly presented to the client in the form of a graphic manual, which generally covers logo usage, font usage and basic rules about layout. However, this does not mean that these guidelines are necessarily fully adhered to. ¬ **Handing over** ¬ Where an identity is flexible or continually evolving, someone needs to manage how, where and when it is applied. Inevitably this involves handing over to other designers, often in-house. As Stefan admits, this can be difficult. Even if someone with sophisticated sensibilities becomes the caretaker of the identity and applies it with care, he is never as satisfied as he would be with his own work. He compares this experience to getting a babysitter: »You have to trust them and that they can do the job, but you know you will always be the better parent.« ¬

The client was »really happy« with the logo. But perhaps a source of greater personal pleasure was that Rem Koolhaas liked the identity so much he asked to meet Stefan, a request that clearly touched him. When asked if he is pleased with the final results, Stefan answers with a measured satisfaction: »It is the right identity. For now it is done.« ¬

28/11 ¬ Lecture in Cankarjev Dom ahead of exhibition opening tomorrow of »Things I Have Learned In My Life So Far« at Galerija Avla NLB in Ljubljana. ¬

The books »Formulare Gestalten« and its English edition »The Form Book«, were created out of designer/author Borries Schwesinger's (born 1978) love of one of graphic design's more humble outcomes: the form. Beginning life as his college thesis, the original book and its subsequent English edition examine a wide array of documents that have one thing in common – they are all designed to be filled in. ¬ In his book of 1935, »Asymmetric Typography«, Jan Tschichold illustrated the close relationship of abstract painting to typography by showing examples of design work that included tables – the contrasting weights of rules and type, powerfully offset against acres of unfilled white space. Information design still holds an appeal for many designers, combining as it does systematic thinking with a necessarily minimal aesthetic. It is almost an invisible badge of honour among »serious« typographers to spend time designing timetables and forms, and it was this secret world that Borries wanted to explore. ¬ We were intrigued, partly because of the book's rarified subject matter and partly because this was a self-initiated and self-authored project. Borries' thesis was initially taken up by a German publisher, and then by a British publishing house; so how difficult was it for Borries to engender enthusiasm for his proposal not once but twice? Once underway, did he manage to retain creative control, and how did being both author and designer shape the process? We follow Borries in transforming his academic study into an award-winning and lovingly-realized book. ¬

Form design is a niche area of graphic design practice that is easy to dismiss as worthy but dry. Embarking upon academic research into this field requires self-discipline, scrutiny and rigour. Persuading a publisher that the findings will result in an engaging and visually sophisticated book requires flair, coupled with a passionate disposition. So, what informs Borries' approach? Does he see himself as an information designer or is this just one of many design skills and enthusiasms? ¬

In the genes ¬ Borries is the only child of two graphic designers. Far from being inspired by what he saw, he »knew all about it, which made it less attractive«. His parents didn't expect him to be a graphic designer so, even after his foray into urban planning, Borries was fatalistic about it as a possible career path. He entered a local graphic design competition – which he won – and at twenty-one applied to one graphic design course in Berlin and one in Potsdam. Borries' insider knowledge made him realistic about the prospect of failure, so he was pleased to be accepted by the University of Applied Sciences in Potsdam for a four-year course in graphic design. ¬

Desk-bound ¬ Unsurprisingly for a graphic designer interested in modular structures, Borries spent his secondary school years wanting to be an architect. Upon closer consideration he turned his attention to urban planning, thinking that focusing on the system that underpins the built environment was the way to go. It seemed »more important«, he explains. After two years at college Borries reconsidered – he feared he would be chained to his desk, with decision-making determined more often by the impenetrable relationship between developers and local officials than any planner's vision. It was back to the drawing board for Borries. He smiles wryly as he observes that as a graphic designer, his is still a desk-bound job. ¬

Work-shy ¬ Borries is a humble designer, but not without ambition. In 2004, while still at college, he collaborated with two fellow students, Svenja von Döhlen and Steffen Wierer, and set up a small studio in Berlin called Formdusche. Their projects included corporate and identity work as well as projects from the cultural, educational and scientific sectors. Borries also had some foreign work experience as a student, spending six months in Milan. Eighteen months after graduating he decided to work abroad again, this time moving to the UK to improve his grasp of the language and learn more of the British and their design sensibilities. Starting from scratch in a foreign country could have been a solitary experience were it not for the fact that he maintained regular contact with one particularly like-minded graduate from his course, Judith Schalansky: »We are often in very similar situations. She's still in Berlin but we phone every day – it's like having an office partner – and we email things. We always give each other direct, open and honest comments on these things. This feedback is very important.« ¬

Is God in the details? ¬
Underpinning Borries' design
philosophy is a belief that
the outcome grows from
the content. If this is analyzed
correctly, then »A new set
of appropriate design rules
will follow«. For every project,
Borries aims to develop
a system that will help elucidate
meaning and make the design
process more streamlined.
This systematic approach
is hugely important to him.
Borries focuses on every
detail – not just the structural
considerations of format,
grid, hierarchy, type sizes and
spacing, but also what might
seem design minutiae
like kerning, tracking and line
breaks. It's painstaking work
but Borries believes that,
»Even if the detail isn't always
noticed you can feel it – feel
the effort – and this makes
the whole project more cared
for and special.« ¬

Background noise ¬ It almost
goes without saying that
Borries is an exponent of
the modern movement.
But as a fairly unassuming
designer he is wary of designer
adulation: »I couldn't name any
design idols.« The later
modernists impress him though,
and Borries aims to emulate
Paul Rand's approach to client
presentations by developing
inventive techniques to
elucidate the design process.
He admits to flicking through
design magazines, and happily
visiting galleries and
exhibitions, but sees this
as research rather than
inspiration: »It's a backdrop,
but I rarely see something
and want to repeat it. It would
generally be inappropriate
to do so anyway.« For Borries,
an hour spent clearing
his head walking or cycling
is as important as looking
at a design book – he finds
that the latter may thrill but
can just as easily distract. ¬

Designing information ¬
Perhaps because the activity
is still in its infancy, the
terminology that is supposed
to define graphic design
is woefully inadequate
and misleading. Borries is
understandably wary of being
defined as an »information
designer«, because it has
become an over-used and
under-defined term. On the
one hand it is synonymous
with serious work designed
to impart practical and useful
knowledge – so wayfinding
systems, timetables and
diagrammatic representations
of all kinds fall into this
category. On the other hand,
as the function of most graphic
design is to impart information
of some kind, the majority
of projects – however
ephemeral, visually delightful
or simply entertaining –
could loosely be described
this way. »Where does
one draw the line between
a book designer, typographer
and information designer?
Often I call myself a
communication designer.« ¬

Borries Schwesinger
Matrikel Nummer 3798

Diplomexposé

Thema
Formulare gestalten

Formulare gehören zu unserem Alltag. Mitunter sind sie das einzige Medium, über das Kunden mit Firmen oder Bürger mit ihrem Staat kommunizieren. Formulare sind Teil eines hoch sensiblen Kommunikationsprozesses. Der Gestaltung von Formularen wird aber von ihren Herausgebern und auch von vielen Gestaltern oft nur wenig Beachtung geschenkt. Auch in der Literatur, in Designbüchern und Gestaltungsratgebern finden sich nur wenige systematische Analysen dieses Designfeldes und kaum Kriterien an denen sich der Gestalter orientieren kann.

Diese Arbeit will dieses Problem skizzieren und Lösungen entwickeln. Auf der Grundlage einer Sammlung von Formularen aus verschiedenen Bereichen, Zeiten und Regionen wird zunächst eine Typisierung dieses Gestaltungsfeldes entwickelt. Die vorliegenden Formulare werden anhand einer zu entwickelnden Systematik analysiert und eingeordnet. Dabei sollen sie auch im Kontext eines uns umgebenden Alltagsdesigns gesehen werden.

Bisher erschienene Schriften und von Gestaltern, Typografen, aber auch von Sprachwissenschaftlern geäußerte Meinungen und Auffassungen zur Formulargestaltung werden gesammelt, in einen Kontext gestellt und Grundlage für eine weitergehende Analyse sein. Daraus wird der Ansatz einer graphischen Semiologie der Formulargestaltung entwickelt. Dies kann Grundlage für die Formulierung von Gestaltungsgrundsätzen sein und in der Darstellung eines beispielhaften Kanons an Gestaltungselementen und -prinzipien enden.

Neben dieser formalästhetischen Analyse wird auf die kommunikative Bedeutung von Formularen eingegangen. Dabei kann ihre Bedeutung als Schnittstelle zwischen Staat und Bürgern bzw. Firmen und Kunden sowie ihre Rolle in der Entwicklung einer Corporate Identity untersucht und dargestellt werden.

Ein Ergebnis dieser Auseinandersetzung kann der Entwurf einer Publikation sein, die sich vor allem an Gestalter aber auch an Herausgeber von Formularen richtet, diese für das Thema sensibilisiert und Orientierung für die Gestaltung bietet.

One evening, Borries was sitting in his girlfriend's kitchen in Zurich mulling over possible topics for his thesis when he spied an A5 pad of forms for taking telephone messages. Borries was charmed by the unlaboured layout – the handless clock awaiting completion, the instructions in both German and French, the lengths of its ruled lines. As he examined it more closely, Borries started to wonder if his thesis could investigate this and other similar kinds of functional but aesthetically pleasing items of ephemera. ¬

Borries had to submit a research proposal before he could embark on his thesis. He outlined his intention to analyze the design and semiotics of forms to arrive at a set of design principles by which form design might be reviewed. His proposal is shown here, bound together with various other items of background material to form what Borries calls his »process book«. This was submitted as part of his final presentation although it was not marked. ¬

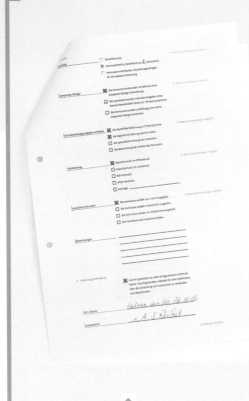

The thesis ¬ It's not unusual for art and design books to start as unsolicited proposals drafted by would-be authors or author/designers. It is unusual though for a student-written and -designed thesis to be published commercially in an almost unedited form. ¬ When Borries started thinking about his final-year research project he had no idea that the eventual outcome would be a book. Rather like a fine artist he started by defining the problem he wanted to solve and then considering what form the solution should take. ¬ Despite being a year-long college project the pressure was immediately on as, »for many students the aim is to produce a masterpiece!«. He narrowed down his ideas to an investigation into the design of forms – a specialist area of information design into which there had been little research. Borries wanted to define the activity and the output. What constitutes a form? Are there different categories? Is there any specific design-related terminology? What are the design variables and constraints? Borries' tutors greeted his proposal enthusiastically but were not themselves experts in this field. He updated them on his progress five or six times but this was essentially a self-directed project. ¬ At Borries' college the convention was for final-year design projects and theses to be conceived as separate entities, but Borries wanted to combine the two. He contemplated putting what he researched into practice by designing some forms, but these would still have had to be accompanied by the research document itself. One evening, as Borries started grouping his research into distinct sections, he imagined the outcome as an illustrated book and decided that this was by far the most honed and efficient solution. ¬

Borries researched past and present forms, citing a fifteenth-century letter of indulgence as an early example (indulgences were awarded by the Medieval Church as a remission of sin and consisted of a pre-printed document with an empty space to be filled in with the name of the purchaser). For the current examples, Borries asked 25 contemporary designers to submit their design work for analysis and inclusion in his thesis. Almost all responded positively – eventually. Borries was interested in including as wide an array of examples as possible – loosely defining a form as anything that includes an area to be filled in by hand or by machine, on paper or on screen. He asked not only for business and administrative forms, but also for postcard answers to mailings, tickets, questionnaires, certificates and so on. He was of course interested to see examples before and after being filled in – the latter being the final test of a form's success. ¬

↑
Once he was signed up with his German publisher, Borries went through this process again, this time sending out a more formal call for entries, shown here, that was in itself a form of course! The British version required further research so that the book would appeal to American, Australian and other English-speaking readers. To ensure as long a shelf life as possible, both books include more than 300 contemporary and historical examples. ¬

07/06/05 ¬ First discussion with Professor Beyrow about my proposed thesis – he likes it very much. ¬
10/06/05 ¬ Same discussion with Professor Müller – now the project is approved. Official starting day is 24/08/05. Thesis due to be handed in exactly six months later. ¬
09–15/06/05 ¬ Been in Potsdam all day, supervising the »Einstein project« – for a client we plaster the whole city of Potsdam with his iconic e=mc². ¬
22/06/05 ¬ Corina arrives from Zurich for a week. Won't go to the studio. ¬
05/10/05 ¬ First consultation with my prof – went well. We agreed that I should make a book out of it. ¬

Design Diaries

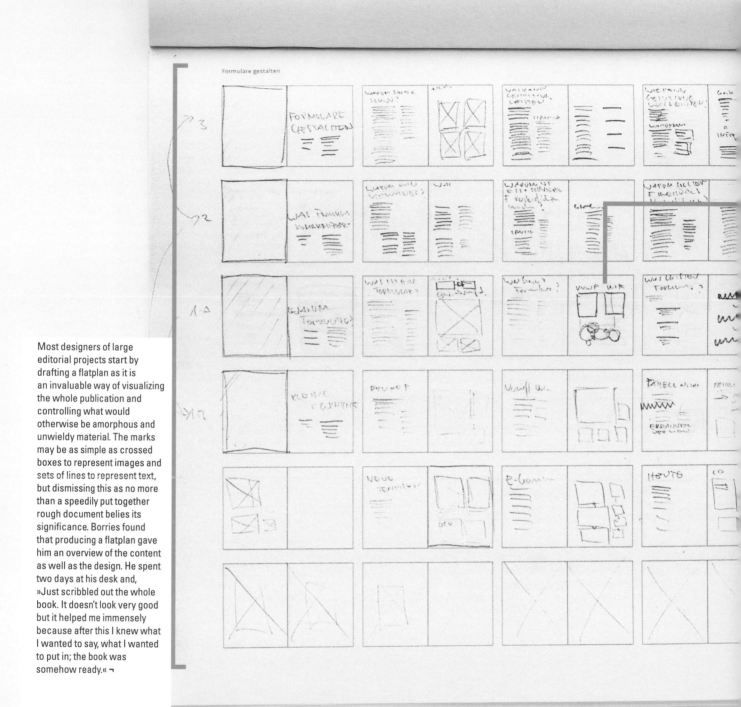

Formulare gestalten

Most designers of large editorial projects start by drafting a flatplan as it is an invaluable way of visualizing the whole publication and controlling what would otherwise be amorphous and unwieldy material. The marks may be as simple as crossed boxes to represent images and sets of lines to represent text, but dismissing this as no more than a speedily put together rough document belies its significance. Borries found that producing a flatplan gave him an overview of the content as well as the design. He spent two days at his desk and, »Just scribbled out the whole book. It doesn't look very good but it helped me immensely because after this I knew what I wanted to say, what I wanted to put in; the book was somehow ready.« ¬

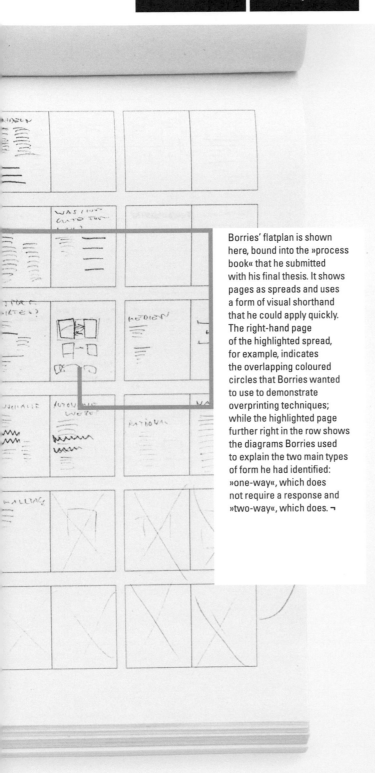

Borries' flatplan is shown here, bound into the »process book« that he submitted with his final thesis. It shows pages as spreads and uses a form of visual shorthand that he could apply quickly. The right-hand page of the highlighted spread, for example, indicates the overlapping coloured circles that Borries wanted to use to demonstrate overprinting techniques; while the highlighted page further right in the row shows the diagrams Borries used to explain the two main types of form he had identified: »one-way«, which does not require a response and »two-way«, which does. ¬

Writing and designing ¬ Even for an experienced author/designer, the scale and potential of a book project is daunting. Perhaps this is partly because many graphic designers revere books, offering as they do the chance of immortality. Just like for Sisyphus, who was condemned to an eternity of pushing a rock up a mountain, only to have it roll back down again, the task can seem unending, with the time needed incalculable and yet disproportionately high, relative to the page count. ¬ Having applied logic to his original step-by-step plan and schedule, Borries found that the writing of his thesis and the designing of the book came together far more organically than he had anticipated. His intention to compartmentalize activities faded fast, as contributors responded erratically and colleagues and friends mercilessly critiqued his analysis and texts. ¬ Borries found his design time diminishing; a panic-induced fug descended while the text was reworked and refined. The only way to regain control was to start the design process, even though only half the text was complete: »This was good for my feeling, to see something concrete. In the end I decided on the design and then I wrote into it. I needed two pages on such-and-such topic so I knew I had to write three paragraphs or a certain number of words.« That said, Borries admits that both activities induced crises of confidence: »If you're not used to writing you think, ›Ah, writing's so hard, I would so much more like to design, it's much easier and I can do it because I have the skills and know how to do it.‹ Then you start thinking, ›Oh my God, designing is so hard, maybe better get back to writing the text!‹« ¬

12/10/05 ¬ Four-hour meeting with our client from the theatre. Outlined a new image campaign. ¬
27/10/05 ¬ Off to Heidelberg for the MFG award show – dedicated especially to good form design. Then on to Zurich for the weekend. ¬
16/11/05 ¬ Met renowned Swiss designer Beat Müller in Basel to talk about his ideas concerning form design. ¬

Borries is most stimulated
when he is applying logic
and reason to his work.
He believes that the »right«
solution is often the result
of an unlaboured approach,
that answers will present
themselves if the brief
is analyzed and understood
fully – but he struggled when
it came to choosing the format
for his book. He knew that
A4 was the obvious choice
because so many forms are
this size, but it wasn't ideal:
»It's not a very attractive
format. I knew I couldn't show
things at actual size, that
it's quite big and cumbersome
and that the proportions are
not good, but then it's a book
about form design so A4 was
the right choice.« Shown here
is Borries' grid for his thesis
and the German-language
edition of his book. In addition
to its six columns, intercolumn
spaces and margins it
indicates the hanging height
of main heads or chapter titles.
Some designers also subdivide
the page horizontally into fields,
used generally to position
and size images. Borries' grid
is measured in millimetres
across the page and points
down the page. ¬

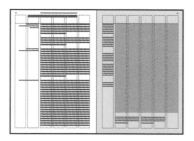

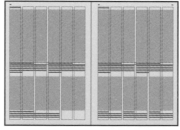

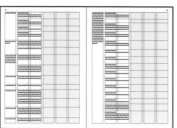

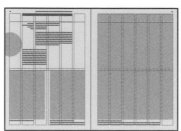

As these diagrams show,
Borries' grid is a flexible
multi-column structure.
As author, he was keen
that the text be easy to read.
He considered carefully
the relationship of type size
to optimum word count
per line. The narrowest
column of his grid is used
for captions while these
columns are combined
to give a wider text measure
for body text and images. ¬

First design ideas ¬ Although a gross oversimplification, graphic designers seem to fall into two camps: the list-makers whose black notebooks are generally unruled but whose initial jottings are nevertheless evenly spaced; and the collectors who gather inspiration from the flotsam and jetsam about them into richly-packed and bulging sketchbooks. Designers who write often seem to fall into the first category. »I'm not really a sketchbook person«, explains Borries. »My scribbles are never very sophisticated. We're not trained to do this in Germany – you know, where you gather bits and pieces and stick them in.« That said, Borries acknowledges that he has to make quick drawings of a page layout or cover to make it feel real: »I have to see the problem somehow, but I write down a lot – words, lines from the brief – or I make a small graph connecting things. But design is so visual that really I start at the computer.« ¬ Designers often refer to the vernacular for inspiration – rather than applying a design philosophy that has its own visual language, they reinterpret the everyday design around them as appropriate for a particular brief. Borries started by testing how much the design of his book should reference the language of form design. It seemed a rational solution: »I felt from the beginning, if I don't design any forms as part of my thesis then the book should be like a form. I tried out defined spaces for the annotations, texts and illustrations. But it was actually too contrived-looking. It's a book, not a form, so why make it look like a form? It constrained me too much and every page looked the same.« ¬

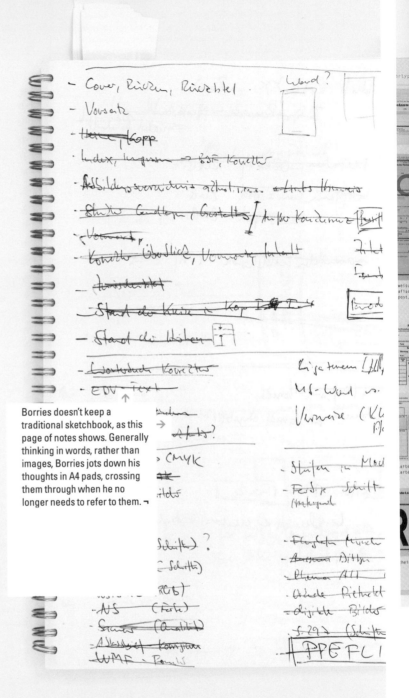

Borries doesn't keep a traditional sketchbook, as this page of notes shows. Generally thinking in words, rather than images, Borries jots down his thoughts in A4 pads, crossing them through when he no longer needs to refer to them. ¬

09/12/05 ¬ Attended talk by Austrian information design researcher Gerhard Dirmoser. ¬
22/12/05 ¬ Meeting with form designer Peter M Scholz in Berlin. He agrees to contribute samples of his work to my thesis. ¬
15/01/06 – 29/02/06 ¬ The last four or five weeks I didn't go to the office anymore. I stayed at home and just worked on my thesis. ¬

Design development ¬ Having jettisoned the idea of using the visual language of form design as inspiration for his overall approach, Borries decided to reference forms more subtly in his design. He used a mono-spaced font for his headings, FF Letter Gothic, combined with a rather insipid green used on German tax forms. His intention was to give the book »a sort of unaesthetic aesthetic« – an attempt to show the beauty in the everyday, even the design of bureaucracy. ¬ **Printing and finishing** ¬ Just as Borries carefully considered the design, he also experimented with production processes. Initially he hoped to give the project an authentic patina by incorporating 1970s matrix printouts and carbon-copy paper in its production. Finding the equipment for this became a bit of an obsession for Borries. He travelled around Berlin on a hunt for these antiquated printers and, at great expense, found two huge machines that took up residence in his tiny flat while he got them working. But this was a detour into a conceptual cul-de-sac: »I felt there must be something special I could produce to add to the book – but no ideas came to me. I bought large quantities of the paper but eventually used it for the introduction – not the outcome I had in mind. Even today I think I overlooked something – but perhaps not, as nobody else has done it!« ¬ Borries decided to reinforce the bookish quality of his thesis by having it cloth bound with a hardback cover – a method of finishing that he developed further when the thesis was eventually published commercially. Eventually, five copies of Borries' final thesis were printed digitally through a high-quality printer and bound by hand. Three of these were kept by his college. ¬

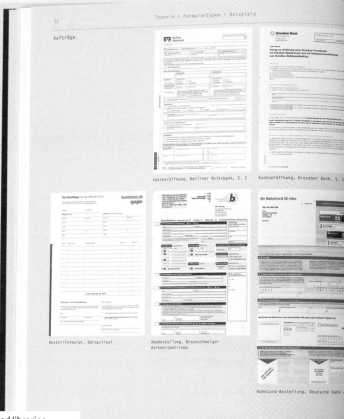

Borries scoured libraries, archives and the Internet for image references, and asked friends for more personal records. Reproduction quality was variable but as his thesis wasn't being professionally printed this wasn't a major concern. Borries photographed some material, other items were scanned and he was lucky to have some images in digital form. ¬

Some of the images had to be retouched to remove people's names or other personal data. Borries tried to be as subtle as possible: »No blurring or black overprinted bars«; instead he tried to invisibly amend numbers and names. ¬

Theorie › Formulartypen › Beispiele   33

oben › Zahlkarte, DDR-Post, ca. 1980
te › Einzahlungsauftrag, DDR-Post, ca. 1980
en › Postanweisung, Bundespost, 1963

oben › Postanweisung, DDR-Post, ca. 1955
unten › Telegrafische Postanweisung,
Bundespost, 1963

PACKCHEN

POSTPAKET

› Päckchen, Deutsche Post AG
› Postpaket, DHL

oben › Paketkarte, DDR-Post
unten › Paketkarte, Bundespost, 1963

Postprotestauftrag, 1963

AR

Antwort-Rückschein, Deutsche Post AG

oben › Anschriftenprüfung,
Bundespost, 1963
unten › Anschriftenprüfung,
Deutsche Post AG

Borries used Dolly as his text font. Designed by Bas Jacobs, Akiem Helmling and Sami Kortemäki and released in 2000, Borries chose it for its legibility and newsy, but human, feel. He used a strict 3pt baseline grid, setting his main text to 11/15pt, making the leading five baseline units, with captions set at 8.5/12pt. All internal horizontal spacing is a multiple of this 3pt unit. So, spaces between images or headings, rules and paragraphs are all determined by this unit of measurement. ¬

16

Funktionen

Formulare haben verschiedene Funktionen. Die Verwaltun
wissenschaftler Hans Brinckmann und Klaus Grimmer un
zwischen *Interaktions-*, *Organisations-* und *Subsumtionsfunk*
die im Folgenden kurz beschrieben werden sollen. Die me
Formulare, vor allem jene in Verwaltungsverfahren, müss
drei Funktionen, mit ihren jeweils unterschiedlichen Ans
an Inhalt und Gestaltung, gerecht werden.

4 Vgl. BRINCK-
MANN, GRIMMER
u.a.: Formu-
lare im Verwal-
tungsverfahren,
ff.

Interaktionsfunktion

Formulare dienen dem Informationsaustausch zwischen F
herausgeber und Klient. Dieser Austausch von Informatio
ist eine durch das Formular gesteuerte und geregelte Inter
die in Aktion und Reaktion unterteilt werden kann. Die Ak
liegt auf Seiten des Herausgebers, er erstellt das Formular
tiert es dem Klienten. Dieser reagiert darauf, indem er das
zur Kenntnis nimmt (*uni-direktionale Formulare*) bzw. ausf
(*bi-direktionale Formulare*). Das Formular ersetzt in seiner I
tionsfunktion andere Interaktionsmöglichkeiten, wie zum
ein persönliches Schreiben oder ein Gespräch. Daraus leite
Ansprüche vor allem an die Verständlichkeit des Formular
die Benutzerführung ab. Das heißt, der Klient muss sowoh
mittelten Informationen verstehen und einordnen können
dazu gebracht werden, die im Sinne des Herausgebers rich
Informationen einzutragen.

he Seite 20.
mulartypen.

Organisationsfunktion

Formulare haben, neben ihrer interaktiven Funktion, vor a
Aufgabe, Arbeitsabläufe zu organisieren und die räumliche
zeitlichen Distanzen zwischen einzelnen Bearbeitern und A
zu überbrücken. Indem sie den Informationsfluss formalis
und schriftlich festhalten, ermöglichen Formulare sowohl
teilung als auch die räumlich-zeitliche Trennung von Erfas
Präsentation, Auswertung und Speicherung der Informatio
In Formularen wird das Verwaltungshandeln erst sichtbar u
so, zumindest theoretisch, für die Nachwelt nachvollziehba
   Vordergründig sind Formulare dabei nur Mittel zum Zwe
Verwaltung bedient sich ihrer, um die Arbeit zu rationalisi
Was vorgedruckt ist, muss weder selbst geschrieben noch h
werden. Wiederholungs-, Denk-, Schreib- und Sucharbeite
werden vermieden.

19/02/06 ¬ Tonight I sent the whole thesis off for proofreading. Will care about the images in the meantime and think about a cover. ¬
   28/02/06 ¬ Last night of working on the thesis. Worked until 4am, then slept four hours, got up, still had to convert all images to cmyk, then went to the printshop around noon. ¬

Zusammenfassung der am 3. Mai 2006 besprochenen Manuskript-Änderungen des Buch-Projekts »Formulare gestalten.«

Grundsätzlich: Wir machen das beste Formular-Buch.

ALLGEMEINES ZUM INHALT

- vermitteln, dass zu (fast) jeder Frage der Formulargestaltung eine Antwort gegeben wird
- anschaulicher, »netter«, Leser-orientierter schreiben
- den Leser nicht mit wissenschaftlich-analytischen Abhandlungen überfordern, sondern immer den Bezug zur Praxis der Formulargestaltung herstellen
- den Leser »an die Hand nehmen«

ALLGEMEINES ZUR GESTALTUNG

- kleinere Schriftgröße der Headlines (Letter Gothic)
- Lesbarkeit der Letter Gothic bei größeren Textmengen verbessern
- Abbildungen größer

KONKRETES ZUM INHALT

Prolog

- ja/nein-Idee trägt nicht über mehrere Seiten
- wenn möglich neuen Prolog/Aufmacher finden
- Text über Schönheit der Formulare ist gut > aber lesefreundlichere Gestaltung

Inhaltsverzeichnis

- Zuordnung der Einträge zu den Seitenzahlen optimieren
- Register hinten anfügen

- wissenschaftlichen Anspruch vermindern, anschaulicher, pointierter erklären
- Definition weniger abstrakt und sich weniger ernst nehmend formulieren
- auf Systemtheorie nur nur verweisen, Bilder, Metaphern finden
- eingeführte Begriffe (z.B. uni-bi-direktional) sind zu abstrakt und wenig anschaulich, bessere finden
- Typologie als Typologie von Gestaltungsprototypen entwickeln (z.B. Auftragsformulare, Fragebögen, Antragsformulare, Response-mailings) und anhand ihrer spezifischen Probleme erläutern
- Typolgie mit Beispielen verknüpfen
- Beliebigkeit der Formularsammlung vermeiden, Schwerpunkte bilden, mit verschieden Bildgrößen arbeiten
- zeitgenössische und historische Beispiele nicht vermischen

...hte

- ...r Geschichte der Satz- und Reproduktionstechniken verknüpfen,
- ...le aus verschiedenen Epochen zeigen (z.B. Formulare der 20er, ...40er Jahre etc.)
- ...llung des E-government-teil ist nicht wirklich objektiv, entweder ...tiver darstellen oder subjektive Sicht mehr herausarbeiten

...nikation

- ...unikationsintentionen der Formularherausgeber differenzierter ...ellen,
- ...cher Situation begegnen einem welche Formulare und was ...et dies für die Gestaltung?

Gestaltu...

- grunds... ...ellen, da Zielgruppe nicht n...
- Checkl... ...ng entwickeln
- Gestal... ...ziehen
- Möglic... ...e-Formularen genauer darste... ...rung, Validierung von Eingaben etc.
- Gestaltgesetze anschaulicher, plastischer darstellen
- Graphisches Zeichensystem eventuell weglassen, dafür ausführlicher auf Gestaltungselement »Farbe« eingehen
- mehr zu Schrift und typografischen Grundlagen
- ausführlicher auf Papierformate eingehen
- mehr zum Gestaltungshilfsmittel »Raster«, Varianten zeigen
- Formulartektonik genauer zeigen und besser beschreiben
- mehr Varianten von Formularstrukturen zeigen
- Formularprotagonisten mehr erläutern, mehr Beispiele
- mehr Varianten und Witz in den Beispieltexten

Beispielteil

- viel mehr Beispiele
- auch Details zeigen
- vielleicht nach Inhalt und Gestaltung ordnen
- mehr kommentieren und mit Ratgeberteil verknüpfen bzw. darauf verweisen

Would-be authors and author/designers often submit proposals to publishers. These include biographical details, a brief book synopsis and a list of possible chapter headings with an indication of content. Publishers also approach authors and author/designers with proposals themselves, in which case the proposal acts rather like a brief. Borries' publishing arrangement was unusual, however, as his book already existed in the form of his thesis and so a conventional proposal was unnecessary. Instead, the publishers went through the thesis carefully and then outlined the changes necessary in order to publish it as a commercially viable book. ¬

Borries met with the publisher and then sent this three-page letter confirming what he had understood from the meeting. Requested design changes included adding illustrations to the introduction, shown top right, and running the continuous text in a conventional type size instead of treating it as display. Content changes included adding an explanatory spread on each different type of form that Borries had identified, instead of the single spread shown here, and drafting extended captions for each of his contemporary and historical examples. Overall the publishers wanted Borries to add more case studies to the book so that it would become a more comprehensive survey of the subject. ¬

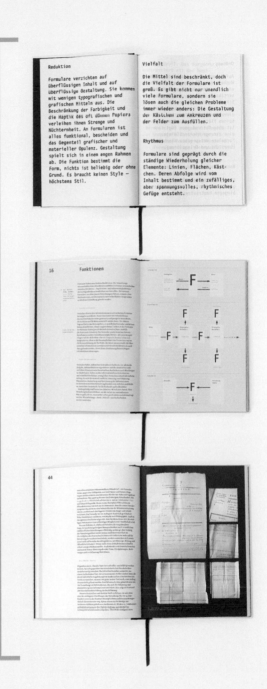

Approaching the publisher ¬ Designers are often required to impose order amid chaos so it is ironic that serendipity plays such a significant role in their working lives – as Borries learnt early in his career. ¬ While working on his thesis Borries had the occasional flight of fancy: »How great it would be to have my book published by the renowned typographic publisher Verlag Hermann Schmidt Mainz«. This was quickly countered by, »But who am I to think like this?«, at which he more or less forgot his dream. ¬ Hishopes were ultimately dashed when he heard that another designer was working on a similar topic. It is part of a designer's job to anticipate the zeitgeist, so it is hardly surprising when several designers come up with the same idea simultaneously. But Borries felt profoundly disappointed at the realization that his book would never be published. ¬ At about the same time a fellow student was working on another typographic book and secured a publishing deal with Verlag Hermann Schmidt Mainz. One day she seized an opening to mention Borries' thesis. The publishers expressed interest so it was with some anticipation that Borries sent off a copy of his completed project and then later telephoned the publisher: »Somehow it was clear during the discussion that we were making a book. I asked if they were publishing anything else on this topic and they said not.« Borries was of course overjoyed by this opportunity. ¬

22/03/06 ¬ Public presentation of my thesis at the college. Sixty visitors. Went very well. Feeling relieved. Same evening party at Judith's place, celebrating her book and my finished thesis. ¬
05/04/06 ¬ First phone call with the publisher, feels good, but it will be a long way to go for the finished book. At the same time, working long shifts on the new theatre season book. ¬
10/06/06 ¬ Phoned again with the publisher to clarify some contract details. ¬

Many months before the
publication was due Borries'
publishers produced their
bi-annual catalogue, which
featured »Formulare Gestalten«.
At this stage he was asked
to develop a new harder-
hitting cover – the text-only
cover of his thesis, shown
right, was considered too
subtle to attract buyers in
the competitive environment
of a bookshop. »It was an
anti-cover. I have to admit
I'm not so good at covers.
It was obvious the thesis cover
couldn't be the cover of the
book. I mean, nobody would
buy it. Not enough people,
at least, would buy it.« ¬

Formulare gestalten.

Borries Schwesinger

Preparing visuals ¬ Borries' initial experience as a professional book designer was unusual. He didn't have to present visuals to his publisher, for example, because his thesis gave an accurate indication of how his book would look. Generally, however, once an author is contracted, a designer is commissioned whose first task is to develop a design approach outlined in a series of sample spreads and cover alternatives. These use material supplied by the author that is indicative of the final content of the book. ¬ **The blad** ¬ Dummy pages form the basis of a blad – a piece of promotional material circulated to booksellers and possible foreign language partners many months before a book's publication. Some publishers place a great deal of emphasis on selling foreign language rights to other publishers to make their enterprise fully viable. The blad is vital in generating interest, giving as it does a fairly accurate foretaste of what is to come. Blads can be short and professionally printed, or amount to many spreads run out digitally. Borries' ran to 54 pages. It included sample text and image pages from each chapter of the book. Blads are sometimes presented with a blank dummy so that possible partners can get a real sense of the paper quality, intended binding and the 3D characteristics of the proposed book. ¬ Borries' blad was shown most notably at Frankfurt – the biggest book trade fair in the world where more than 7,000 exhibitors from more than 100 countries present their forthcoming wares. It attracted a great deal of interest. ¬

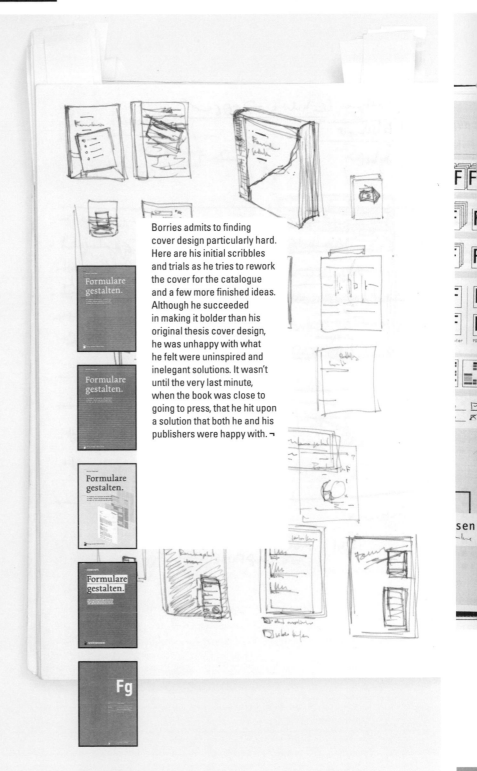

Borries admits to finding cover design particularly hard. Here are his initial scribbles and trials as he tries to rework the cover for the catalogue and a few more finished ideas. Although he succeeded in making it bolder than his original thesis cover design, he was unhappy with what he felt were uninspired and inelegant solutions. It wasn't until the very last minute, when the book was close to going to press, that he hit upon a solution that both he and his publishers were happy with. ¬

19/07/06 ¬ Went to the Museum of Communication in Berlin. Crawled through the archives desperately looking for the first published OCR form – nothing, only some new hints. ¬

10–12/06 ¬ Go to the studio every day and try to squeeze in the work on the book into the normal office duties. ¬

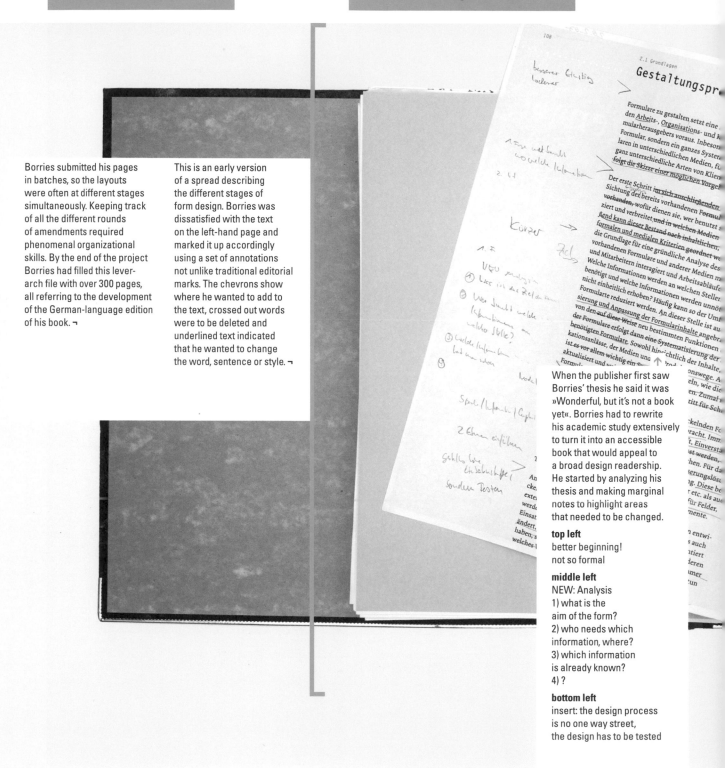

Borries submitted his pages in batches, so the layouts were often at different stages simultaneously. Keeping track of all the different rounds of amendments required phenomenal organizational skills. By the end of the project Borries had filled this lever-arch file with over 300 pages, all referring to the development of the German-language edition of his book. ¬

This is an early version of a spread describing the different stages of form design. Borries was dissatisfied with the text on the left-hand page and marked it up accordingly using a set of annotations not unlike traditional editorial marks. The chevrons show where he wanted to add to the text, crossed out words were to be deleted and underlined text indicated that he wanted to change the word, sentence or style. ¬

When the publisher first saw Borries' thesis he said it was »Wonderful, but it's not a book yet«. Borries had to rewrite his academic study extensively to turn it into an accessible book that would appeal to a broad design readership. He started by analyzing his thesis and making marginal notes to highlight areas that needed to be changed.

top left
better beginning!
not so formal

middle left
NEW: Analysis
1) what is the
aim of the form?
2) who needs which
information, where?
3) which information
is already known?
4) ?

bottom left
insert: the design process
is no one way street,
the design has to be tested

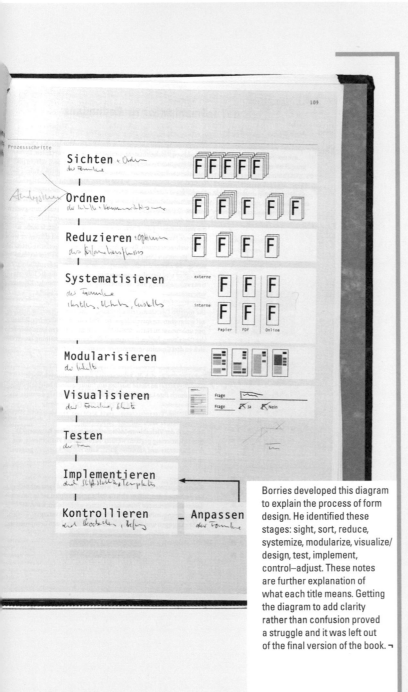

Borries developed this diagram to explain the process of form design. He identified these stages: sight, sort, reduce, systemize, modularize, visualize/ design, test, implement, control—adjust. These notes are further explanation of what each title means. Getting the diagram to add clarity rather than confusion proved a struggle and it was left out of the final version of the book. ¬

The amendment stages ¬ As author/designer, Borries' experience of book production was more integrated than that of most designers. The process usually starts several months after visuals are approved, when designers receive edited, marked-up text and images from the book's editor. The mark-up indicates the hierarchical relationship of headings and highlights different types of text matter – main text, pull-out quotes, captions and so on. This material is often accompanied by a page plan showing how the editor imagines text and images will fall. ¬ Layout One is the first time that everyone sees the final material as a real book, so text and design amendments can be heavy. Most books go through at least three major layout stages – each stage incorporates comments made by the publisher's editor/s, the author and eventually a proofreader. The editor acts as an intermediary once comments are received. These are either marked up on printouts and taken in by the designer, or the editor makes the text corrections directly to the artwork files prior to the designer making design changes. ¬ For author/designer Borries the amendment stages were unusual as his manuscript was a previously designed thesis. He recalls the process with humour: »I rewrote the thesis once in response to the publisher's comments, then I gave it to other people, who tore it apart. I tore it apart and rewrote it. Then I submitted it to the publisher. He annotated the text with his corrections and comments – add this, delete that. I rewrote it and submitted it a second time. It was proofread, the corrections came back, I made them and submitted it another time. They checked the corrections were done, made some new ones and I took these in too. So there were three big correction stages and then lots of last-minute smaller corrections because with so much content many things change at the last minute.« ¬

15/01/07 ¬ The whole studio moved into new rooms in Chodowieckistrasse. Lovely – spacy and light. Feels good working here. ¬
29/01/07 ¬ Two-page letter has arrived from the publisher outlining changes to my new version of chapter 1! ¬

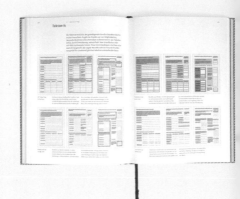

From the tactile quality of the paper to the colour of the bookmark, Borries was very precise in every detail of the production of his book: »I spent a lot of time searching for a good book paper for example, good to read, with a nice feel that fits the topic. It had to have a little roughness – most book papers are a little too nice. This needed to feel utilitarian.« Borries chose a 130gsm white Munken Polar for the main body of the book. It had a 1.5 volume, which means that it was less compressed than other papers of the same grammage and bulked up well. The paper was expensive, but Borries' publishers were pleased that its environmental credentials were good. The introduction was printed on 60gsm PlanoPak, a stock reminiscent of the blue carbon paper used in the original thesis. ¬

Like Borries' thesis, the book is an A4 hardback with a cloth spine. It is printed in cmyk, plus one additional colour throughout. Although cmyk is also referred to as full colour, the palette is actually very limited. The green of the German tax forms, that Borries was so keen to evoke, could only be achieved as a fifth working colour, HKS 62. The HKS colour system is the German equivalent of the Pantone Matching System and is comprised of 120 spot colours. »Spot« colours are also often referred to as »specials«. ¬

Borries believes that it is the care and attention given to detailing that can make an assignment truly special. The reader may be unaware of what is entailed, but Borries is sure that they feel the love that has gone into the project and therefore enjoy and value the outcome more fully. Once all the text amendments were signed off, Borries was lucky in being able to enlist the help of his designer father as a fresh pair of eyes to check the line endings for widows, orphans and clumsy word breaks that could disrupt the easy reading of the text. Widows and orphans are single lines at the beginning or end of paragraphs left to sit alone at the top or bottom of a column. Widows are also commonly understood to be single words that form the last line of a paragraph. ¬

Borries was faced with the daunting task of seeking formal permissions and sourcing high-resolution image files for the book, neither of which had been necessary for his thesis. Some of the photographs used originally were impossible to find at good enough quality to reproduce, so Borries had to find alternative illustrations. For other images, like the form designed by Kurt Schwitters shown at the bottom of the black right-hand page opposite, Borries had to negotiate usage and copyright fees. Most of the scanning, retouching and image manipulation was done by a reprographic house in Mainz, although Borries did some of this work himself. ¬

Production values ¬ Although profitable, publishing is a financially risky business, with one successful book often subsidising several less lucrative ventures. Author and designer fees are paid out long before sales are made, as are the bills for print and production. One way for publishers to reduce these costs is to have a stake in the printers of their books, and another is to outsource production to cheaper parts of the world. ¬ Borries had wisely identified Verlag Hermann Schmidt Mainz as his favoured publisher: »They pride themselves on producing beautiful books.« All their books are credited as, »Printed in Germany with love« – and they certainly seem to be. The publishers own the printers, are exacting in their quality control and give designers a freer reign than is usual in recommending papers and experimenting with different types of binding and finishing. ¬ Borries felt advantaged by publishing initially in Germany because more expensive books, aimed at a small and select readership, are not unusual there: »The publishers are not worried that their books are more expensive than most – because people buy them.« The print run of the German edition was 5,000 – an average quantity for an art and design book. ¬

09–11/02/07 ¬ Flew to Amsterdam to talk to the great form designers of Eden design. They contribute some of their work, too. The night I spend in the pub with my old friend Pia. I think about how you can learn a lot about me in both the thesis and the book, and about the time in which the book was made – there are receipts from restaurants, a boarding pass from this time and a cinema ticket! ¬

The cover ¬ All publishers pay particular attention to cover design. Covers are considered to be the book equivalent of a magnet, designed to be irresistible to the interested reader. Generally designers only present one overall concept for the interior of the book, but three or more covers. ¬ By his own admission Borries made several aborted attempts to design a cover that satisfied his client and himself. It wasn't until the book was about to go to press that he hit on the right solution: »The plan was that I would get the last round of corrections on Friday and do them over the weekend, but then the proofreader was ill. So I had time to do the cover another time – to revisit the terrible cover I had done before. Suddenly the stripes came to me, and this sticker idea, which looks a bit like a till receipt applied to the corner of the cover.« ¬ **The binding and finishing** ¬ The latter part of the publishing process was quite overwhelming for Borries. He was taking in final amends, checking typographic detailing and trying to make important production decisions all at the same time: »I couldn't see anymore, it was just ridiculous«. He tried to remain true to one of his original objectives, though – that this should be an archetypal book. This was his rationale for its being a quarter-bound hardback book with endpapers, a headband and bound-in bookmark. ¬

»Formulare Gestalten« is a quarter-bound hardback. This means that the spine and a small part of the cover are in a different material, in this case cloth, to the rest of the cover boards. Borries' book was printed in sections that were sewn together. It has a headband – a cloth band that projects slightly beyond the head and tail of the book. Although now more ornamental than functional, headbands were originally a thong core around which the ends of the threads of a sewn book were twisted as a way of neatly securing them. ¬

Borries' publishing contract initially specified that the book would be hardback with some embossing on the cover – Borries assumed that the publisher thought this would give added value to the book. He decided to recess the area for the sticker, which was printed in three colours on a gloss stock to contrast with his unlaminated, uncoated cover. The sticker is applied by hand – a costly process that added one Euro to the production cost of each book. Borries wanted the sticker to wrap round the edge of the cover but this was too expensive. ¬

At the last minute the publishers advised Borries to revisit the colour of his black cloth binding, »We went through these catalogues of linen and came to the feeling that this was somehow not a black book or a blue book but a green book. Inside it's green and the cover is green, and so it had to be green on the shelf. We found a matching bookmark and these yellow headbands as a contrast. Lastly we chose the blue endpapers. It was a strange moment in the print shop deciding all these things very fast, within half an hour or so.« ¬

Endpapers are glued between the cover and the text block, or body of the book, to cover the raw edges of the covering material if it is turned over the cover boards, as well as the inside surfaces of the boards themselves. ¬

»Formulare Gestalten« has won five international awards, including the TDC New York Award for Typographic Excellence 2008 and the Tokyo TDC Book Design Prize 2008. »I didn't expect this«, says Borries modestly, »I enjoyed it«. This adulation has its downside though. Borries is more aware now of how his work is perceived. »A book that's printed 5,000 times — 5,000 people will have it in their hands and think something about you, more or less. Maybe only a little but this awareness influences the whole process.« ¬

20/07/07 ¬ Friday the corrections didn't arrive. I redo the cover. The following Wednesday I go to the print shop in Mainz, choose the linen for the binding, the endpapers, the bookmark. Then take in more amends, then I catch the last train to Zurich at 6pm — to see my girlfriend — and said to the printers: »Goodbye, do something with it, make a book out of it!« ¬
01/09/07 ¬ It's published! ¬

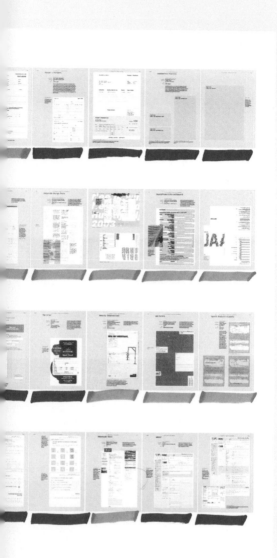

Borries' colour-coded flatplan
for the English language version
of »Formulare Gestalten«,
showing the number of new
case studies requested by
the publisher to turn it into
»The Form Book«. ¬

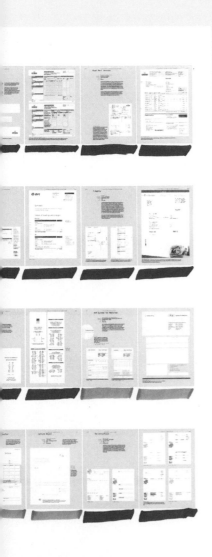

Co-editioning ¬ It's common for art and design books to be published in more than one language, either simultaneously or after the initial publication. Often, the original book is reprinted under the new publisher's name with the translated text replacing the original copy but the design unchanged. To make this economical, publishers often specify that all text in the original language is printed in black, so that only one plate change is necessary in translation, and that layouts are designed to allow for the variable lengths of different languages. ¬ It took over two years for »Formulare Gestalten« to hit the shops in the English-language version published by Thames & Hudson. Borries' initially revisited the text – adding new case studies to resonate with an English-speaking audience – and then redesigned the pages to accommodate this new text. »I was definitely enthusiastic about having an English edition, but of course it was hard to work again on the same thing, especially as it was the third time!« ¬ »The Form Book« retails at approximately two-thirds of the price of its German counterpart, making it accessible to a wider audience, although its production values are less high. Borries is aware that in professional practice the case is constantly argued for both approaches. »I know there are many things I could have done differently«, says Borries, reflecting on the process of turning his thesis into two books. »It was such a long project, after a time the thing becomes autonomous so I learned to let it grow by itself. It took a certain direction and I had to support it, even if sometimes it was not as perfect as I wanted it to be!« ¬

Borries considers if he is ready to embark on such a huge project again: »I would never do something like this alone again. You become crazy – but the financial constraints mean that you can't afford to get help, of course!« Borries is not alone in vowing never to embark upon another book project. But most author/designers find that the memories of panic-induced late nights and terror-fuelled working weekends fade. The sense of gratification in rediscovering each page endures, as does the admiration from peers who are more than aware of the exertion required in producing a book like Borries'. ¬

28/04/08 ¬ Met Jamie Camplin, managing director of Thames & Hudson in London. Outlined changes to the book to make it work in English. Start again… ¬

Warsaw-based design duo Homework's
specialism is designing theatre and film
posters – a revered national practice.
For the greater part of the last century Poland,
along with fellow Eastern European countries
Hungary and the former Czechoslovakia,
developed an approach to film and theatre
poster design that was quite unlike that of
its Western counterparts. Instead of featuring
images of the lead actors combined with
typography determined by star-power alone,
rather than by any design considerations,
each Eastern European design was conceived
as an artwork in its own right. Although
prevailing art movements informed these
designs, the posters shared a clever and
arresting use of visual metaphor that assumed
visual literacy in their audience – a trait still
unrecognized by film distributors in the West. ¬
Joanna Górska (born 1976) and Jerzy Skakun
(born 1973) design around 30 theatre and film
posters every year. They are speedily and
inventively executed, and the results are hugely
varied but always striking, and distinct from
posters produced elsewhere in the world. We
were interested to know how Joanna and Jerzy
maintain these high standards, how they generate
ideas so quickly and whether they see themselves
as working within a continuous design tradition.
We followed them designing a poster for the
Czech film »Pupendo«, during several dark winter
days in their studio in Warsaw. ¬

Designing film posters sounds glamorous, but for Joanna and Jerzy, brought up in the former Eastern bloc and working within a long and respected design tradition, it is a far more subtle and loaded activity. Does politics influence their work in any way? How did their design education shape them, and what continues to inspire and engender delight? ¬

Looking beneath the surface ¬
Joanna and Jerzy are most concerned about the appropriateness of their work. They consider their posters to be unsuccessful if they don't communicate a film or play's central theme: »Without a concept, a poster can be beautiful but is only a decoration.« Their inspiration comes from analysis of the source material: »When we make a poster for a theatre, we read the text of the play and talk with the director. If we make a film poster we watch the film first. When you see a poster you can say it is beautiful, nice, ugly, strong, weak and so on, but you need to see the film or go to the play to know if it adequately reflects the content.« ¬

Followers of fashion ¬
Homework's design stands apart from other work because it cannot be easily identified by style or period. Joanna and Jerzy do not concern themselves with categorizing their work and do not adhere to the principles of any particular movement. They describe »avant-garde«, »modern« and »fashionable« as referring to ephemeral and irrelevant qualities, particularly in this culturally interconnected world, and pride themselves on developing varied solutions that are not determined by faithfulness to any particular style: »We think it is uninteresting to make all things in a similar style, especially if you create many works.« Jerzy adds that graphic design's appeal is that it gives the opportunity to »make lots of different things. You don't have to do the same thing your whole life«. ¬ The duo cite a range of designers from across Europe as influences: Uwe Loesch (German), Anette Lenz (French), Andrey Logvin (Russian) and Roman Cieslewicz (Polish) – all of whom are known for highly graphic and varied poster design. ¬

Like-minded clients ¬ Joanna and Jerzy's clients are generally from the cultural sector. This wasn't planned at the outset but they are pleased that arts-related publicity is their specialism, saying that their clients are highly receptive to design and often become their friends. Joanna and Jerzy's clients are confident in decision-making and are happy to follow their instincts without focus group testing, the reassurance sought by many marketeers: »We do not usually work with the stress of sales charts or market research.« The fees are not high but are enough to make a living, »but we do work a lot.« Homework has built up a regular clientele, with some jobs repeating each year. Having designed the identity for the Teatr Polski in Bydgoszcz, both designers are responsible for implementing it in all the theatre's publicity. They have designed stamps for the Polish postal service and continue to produce posters and exhibition catalogues for the Casimir Pulaski Museum in Warka. ¬

Coming in from the cold ¬
Both designers were brought up in communist Poland and as children were aware of the economic problems associated with the regime. »Even today we are catching up with Western Europe, and that is in all domains, graphic design included.« That said, much of Poland's design legacy is thanks to the state-owned publishing house Wydawnictwo Artystyczno-Graficzne that acted as patron to many graphic artists working after the Second World War, and which recognized film poster design as a form of egalitarian visual art that was to be encouraged. ¬

A touch of pragmatism ¬
There is a long-standing
practice among international
poster designers of producing
work specifically for themed
design competitions. While
at college, Joanna and Jerzy
entered their posters into
competitions as a profile-raising
exercise – the winning entries
were printed and displayed
publicly. Now they send live
projects to various biennales
instead. Seeing their projects
alongside entries from their
peers helps them re-evaluate
their work – and it reassures
clients that commissioning
Homework was right when they
see the results in a wider design
context. In 2008, Homework
was awarded a Gold Medal
at the tenth International
Poster Biennial in Mexico.
Their winning entry was
a theatre poster for »The
Danton Case« and was judged
in the cultural poster category.
Although very pleased, both
designers are relaxed about
the process: »We do not put
much weight on competitions.
The jurors are always different,
obviously, so works that
are awarded in one competition
might not even be accepted
in another. We treat it more
as fun.« ¬

Licence to be poetic ¬
Homework considers poster
design as akin to writing poetry.
Poets use rhetorical devices
to catch their reader's
imagination. They play with the
sounds and meanings of words,
and the syntax of verse, to lend
beauty and elucidate meaning.
In a similar way, Joanna and
Jerzy are the past masters
of using the visual metaphor –
images of one thing that are
used to mean something else.
This is very much in the Eastern
European tradition of poster
design: »We have some
Polish-school roots, although
we do not think consciously
about it much. Somehow
it comes naturally because of
our Polish education. It's mostly
to do with a way of thinking
and an approach to simplicity
rather than any style.«¬

Different perspectives ¬
Joanna and Jerzy met at the
Fine Arts Academy in Gdańsk,
where both took a five-year
graphic course in the Painting
and Graphic department.
Here they developed the
mark-making skills that would
give life to their ideas, but on
graduation they felt unprepared
for professional practice:
»In Poland there were no
courses in typography. We did
a lot of painting, drawing,
classical graphics – engraving,
linocut – and about eight hours
a week of graphic design, when
we did posters, logos and so
on.« Both designers felt that
they needed to supplement their
education and went on to study
abroad – Joanna in Paris and
Jerzy in St Gallen, Switzerland.
It was here that Jerzy designed
typography with a computer
for the first time, while Joanna
won a scholarship and went
for a year to ESAG Penninghen
(École Supérieure de
design, d'art graphique
et d'architecture intérieure)
in Paris. Here she studied
poster design under Michel
Bouvet, typography with
art director and designer
Étienne Robial and photography
with Italian-born fashion
photographer Paolo Roversi.¬

Time and space ¬ Homework
is a prolific studio. It often
produces a poster design in
a matter of days and generally
only has work planned two or
three weeks ahead. Joanna and
Jerzy like this fast turnaround;
they find that the time
constraints help focus the mind.
Since setting up in 2003, they
have developed organizational
skills to ensure that their
working hours are used most
productively and that private
time isn't compromised:
»We do not work at night.«
Named Homework because
they work at home, the duo
work in separate rooms, but
within easy chatting distance.
Their work incorporates
hands-on making, so the
studio includes a photographic
corner and a table for building
models: »We dream about
a bigger space.« ¬

»Pupendo« is a Czech-made tragicomedy, a portrait of two Prague families one summer during the early 1980s. The first family stands by its political principles and is persecuted by the regime, the other is happy as part of the mainstream. Homework took inspiration from the story of Bedrich Mára, the father of the first family – a renowned but ostracized sculptor who is deprived of his job at the Academy of Arts and reduced to making kitsch forms of ceramics, most notably piggy banks that look like buttocks, because he won't kowtow to the authorities. Then Mára is given a humiliating commission by the state, to sculpt a comrade army general. »We liked this film«, comment Joanna and Jerzy. »We often have to design posters for films we like less. Liking the film isn't significant for us.« ¬

»Aside from the film itself we do not have any additional brief from the distributors and we do not consult with them. We watch the film ourselves and then talk about it briefly. Sometimes the first associations or ideas are best. We seldom watch the film again, though Jerzy does research, looking for interesting stills that act as reminders and prompts.« ¬

Film poster design ¬ Film and theatre poster design is unlike most other areas of graphic design. The scale, coupled with the significance placed on imagery, means that these posters have the potential to be valued as artworks in their own right. Their primary function, however, is to evoke a story, to sum up the essence of a film or play. They have to be attention-grabbing at a distance, but merit a second viewing close at hand. They have to be intriguing, but easy to assimilate at speed and simple enough to lodge in the residual memories of people passing by. These considerations form part of the brief for any film poster design project. Homework stumbled into this area of graphic design by accident but consider all these factors in their work. ¬ **The client** ¬ Having designed one poster for a Latin American film festival, recommendations followed and now over half of Joanna and Jerzy's projects are cinema-related. Most are commissioned by independent distributors Vivarto, who specialize in distributing European films for screening in a network of art-house cinemas all over Poland. More commercially orientated distributors use the original poster artworks and simply translate the wording into Polish, but Vivarto is keen that its posters are unique. ¬ **The film, audience and schedule** ¬ »Pupendo« is a Czech film, distributed in Poland by Vivarto, who commissioned Homework to design the poster, invitations to screenings, press adverts and flyers. A DVD of the film acted as Homework's brief. Joanna and Jerzy had a maximum of four days to design the poster and were working on three other projects concurrently. ¬

20/12 afternoon ¬ We're asked if, and how quickly, we could do the poster for »Pupendo« (18/01 is the premiere). ¬ **evening** ¬ Christmas gift packing. ¬ **21/12 morning** ¬ Coffee and corrections for Dramatyczny Theatre Book. ¬ **afternoon** ¬ Messenger brings DVD of »Pupendo« film. ¬ **evening** ¬ Film watching. ¬ **22/12 morning** ¬ Appointment at Vivarto; we are asked to design a set of posters for »classic cinema«, with deadline next month. ¬ **afternoon** ¬ First sketches for »Pupendo«. Checking Internet for previous promotion of it. ¬ **evening** ¬ Mail our Christmas card. ¬

The original Czech poster uses a still from the film showing a pale and flabby bather, timid and lost in the middle of Hungary's Lake Balaton. In the film, Mára and his family take their holiday here – their original plan to visit the seaside in Yugoslavia having been thwarted. There is a real sadness about this image but the poster lacks visual dynamism. ¬

Given the speed at which the duo work it's hardly surprising that they describe their studio as »rather messy«. Joanna and Jerzy draw upon a wealth of different references, and make sure that a diverse range of books is close at hand. ¬

This spread from Jerzy's sketchbook shows on the left-hand page ideas for another project that was running simultaneously to the »Pupendo« brief. The page on the right shows some initial ideas for the »Pupendo« project – none of which are directly reflected in the final poster. A recurring image in the film is the pottery piggy banks that the blacklisted sculptor produces to make his meagre living. These are crude, and their smooth curves resemble buttocks. Here Jerzy explores whether this demeaning metaphor can be expanded upon to become the poster's central image. ¬

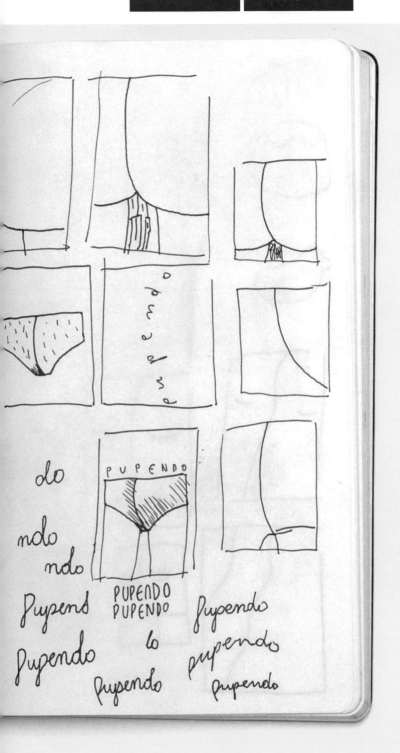

General approach ¬ Homework's approach to film poster design is similar to the famed artist/designers of the Polish school. They think of a film poster as an autonomous piece of art and design – the film is purely its inspiration. Of course a bi-product is that the poster raises awareness of the film by conveying something of its essence, but the objective is to do this via imagery and typography that is a response to the film, and goes beyond merely showing stills or portraits of the stars. Their client Vivarto, »Pupendo«'s distributor, was confident that by commissioning Homework it would have a poster that worked effectively as a promotional tool. Vivarto knew that Homework's design would be a strong contrast to the crowd of photographic posters alongside it: »It will be recognizable.« ¬

Generating ideas ¬ Having watched and discussed the film, Joanna and Jerzy start by scribbling down their first thoughts in their sketchbooks. They work separately and then share ideas. This process isn't competitive; it's simply the most unencumbered way for Joanna and Jerzy to focus on a new project. If they have some kind of creative block they allow themselves a break, or use a new tool. Just as different verbal languages allow people to formulate entirely different ideas, Joanna and Jerzy find that turning from drawing on paper to using the computer or taking some photographs can stimulate new design thinking. Sometimes they simultaneously research online, watch extracts of the film again or check out the posters that have been created for earlier screenings of the film. ¬

23/12 ¬ Travel to Sopot for Christmas break. ¬
24–30/12 ¬ Some family time at Joanna's parents and with mine in Olsztyn. ¬

Developing ideas ¬ Joanna and Jerzy are a prolific and highly inventive team, producing posters that can be shocking, sinister and disturbing or delightful, dreamlike and mischievous in equal measure. Despite the rich variety of their work, some generalizations can be made. Homework's posters are usually image-led. Joanna and Jerzy specialize in generating simple and bold graphic forms that refer as much to pictograms or icons as to illustration. Occasionally, their own photography is integrated into the designs, but these images are generally combined with other elements to maximize their graphic potential: »We rarely refine our ideas typographically at this stage. Usually after selecting the sketches we think are worth developing we start working on a computer, and sometimes we start sketching straight away in Illustrator. At first we focus on the illustration, then we look at adding type. We use existing fonts, sometimes then altering them a bit.« ¬ Joanna and Jerzy narrowed down their ideas for the »Pupendo« poster to two, which they then developed for the first client presentation. One idea was to use an image of a communist general, »with his breast full of medals and a butt-like head similar to a pig«, reflecting the demeaning work of the film's central character. They were searching for an image of a general as reference and found a picture of Leonid Brezhnev on the Internet. Brezhnev was General Secretary of the Communist Party of the Soviet Union, and therefore political leader, from 1964 to 1982. This image acted as a particularly apt starting point for some of Homework's presentation visuals. ¬

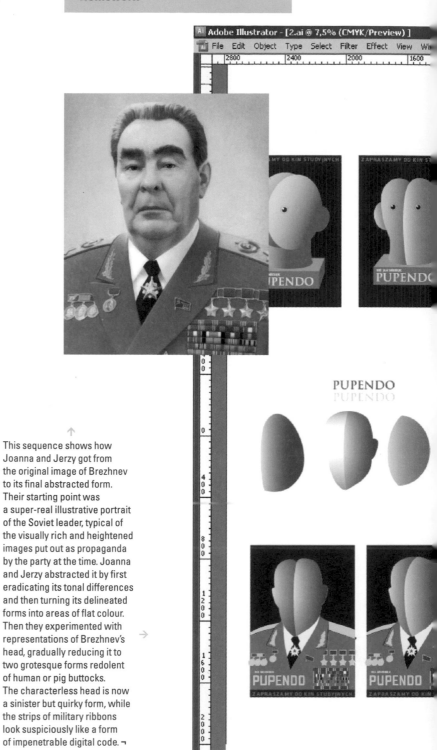

↑
This sequence shows how Joanna and Jerzy got from the original image of Brezhnev to its final abstracted form. Their starting point was a super-real illustrative portrait of the Soviet leader, typical of the visually rich and heightened images put out as propaganda by the party at the time. Joanna and Jerzy abstracted it by first eradicating its tonal differences and then turning its delineated forms into areas of flat colour. Then they experimented with representations of Brezhnev's head, gradually reducing it to two grotesque forms redolent of human or pig buttocks. The characterless head is now a sinister but quirky form, while the strips of military ribbons look suspiciously like a form of impenetrable digital code. ¬

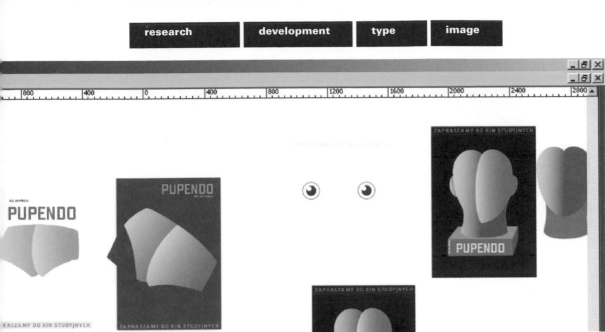

A screen grab from Joanna and Jerzy's pages of roughs which gives an idea of how their work progresses. Their initial sketchbook scribbles are worked up, before being significantly rethought to form an abstracted version of a sculpted bust and the general's head. Rather like a kit of parts, various illustrative elements and pieces of typography are repeated or combined in subtly different ways as the designers experiment to see which grouping is the most dynamic. ¬

31/12 ¬ Back in Warsaw for New Year's Eve. We spend it with friends. ¬
01/01 ¬ Resting, Joanna has some health problem, a fever. ¬
02/01 morning ¬ Our daughter Ewa is going back to kindergarten, we get back to work. ¬ afternoon ¬ Hard to get back to work. »Pupendo« project, finishing book for Pulaski Museum in Warka. ¬ evening ¬ Joanna still has fever. ¬

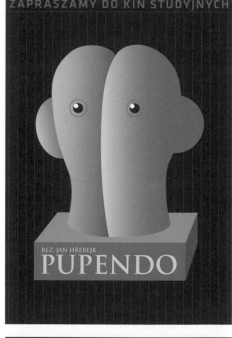

Homework presented two ideas of the »Pupendo« poster to their client, with two versions of each. The first approach took → sculpture more obviously as its theme, while the second → design developed their idea of a general with a pig-like head. Vivarto chose the latter idea and didn't request any changes, but Joanna and Jerzy »wondered for a long time whether we should give eyes to the general or not«. They removed the eyes on the final poster, thinking that this made the figure look more inhuman. ¬

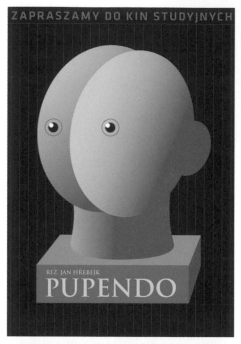

Client visuals ¬ Homework has an extremely good relationship with its client Vivarto. Joanna and Jerzy generally present them with three initial ideas. The number is entirely up to them and they have been known to show just one, »when we were sure it was the one we liked«. Given the speed at which these jobs have to be completed, there is no formal presentation. The poster visuals are emailed to the client as pdfs without any explanatory notes. Joanna and Jerzy presented four visuals for the »Pupendo« poster and the initial response was positive. A design was quickly chosen and accepted without changes. ¬ **Production** ¬ The printers of the »Pupendo« poster were chosen by the client and unfortunately budgets didn't allow for wet proofs. Joanna and Jerzy make sure that they run out reduced size tests at high quality before sending their jobs to print. These act as some form of quality control, although they are aware that no form of digital proof is as accurate as a printer's proof on the actual stock. Before the artwork is signed off Joanna and Jerzy add various obligatory elements at the bottom of the poster. These include funding logos and the wording »tylko w kinach studyjnych« (only in art-house cinemas). The »Pupendo« poster measures 680 x 980 mm (26.5 x 38.5 in) and was printed in cmyk on an uncoated paper. The print run was 1,000 copies. In addition to the posters, Homework designed other items of publicity material, including digitally printed banners measuring 1200 x 1800 mm (47.25 x 71 in), and flyers. ¬

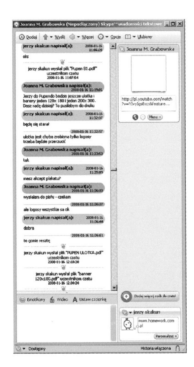

Joanna and Jerzy often use instant messaging (IM) or real-time text-based communication to liaise with their clients. The advantages over the telephone are that it's handsfree, a record of the »conversation« can easily be kept and it is a constant stream of communication that isn't distracting. Attachments can also be added to each message as necessary. Overall, it's as close to being in a remote office as is possible without having to use an expensive conferencing system. ¬

03/01 morning ¬ Take Joanna to the doctor. Medical examination is not looking good – antibiotics and week in bed. ¬ **afternoon** ¬ Book for museum sent to print. Snowing; I build snowman with Ewa on our terrace. ¬
04/01 morning ¬ Mail jpg of »Pupendo« project to client. ¬ **afternoon** ¬ They chose »general«, with no eyes. ¬

The »Pupendo« poster
on display in the foyer of
one of the cinemas in which
it was used. Its bright colours
and abstract forms contrast
perfectly with the plush and
richly coloured interior of the
Kinoteka. This opulent-looking
cinema is in the rather severe
Soviet-built Palace of Culture
and Science, Warsaw, shown
on page 050. ¬

Distribution ¬ The »Pupendo« poster
was used in 55 cinemas in 36 cities in Poland
for about a year. At any one time, at least ten
different poster designs by Homework are
in circulation. Joanna and Jerzy still feel thrilled
to see their work on display and have recently
discovered that there is a developing market
among collectors for their old posters. Jerzy
set up a blog on the Homework website, »a sort
of photographic diary as I make lots of photos«,
which over time has become more of a forum
for exchange about their graphic design. The
responses to Homework's projects are generally
favourable. By the »Pupendo« post someone
commented: »It has to be a good film!« ¬

05/01 morning ¬ We get text for »Pupendo« flyer, invitations and list of logos to include. ¬
afternoon ¬ Told that the »classic cinema« posters should be ready for next week, first three are for Chaplin movies. ¬
06/01 morning ¬ All the »Pupendo« materials sent to Vivarto, last changes made in the logo strip. ¬ **afternoon** ¬ Mail with text for »The Danton Case«
drama arrives; we have a month to do a poster. All the »Pupendo« materials sent to print. ¬ **evening** ¬ It's getting warmer, snowman melts. ¬

When we set about writing this book, one of our objectives was to include work about which we were truly curious. The design of a monthly magazine was one such project – how is it possible to maintain high standards of design, production and, of course, content in such a fast-turnaround environment? How much creativity is really involved when working within strict design, marketing and time constraints, and what kind of creative process takes place? ¬ »Wallpaper*« magazine was started in 1996 in London by Canadian journalist Tyler Brûlé, and even before it was a year old it had been hailed as a zeitgeist-defining publication and an influential trendsetter in global design and luxury modern living. The magazine celebrates fashion, architecture, art, travel, technology and all aspects of design. It is an unashamedly luxurious publication, proud of its position as a bible of contemporary style. ¬ In 1997 Brûlé sold »Wallpaper*« to Time Warner, the world's largest media organization. Tony Chambers, a former creative director of the magazine, was appointed editor-in-chief in 2007. In 2008 »Wallpaper*« moved from ten issues a year to twelve. ¬ Having joined »Wallpaper*« in 2003, Meirion Pritchard (born 1978) is its current art director. Alongside the editor-in-chief, he is responsible for ensuring the creative direction, design and production of every issue of »Wallpaper*«. So, we wondered, what is the creative process of this magazine, and how does an issue come into being? ¬

Clients may be unaware that in choosing a designer they are frequently also choosing a design philosophy. In the case of »Wallpaper*«, though, its readers are design-literate and know exactly what they are looking for. They want to be visually surprised and excited and they want to be made aware of current fashions and trends. They are likely to know the distinction between modernism and postmodernism and to have a broad understanding of where one design philosophy may feed into the next. So, what does »Wallpaper*« art director Meirion Pritchard make of all this? Does he nail his colours firmly to one design mast? What informs his approach and where does he go to be inspired? ¬

The glossies ¬ Meirion cut his editorial design teeth at Redwood Publishing and first showed his work to Tony Chambers, now »Wallpaper*« editor-in-chief, while Tony was at »GQ«. When they subsequently bumped into each other at a party, Tony suggested Meirion come and see him at »Wallpaper*«, where he had become creative director. After a number of »pretty informal« meetings, he offered Meirion a job as a designer and in 2007 Meirion was appointed art director. The great thing about »Wallpaper*«, he tells us, is that he gets to do graphic design; not only is the subject matter design-based but each issue also involves a range of graphic design skills and applications, including branding, events and working with the bespoke department which produces special features, advertising and events. From its content to its design and production, the magazine »is about details«, and in this regard he is only too aware that not all magazines are equal. ¬

Beautiful buildings ¬ Coming from a family of teachers, Meirion thought that art »would make a nice change«, and initially wanted to be an architect. Following a stint of work experience at an architectural practice in west Wales he admits to being put off by the length of training required and turned his attention to graphic design. Working at »Wallpaper*« he gets to indulge his love of architecture and has extended his knowledge and first-hand experience of some of the great contemporary buildings around the world. ¬

More than the big idea ¬ In 2001, Meirion graduated from Kingston University, where he studied graphic design. As a designer who loved coming up with the big idea, but who also valued the craft of typography, layout and the finer points of graphic design, he wanted a job that would utilize these skills as integral tools of communication. As art director at »Wallpaper*«, he is involved not only in overseeing all aspects of the magazine design, but also in developing concepts and branding for special projects, events and exhibitions. ¬

Valley boy ¬ As his name and still perceptible accent reveal, Meirion is Welsh. Although a distinctive name can be useful in this business, he rolls his eyes as he tells of the mail he receives addressed to »Ms« Pritchard. Born and brought up in Wales until he left for art college, he now lives – perhaps not unexpectedly – in Shoreditch, one of the more fashionable and design-centred areas of London. He cycles to work across the river, to the imposing new building where all IPC publications are based. It's a strangely corporate environment for such a trendsetting magazine and, as he points out, the best thing about being there is the view. From his desk he can look straight into the members' lounge of Tate Modern and past this to the dome of St Paul's Cathedral, the Barbican towers and the City beyond. ¬

Crouwel, Gerstner and Vasarély ¬ Meirion describes his early working relationship with Tony Chambers as a kind of semi-apprenticeship. This involved the handing on of the knowledge and rigorous design training that Tony had received while studying at the Central School of Art and Design (now Central St Martins) in London and working at »The Sunday Times Magazine« under Michael Rand. The modernist principles that characterize his approach to graphic design are evident in Meirion's love of typographic detail and his delight in the beauty of the grid. The influences he cites reflect this, from Victor Vasarely's colour explorations to Wim Crouwel's typography and the work of Karl Gerstner, a consummate exponent of the possibilities of the grid. Meirion reserves a special mention for former colleague Loran Stosskopf, from whom he learned about »giving it all«. He recalls his exacting eye for detail and working a 24-hour shift together to complete a centre spread for »Kilimanjaro« magazine. ¬

People, places and private views ¬ »We're notching up some pretty good artists«, says Meirion proudly of the stellar cast of contemporary artists, photographers and designers whom he has commissioned in the last year. An integral part of his role as art director is management and networking. He is constantly interacting with other people, including the movers and shakers of the worlds of art, design and fashion. When deadlines allow he enjoys the socializing his job involves, and the rounds of private views, launches and fairs to which he is invited. Having his finger on the pulse of what and who is happening means managing a hectic diary that frequently includes travel – during this issue he has visited Milan twice, and attended a photography and fashion fair in Hyères. ¬

Thursday football ¬ At one of our first meetings Meirion was rueful about having to miss playing football that night because of overrunning deadlines. Football looms large in the social networks of many male London-based designers and he has met clients, colleagues and competitors on the East End astroturf where he plays every week. He has found being a sportsman a good leveller. It helps him let off steam, but also provides an easy social language and context to cement working relationships – and even commission work. ¬ Meirion explains that playing football with Norwegian photographer Sølve Sundsbø made it easier to ask him to shoot the Norwegian Opera House piece for the issue featured here. ¬

Paddling furiously below ¬ The pace of work at »Wallpaper*« is, Meirion says, »relentless«, and, although he evidently thrives on the adrenalin, it is striking how steady and unflappable he appears to be. When asked about this, he gives a wry smile and quotes the old saying about a swan – that it glides gracefully above water while all the time its feet are paddling furiously below. When asked what keeps him going he says, »As long as I keep eating I keep calm – I'm OK.« ¬ Meirion also attributes his confidence to the strength of his design team; art editor Sarah Douglas, senior designer Lee Belcher and designer Dominic Bell. He reflects, »I'm lucky to have such a talented team.« ¬

The flatplan is a diagram showing each page as a numbered thumbnail. Pages are shown in pairs as spreads. It is used to work out and map the running order, content and essential structural and production information of the magazine. The editorial team meets on Monday mornings to discuss content and progress, where they add to and amend the flatplan accordingly. The flatplan is updated as advertising space is sold or changes to the editorial content occur – both can continue well into the design of an issue. The flatplan plays a crucial role as an easily understood overview that shows each component as part of a coherent whole. In conjunction with a miniboard on the wall of the office, it helps the design team check the flow of the issue and easily cross-reference with other departments. ¬

Advertising space is sold and priced in relation to its position in the magazine. Opening spreads and pages in the first third of the magazine come at a premium and right-hand pages cost more than those on the left. The flatplan shows the tally of sales for double page spreads (DPS), left-hand pages (LHP) and right-hand pages (RHP) and those still to be sold remain white. As new advertising comes in, the editorial team can commission new features and extend the page count for stories. The editorial team has some control over where advertisements fall, although there are constraints on this if the advertising space has been sold in a specific position in the magazine. Meirion is sensitive to the design clashes advertisements can cause. He works with the advertising department to identify any advertisements that are badly designed and has been known to redesign some that did not come up to scratch. He will find out which advertisements are facing editorial pages before he designs his pages. He has a good relationship with the advertising department and talks of »wrangling and dealing« about which advertisements go where. Although there are obvious restrictions, there is some flexibility because ultimately »we are all on the same team and want the issue to look as good as possible. It's about getting a balance.« ¬

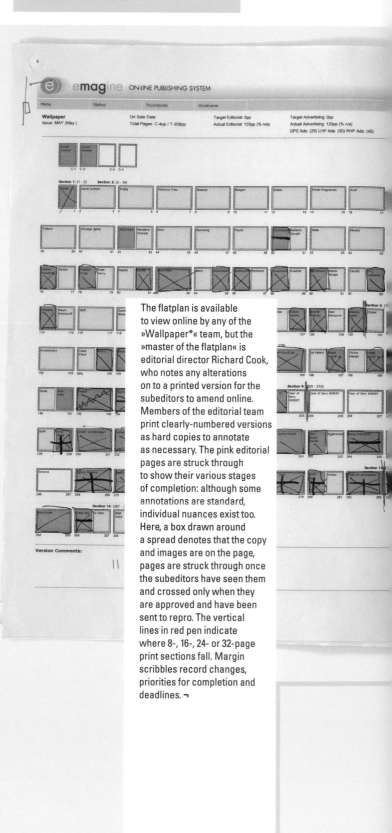

The flatplan is available to view online by any of the »Wallpaper*« team, but the »master of the flatplan« is editorial director Richard Cook, who notes any alterations on to a printed version for the subeditors to amend online. Members of the editorial team print clearly-numbered versions as hard copies to annotate as necessary. The pink editorial pages are struck through to show their various stages of completion: although some annotations are standard, individual nuances exist too. Here, a box drawn around a spread denotes that the copy and images are on the page, pages are struck through once the subeditors have seen them and crossed only when they are approved and have been sent to repro. The vertical lines in red pen indicate where 8-, 16-, 24- or 32-page print sections fall. Margin scribbles record changes, priorities for completion and deadlines. ¬

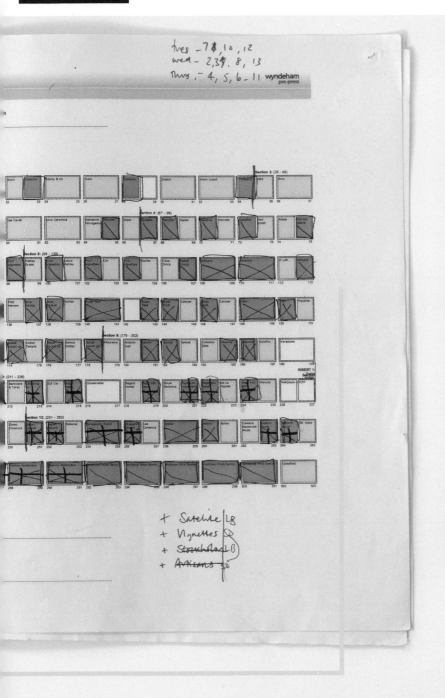

The flatplan ¬ »Wallpaper*« is unusual in not having a brief in the traditional sense. The key considerations that determine each issue include the audience, extent and theme and are explained in more detail here. The flatplan gives visual form to these constraints. ¬ **Audience** ¬ The »Wallpaper*« readership (circulation 113,000+ at the time of writing) is design-savvy and international. A recent survey of their 30,000 subscribers, who are supplemented by news-stand buyers each month, revealed that this demographic includes a high percentage of readers who work in the creative industries, are in their mid-thirties and have an annual income of over £60,000. ¬ **Extent** ¬ The page extent of each issue is directly affected by the amount of advertising space that has been sold – the flatplan opposite shows the page layouts and proportion of editorial articles to advertisements. Although roughly calculated at a ratio of 50 per cent editorial to 50 per cent advertising, this is fluid and can swing to as much as 70 per cent editorial to 30 per cent advertising. These pages are colour-coded on the flatplan in pink and yellow respectively, graphically illustrating Meirion's comment that »ultimately a magazine is a vessel for advertising«. There would, however, never be more advertising pages than editorial. ¬ **Theme** ¬ Each issue of »Wallpaper*« has a theme, which is planned in advance as part of an annual editorial calendar and starts with a storylist. This can include features from previous issues, reassigned according to their newsworthiness and appropriateness to the theme. Once stories are on the storylist, Meirion and his team start chasing contributors for content. Theme choices take into consideration how much advertising they might attract. The theme for this issue was Salone Internazionale del Mobile, the renowned annual Milan furniture fair: an attractive advertising opportunity that led to the late addition of an extra 40 pages. ¬

26/02 ¬ Meeting with Pierre Glandier, the stylist of the interiors section, together with Tony and Richard. He had a nice idea of doing a story for the Space issue about famous sayings – raining cats and dogs, head over heels, etc. ¬
27/02 ¬ Jaguar has invited someone to go and see the unveiling and to drive the new Jaguar in Monte Carlo, private jet there and all. Had to decline as too much on. Meeting with Amy Heffernan about clocks for In the Market feature in the Work issue. All systems go for this one. ¬

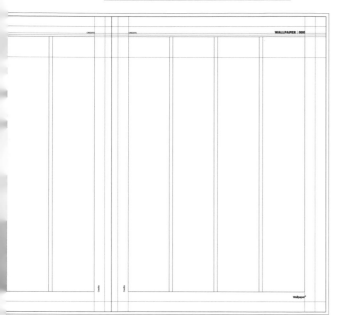
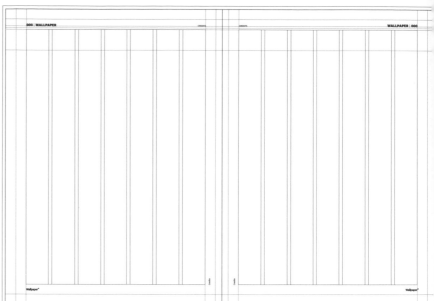

In 2007, Tony and Meirion worked together on designing new grids and typographic identity for »Wallpaper*«. Although never announced as a redesign, these changes reflect their joint ambition: »We'd always said we'd keep evolving things.« While not wanting to do anything that would unsettle the reader, his goal is constantly to improve their reading experience. ¬

»Wallpaper*« uses three grids: three-column, four-column and seven-column. Drawn in InDesign, these grids are measured both vertically and horizontally in points, with all internal dimensions working in multiples of 10pt. This measurement is the basic building block of the grid. The intercolumn spaces and baseline unit are each 10pt, for example, and all positions and shapes are divisions or multiples of this. ¬

The margin running around the page creates a white border that differentiates the editorial pages from the advertisements that run throughout the magazine. The binding process prevents the magazine from opening entirely flat and so it is vital to allow enough space around type and images so that nothing disappears into the gutter. If an image spans a double page spread it is necessary to split the picture and treat the spread as if it were two single pages with bleed, to compensate for what is lost in the gutter. The photographers commissioned by »Wallpaper*« are given the dimensions of where this split occurs and Meirion tells us that it is easy to spot those who have experience of working on magazines as they allow for this when composing their shot. ¬

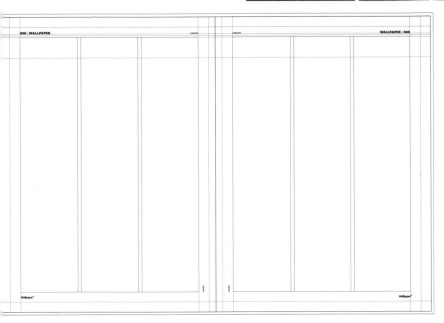

The grid ¬ Like most multi-page documents, »Wallpaper*« is designed using a grid. At its most basic a grid is a series of intersecting lines that divide the page vertically and horizontally. Its purpose is to provide a consistent modular framework to each page. This ensures a degree of visual continuity for the reader and, by helping the designer decide where to place things, simplifies the design process. The page is subdivided into margins, columns, intercolumn spaces and sometimes fields, the sizes of which are determined by the relationship between the size of type being used and the dimensions of the page. ¬ In a magazine, where easy reading is of paramount importance, column widths are chosen partly to achieve an optimum word count per line – conventionally considered to be between eight and ten words – and partly to utilize the space in an economically efficient and visually coherent way. The line length (or measure) affects the way in which we read. A narrow measure is generally associated with newspapers, where short texts are often read at speed. For longer, continuous texts a wider measure is easier on the eye, as demonstrated in the design of books or journals. ¬ »Wallpaper*« uses three grids which are used simultaneously, as if they sit on top of one another. This allows for various combinations of column and measure. The skill of the designer is to use these permutations to manipulate and organize content in a meaningful and aesthetically pleasing way. Meirion and his team are mindful of the need to balance consistency against variety and changes in visual pace. As he observes: »Grids need to be practical; we are ultimately striving for balance and purity.« ¬

The three-column and seven-column grids are used more frequently than the four-column grid, which tends to be used for stand-alone pages. The three-column grid has the widest columns, and is therefore most suitable for features written as continuous text. The seven-column grid has the narrowest columns, which are used mainly for picture captions. The three- and seven-column grids are often combined so that captions can be inserted into the columns of body text. The narrow columns of the seven-column grid are also sometimes combined to make wider columns for extended captions that sit within the images. ¬

Tony and Meirion worked their way through a range of permutations to arrive at these grids. Their trials included a grid that was subdivided into columns and fields based on squares, but Meirion acknowledges that it was too inflexible for a magazine: »You try to follow principles you think are important, but you have to start doing layouts to see if a grid will work.« Despite refinements and attempts to pin things down, he describes how the team use and respect the grid as a »mindset«. This becomes apparent when freelancers use the »Wallpaper*« grids in a different way to the regular design team. ¬

28/02 ¬ A couple of problems still with retouching on the Secret Spaces opener, Armani lounge, worked it out with repro. ¬
29/02 ¬ In Milan today at the Zegna Headquarters and showroom, designed by Antonio Citterio, where we are going to be doing our show during Salone Internazionale del Mobile. It will consist of an exhibition of all our limited-edition covers. HP is going to print them all, possibly on 2 x 3 m (78.5 x 118 in) pieces of Tyvek. ¬

The type ¬ Typography is an essential component of a magazine's visual identity. From eye-catching headlines, using bold and distinctive display fonts, to the subtle changes in tone denoted via the text typography, magazines utilize every kind of typographic detail and design. »Wallpaper*« is a high-end, intelligent and design-driven publication, and as such seeks to project a cool, modern and authoritative tone, a persona reflected in its typographic design. As Meirion points out, »We're not ›Chat‹ magazine«. Although a magazine's typography is instrumental in evoking the appropriate atmosphere, typographic decision-making is not determined by aesthetic considerations alone. In magazine and newspaper design, text has to be legible at small sizes and economic with space, so any text font is chosen as much for its fit as for the personality it gives the text. ¬ The last major redesign of »Wallpaper*« was in 2003 when the creative director Tony Chambers commissioned typographer Paul Barnes to design a new logo and introduce bespoke typefaces as part of a comprehensive overhaul. In 2007, following Tony's rise to editor-in-chief, he and Meirion took the opportunity to develop this typographic identity. As »Wallpaper*« contributing typographic editor, Paul acted as consultant on this and presented an initial selection of typefaces to Meirion and Tony. Meirion then worked with Christian Schwartz, another prominent typographer who had previously designed fonts for the magazine, to commission and introduce further custom-made typefaces. The development of fonts is a gradual process: »As you get used to a typeface you want to experiment with it more«. ¬

»Wallpaper*« uses two text fonts: a serif called Lexicon and a sans serif, Plakat Narrow. Lexicon, designed by Bram de Does for use in Dutch dictionaries, is highly economic with space. Its narrow character width means that more words fit to each line, while its large x-height relative to its body means it is legible at very small sizes. An elegant and restrained sans serif, Plakat Narrow is a development of Plakat, which Christian Schwartz designed for use with his own identity. Plakat has a rounder, friendly character, and is partly based upon Plak, a display font designed by Paul Renner in 1928. Tony commissioned the narrow version to achieve a thoroughly modern feel and a cool authority that sits happily alongside Lexicon and the headline fonts. Meirion explains that the challenge in finding the right fonts is, »To get a balance – we want the typography to complement the pictures and not overwhelm them«. ¬

Plakat Narrow Thin
Plakat Narrow Thin Italic

Plakat Narrow Regular
Plakat Narrow Regular Italic

Plakat Narrow Medium
Plakat Narrow Medium Italic

Plakat Narrow Semibold
Plakat Narrow Semibold Italic

Plakat Narrow Bold
Plakat Narrow Bold Italic

Plakat Narrow Black
Plakat Narrow Black Italic

Plakat Narrow Super
Plakat Narrow Super Italic

Lexicon No. 2 Roman A
Lexicon No. 2 Roman Italic A

Lexicon No. 2 Roman C
Lexicon No. 2 Roman Italic C

Lexicon No. 2 Roman E
Lexicon No. 2 Roman Italic E

Big Caslon Roman Regular

CASLON ANTIQUE SHADED
CASLON ANTIQUE REGULAR
CASLON ANTIQUE SHADOW

»Wallpaper*« employs two display fonts for headlines and drop caps. These are used consistently to signal different sections or types of information. Big Caslon, a recent revision of the eighteenth-century font Caslon by renowned type designer Matthew Carter, was introduced to the magazine in 2003. This specially-drawn italic version with swash capitals and extensive ligatures quickly became the magazine's signature font. More recently, Meirion was keen to refresh the magazine's typography by developing a new bespoke display face to work alongside Big Caslon. He looked at using a headline version of Lexicon, designed for use in newspapers, but felt this lacked elegance and instead commissioned a bespoke version. However, the new font »felt like body copy made bigger« and was never used. ¬

Having tried a range of other fonts, Meirion came back to Caslon: »For some reason only Caslon seemed to work«. This was especially true when applied to the Interiors section, where other fonts added too much character and »looked too Chinese, or too gothic, for example«. Paul started to research in the archive at St Bride's Library, London, and, having been inspired by various examples of wood type, developed a second display face for »Wallpaper*« called Caslon Antique Shaded. Meirion was surprised at how well this worked at small sizes and uses it for headlines on pages which appear in every issue, such as the contributors page, and for graphic openers. Meirion describes this font as similar to, but distinct from, Big Caslon. Continuing the magazine's established and recognizable identity made it »a good stepping-stone« he tells us. »It's Caslon, but it's different.« ¬

04/03 ¬ Hopefully Matthew Donaldson will be able to shoot this. ¬ Hoping to get Dan McPharlin to do the news-stand cover, something really graphic, themed around Milan, and the factory conveyor-belt machine idea. ¬ Satellite, which we are starting the issue with, doesn't look right at the moment so we are thinking of opening with either something graphic or perhaps a sort of archival shot from the past. Still will need some sort of twist. ¬

The cover ¬ »Wallpaper*« is fairly unusual within magazine design, particularly in relation to other glossy and lifestyle titles published by IPC. This is demonstrated by the approach to the cover, which does not adhere to many of the industry rules. This freedom is largely in response to its design-conscious readership, who are less inclined to be attracted to a cover that follows a conventional formula and are more drawn to solutions that are design-led and concept-driven. ¬ »Wallpaper*« is designed and printed in advance of the events it features. This means that an imaginative approach has to be taken to creating eye-catching and appropriate covers that will quickly communicate the theme of the issue. The cover is, in many ways, Meirion's most visible creative canvas and he enjoys using unusual print and production techniques, such as light-sensitive varnish or complex die cuts. He has a good relationship with his printer, with whom he explores and develops cover concepts that use these different processes. ¬ Finding the right cover artist or illustrator for each issue involves a process of research and discussion between Meirion, his design team and Tony, who is presented with a shortlist of possibles from which to make the final decision. Meirion works closely with the features editor on each cover – their challenge is to get the words and image working together effectively. The cover roughs are shown to other members of the team and variations are tested as the idea evolves. The final cover sign-off is often left until the last minute – the artwork for this issue was finalized the day before it went to print – which, although stressful, ensures that each cover is fresh and current. ¬

Meirion persuaded Dan McPharlin, who was already illustrating a gatefold calendar on the fairs of the world for this issue, to produce the cover image too. He proposed an idea based on 3D paper models of machines they had previously seen in Dan's portfolio, and asked him to make a machine that might produce the furniture, objects and art for the Salone fair. The brief for the cover stays very open and informs what Tony Chambers calls the magazine's only cover rule: keep it surprising. The results ensure the magazine stands out on the news-stand and gets seen. This is all the more important, Meirion points out, because newsagents can be confused about where to place »Wallpaper*« on their shelves as it spans interiors, graphics and fashion and could sit in any of these sections. Meirion was »chuffed« that the cover of this issue was picked by the British Society of Magazine Editors as one of the best covers of 2008. The selectors said of their decision that, »In the age of Photoshop it is rare to see something which genuinely stops you in your tracks.« ¬

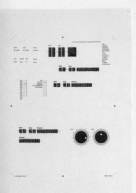

← Starting with the mock-up, using an image from Dan's website, shown top left, Meirion directed the development of a Salone machine. Dan was sent the magazine's bespoke font Plakat Narrow so that even the dials and interface were in keeping with the magazine's typography (top right). ¬

Dan is based in Adelaide, Australia, so communication was mostly via email and had to take the nine-hour time difference into account. Even with the wonders of technology, art directing from the other side of the world has complications. With only one week in which to produce the cover, Meirion's feedback and requests for amendments took on a new urgency. Tony decided that the model needed reshooting from a different angle (middle row) and Meirion art directed this during a Sunday phone call at 3am London time, sending Adelaide-based photographer Grant Hancock scrambling to take the final shots. ¬

← Changes were made, including the angle from which the photograph was taken and the positioning of headlines, shown in the middle row, before the cromalin was run out, shown bottom left. The late addition of new cover lines meant a last minute rejigging of the layout. Having to cut things so fine is a common occurrence and Meirion sees this as a productive part of the creative process. »Knowing that a bike is waiting outside to pick up your artwork can really speed up decision-making.« ¬

10/03 morning ¬ Ultimate Office for next issue, Ben Kempton will work with Lindsay Milne on this and Rick Guest will shoot. Provisional set-ups have been discussed. Twelve pages and a cover try. Nick Compton also writing some features of actual offices from around the world to tie in with it. ¬ Dan has agreed to do the news-stand cover, which is great news. ¬ Seventh image turned up for vignettes, and apparently it's important, credits wise, so need to rejig that layout. ¬

Some features focus on architecture, design or fashion in a more obvious way but these studio shots are more like vignettes – visual stories built around a set of juxtaposed new products and desirable items. The photographer Satoshi Minakawa worked closely with stylist Charlotte Lawton to ensure that the object choices reflected this vision. Stylists bring immense awareness of the field, coupled with a visual sensitivity and understanding of form, colour and composition. For a successful shoot both the photographer and stylist are equally important. Depending on which of them is leading, the stylist is either responsible for realizing the photographer's idea or the photographer needs to follow the stylist's directions to meet their brief. ¬

Bend the rules

At Wallpaper*, we're taking an alternative angle on seven spring/summer trends

PHOTOGRAPHY: SATOSHI MINAKAWA PROP STYLIST: CHARLOTTE LAWTON

Imbalancing act
Symmetry's for squares. We like to throw our kilter off every now and then Clockwise, from left, 'Spin Dry' umbrella, prototype, by Joie de Winter and Machiko Yanagi, for Oof Collective. 'Decale' glasses, £70, by Alain Villechange, from Mint. Wedges, £320, by Marni, from Selfridges. Jacket, £1,620, by Dior Homme. Shoes (and wooden shoe tree, left), price on request, by Doshi Levien Design Office, for John Lobb. Tank Crash watch, £17,250, by Cartier

Wallpaper*

Photography ¬ »Wallpaper*« includes a range of articles and features on a wide variety of topics. Writers, photographers and stylists can all pitch stories – the magazine commissions outside contributors of all kinds as well as using an in-house team. ¬ Photography plays a central role in the reputation and success of »Wallpaper*«. This includes using image-led features by named photographers. The commissioning process at »Wallpaper*« is unusual in not following a strict hierarchy or linear structure. Although the photography editor commissions most photography, Meirion does get involved, »if there's a problem«. He can also be instrumental in commissioning and art directing photoshoots, either on location or studio-based. ¬ the magazine's strength lies partly in the immense diversity of its content and the singularity of how it is displayed, so Meirion has to be aware of what other magazines are doing. He enjoys the creative challenge of trying to stay ahead of the pack. Being inventive in the way images are shot or styled is one way of doing this. ¬ **Laying out text with photographs** ¬ The design of each issue is, Meirion says, »really just loads of problems that need solving«. Once the copy and pictures for a story or spread are in, Meirion and his team will start to work on the layout and design of the page. As most stories are image-led, the design of a spread is usually a response to how the main image works on the page. Meirion is particular in ensuring his designers read all the copy they are handling, so that they are sensitive to its meaning as they design. The magazine adheres to a pre-defined grid and typographic house-style but Meirion enjoys the creative challenge of designing within these established rules. It helps that he worked on the last redesign of the magazine and that the grid and typography are partly of his own making. ¬

An image like this requires careful planning and management, as well as technical skill and artistic flair. The »Wallpaper*« fashion and interiors team worked together to build this set, which required ingenuity to hold the objects at the improbable angles. Some were held in place with sticky tape or adhesive putty while others were pinned or supported by props that were later removed by the photographer, using Photoshop. Getting the lighting right was pivotal too – the colour, tones and depth of the image were dependent upon this and expensive items could be easily cheapened by getting this wrong. ¬

← Although not always the case, these compositions were styled and photographed once the theme had been decided, but before copy lines had been written. A recent news item about the Pope's declaration of seven new deadly sins was suggested as a theme after the late addition of a seventh vignette. The features director was not convinced by trial layouts and felt the relationship between text and image was too obscure. He experimented with various song titles to see if he could find one that was relevant for each image – he and the editorial board then opted for this more straightforward approach. The title »Imbalancing act«, for example, is in direct response to the striking dynamics and diagonals of the composition. ¬

10/03 afternoon ¬ Gatefold needs to be finished. Marked up a few minor tweaks on the image side, text needs to go tomorrow. It's printing much earlier than the rest of the mag because it needs folding etc and then perforating. Need to check with the printers that all is well, especially with the folding. ¬

11/03 ¬ Dan has started the cover, looks promising. Will get Grant Hancock to photograph it again nicely. He is based in Adelaide, Australia. ¬

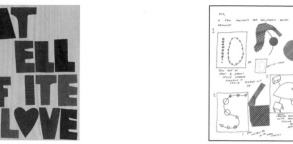

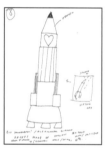

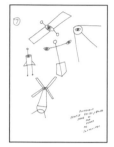

Because Meirion and Nigel have worked with one another before, Meirion's briefing can be very open. He usually starts by sending Nigel the copy to read; in this case he also sent picture references and some rough sketches. A quick exchange of ideas and roughs ensued before the direction Nigel was to follow was agreed. Meirion also sent him a template of the page and included a technical specification – the section always prints in full colour (cmyk) and the image has to incorporate a masthead at the top. The illustration has to fill an area of 182 x 231 mm (7 x 9 in) and is never full bleed. ¬

»Wallpaper*« includes a regular Newspaper section described as a »hot pick of the latest global goings-on«. Meirion commissioned an illustration for its opener, but was unhappy with the interpretation of his brief, feeling it was too typographic when placed against the following pages. At short notice he then turned to regular »Wallpaper*« illustrator Nigel Robinson. This particular Newspaper section was to celebrate ten years of SaloneSatellite, the fringe furniture fair that runs simultaneously with the main Salone fair. As the event had yet to take place, the illustration needed to represent Satellite in a conceptual or visually symbolic way. ¬

Nigel normally produces only a couple of roughs so this job was, he admits, a little unusual. He decided he didn't want to be too obvious and tried to avoid including a satellite in the image. Over the weekend Nigel explored how other types of space imagery, such as rockets, might work and emailed his roughs to Meirion to gauge how abstract his interpretation could be. Meirion felt that some of these had gone »off message« (top left) and was keen to steer Nigel back to his initial image-based ideas. ¬

Black and white sketches are effective in getting the essence of an idea across but sometimes more developed roughs – like this hand-cut colour rocket – are needed to convey accurately the feel and tone of the illustration. ¬

Commissioned imagery, including illustrations, is generally sent to »Wallpaper*« digitally. However, sending original artwork allows the design team to photograph or scan and match exact tones and textures, ensuring good quality reproduction of illustrations and »using everyone to their advantage«. Meirion explains that he will always get »someone good« to shoot artwork as he knows that this will ensure that details such as the depth and shadows of layered paper for example, are captured in the photograph. ¬

For the final image Nigel scanned patterned origami paper and Fablon, an adhesive-backed plastic that comes in various patterns including wood effect, and composed the image in Photoshop. By creating the artwork digitally, changes could be made more easily and quickly than with a hand-cut image. Nigel would normally create an original artwork for »Wallpaper*« to scan or photograph, but because of the tight deadline in this case he emailed his final Photoshop image to Meirion. ¬

Illustration ¬ One of Meirion's roles as art director is to commission work from illustrators as well as photographers. Because photography is used so extensively throughout the magazine, illustration acts as an important contrast. It is cheaper to commission an illustration than organize a photoshoot, but it is primarily used because it is a powerful medium in its own right. Illustration lends itself to abstract and lateral solutions – visual comment that can cleverly punctuate the text. When commissioning, Meirion must remain constantly aware of the overall layout of the issue and he will refer to the latest flatplan to help him see the issue in terms of pace, balance and variety. He commissions largely on instinct, which he says has become easier as »Wallpaper*« has become more sure of what it is. ¬ Meirion describes the commissioning process as a collaboration and is wary of having too much of a fixed idea or specific image in his head when he writes a brief. Most commissions start with a phone call to discuss availability, the idea and time frame and are then followed by emails and more precise specifications as appropriate. Collaboration with illustrators usually involves a dialogue, as roughs are sent back and forth and the idea gradually takes shape. If an illustration does not fulfil the brief or needs altering in response to changes in design or layout, he will recommission accordingly. ¬

11/03 ¬ Vignettes has now been redesigned with the newest images. We will keep one over for another issue. ¬
12/03 morning ¬ Dan sent me through some workings it's going nicely, but needs to go more quickly. Ideally we need to shoot the finished thing on Sunday so that we can send it to repro Monday. ¬ **afternoon** ¬ Dan said he thinks what we discussed sounded good. Using the dials etc to denote the fair, date and type (art, fashion, motoring, etc). ¬ Nick has sent me some cover lines. Need to get them on the page asap. ¬

Colour proofs ¬ For each editorial page of »Wallpaper*«, Meirion and his team scrutinize proofs and tweak and tune what might seem barely perceptible colour levels and imbalances. He tries to spread this task across the team. »Wallpaper*« takes an exacting approach to the reproduction of photographs and will always ask for prints from photographers to act as a guide for colour matching. Along with images that they have commissioned, Meirion and his team have to work with material from PR companies and product manufacturers. These can vary enormously in quality and often require pre-press attention. If the image supplied is not good enough, or one doesn't exist, Meirion will ask designer Dominic Bell to shoot these in-house. ¬ Images are sent to »Wallpaper*« as transparencies, prints or digital files. These are initially put on the page at low resolution and the design team run out in-house colour laser copies of rough page layouts, referred to at »Wallpaper*« as scatter proofs. Scatter proofs are required early in the design process to check the colour and print quality of photographs, and are then marked up with amendments by the editorial team. Once the design and layout are approved a cromalin is run out. Cromalins are colour-corrected proofs produced by the reprographic house and are more indicative of how the final print will look. They are recognizable by the colour bars running along their edge. Art editor Sarah Douglas and senior designer Lee Belcher work closely with the representative from the repro house to check accuracy and quality. ¬

Proofs are marked up by the art editor, chief subeditor and production editor and require a watchful eye as things such as titles – as is the case here – can go awry! ¬

Achieving the correct colour balance and calibration for every photograph is painstaking work, but is vital in a magazine that is so heavily image-led. Specially calibrated screens are used to do this accurately. Here the model houses are marked up as having too much yellow and the saturation levels need to be altered to give the image more punch. ¬

The colour bars on the edge of cromalins usually consist of blocks of cyan, magenta, yellow and black (cmyk), plus any spot colours (otherwise referred to as Pantones or specials) that are being used. These are a way of monitoring the colour as it builds progressively, and keeping the colours consistent across a large print run. Most of »Wallpaper*« is printed cmyk. Each of the four colours is printed by a separate printing plate. The inks are translucent so if one colour is printed on top of the other it will form a third colour. Once on press the colour bars are checked by machine-minders using a densitometer, which measures the density or strength of the ink. ¬

Atelier house

»Wallpaper*« prides itself on its photography and image quality. This attention to detail is demonstrated by this instruction – to retouch distracting variations in the tonal blend of a cloudy sky. ¬

Tight deadlines sometimes mean that pages are run out as cromalins while still awaiting copy lines. Changes, such as line breaks, are made right up to the last minute. ¬

Shed master

12/03 evening ¬ Have talked to Tom at Wyndeham regarding the stacking chairs in the last issue. We think it's as good as it could have been. ¬

13/03 ¬ Vignettes has now gone up to seven pages. Nick Compton doing something along the lines of the seven deadly sins. ¬

Repro ¬ Alongside designing, commissioning, art directing and co-ordinating his team, Meirion is also responsible for overseeing the reprographic process, alongside art editor Sarah Douglas, and ensuring that everything is ready and approved for sending to print. ¬ The reprographic process occurs after the page design has been approved, and involves optimizing the digital files so that they are print-ready. This work is necessary because how a page appears on screen – and even as a cromalin – is not how it will look when printed. The printing process, in particular the type of press and choice of paper stock, can affect print quality and appearance significantly. The role of the repro house is to work with both »Wallpaper*« and the printers to ensure that the appropriate compensations and technical specifications are met so that the files they pass on to the printers will deliver the desired output. Uncoated papers, for example, tend to darken colours while repro might also need to compensate for print phenomena such as dot gain. (All printed images are made up of tiny coloured dots that are too small for the naked eye to see – on some presses, and on some stocks, the dots get slightly larger in size as the ink spreads when it hits the paper. If left uncorrected by the repro house this would make the images look too dark.) ¬ The relationship with a repro house can take time to build – developing an understanding of the exact specifications of what the designer or art director want is crucial, and for this reason many graphic designers like to do the reprographic work themselves. However, for a project of the scale and scope of »Wallpaper*« this would be not only a technically difficult job but also extremely time-consuming. ¬

The proofing process at »Wallpaper*« is rigorous and reflects the importance of quality and high production values for the magazine. The repro house that they use handles seven other IPC titles. But, unusually for IPC, »Wallpaper*« still runs out cromalins – a high-quality proof used to check colour accuracy – of most pages of the magazine. These can go back and forth between the reprographic house and the editorial team a number of times until the editor-in-chief and his team are completely happy and the issue is signed off to print. Each feature or story has its own bag. ¬

These notes are made by the reprographic house and are a record of the changes that they need to make to the files, such as retouching, extending images and matching new proofs. Once the changes have been made the operator signs and dates the bag accordingly and a new cromalin is run out and sent back to »Wallpaper*« to check and mark up again if necessary. ¬

17/03 morning ¬ Newspaper opener still needs more work. Illustrator didn't send a rough, just the final image, which was nice but doesn't work in this context (too similar typography clashing over the page, needs to be more of an image). ¬ Got photos of cover shoot; almost perfect, hopefully they can reshoot tomorrow! ¬

Each issue of »Wallpaper*« is printed in 8-, 16-, 24- or 32-page sections (you can see these clearly identified on the flatplan on pages 068–069). These reels piled up in St Ives' factory are for use in web printing. A reel of paper can measure up to 1,500 mm (59 in) in diameter and weigh 3,500 kilos (7,700 lb). The choice of paper supplied in reels is much more limited than sheets of paper but the economies of scale make it the appropriate printing method for most magazines and newspapers. The inside of »Wallpaper*« is generally printed on 80gsm Star stock and the cover on 250gsm Gallery Art Silk stock. Most of the magazine is printed on a coated paper to heighten colour and maximize contrast. Uncoated papers can produce more subtle results but tend to absorb the ink, which darkens and flattens colour and reduces tonal contrast. The inside pages of this issue of the magazine used approximately 150 reels of paper, weighing a total of 180,000 kilos (396,000 lb). Printing the cover for a single issue of »Wallpaper*« uses on average 50,000 sheets of paper – roughly 7,200 kilos (15,840 lb) in weight. ¬

These large vats contain the inks used in the full colour process. The inside pages of this issue of »Wallpaper*« used approximately 6,000 kilos (13,200 lb) of ink. Most covers use between 80 and 130 kilos (286 lb) of ink. The printer has an in-house ink laboratory with full-time chemist. Regular checks of press chemistry are made to ensure that the inks dry at a temperature that will enhance the colour. ¬

In addition to cmyk, Meirion and his team generally use at least one spot colour or special on the cover of the magazine. Despite its name, full colour is a very limited process. By overprinting combinations of the four inks, secondary colours are made – but it's impossible to achieve many truly vibrant colours this way. A spot colour is pure colour and so if Meirion wants his masthead in an intense luminescent orange, for example, it has to be printed in orange ink straight out of the tin. The same applies to metallics and fluorescents, both of which are impossible even to simulate out of cmyk. ¬

Printing ¬ After the commissioning, design, proofing and reprographic processes are complete the files are sent to print. Meirion tries to send each of his designers to witness this spectacle at some point. He thinks the experience of »seeing it all happen« is important as it reminds the mostly screen-based designers of the alchemy of print on paper and the physicality and scale of the creative process they are involved in. ¬ Changes at this stage are limited, as stopping the printing-presses costs money. However, machine-minders are constantly checking that the colour is consistent and that running sheets are a good match to the signed-off cromalins and proofs. ¬ »Wallpaper*« is printed by offset lithography on both web and sheet-fed presses Web presses print on continuous reels of paper whereas sheet-fed presses print on single sheets passed through the press at speed. Web offset printing is more economical for high-volume print runs, so is used for magazines, newspapers and mass-market books. ¬ The main body of »Wallpaper*« is printed web by St Ives Web in Plymouth on a MAN Roland Lithoman press. The cover is printed sheet-fed by St Ives in Cornwall on a Komori single-sided five-unit press. Four of the units carry cyan, magenta, yellow and black ink. The fifth can carry a spot colour or varnish as needed. The printers have recently bought a Roland ten-unit perfecting press, an investment partly geared towards meeting IPC demands. This press will soon print the cover of »Wallpaper*«. It can either print both sides of a sheet in five colours in one pass (ie at a time), or up to ten colours on one side at the same time. The latter option opens up all sorts of print and finishing possibilities for Meirion and his team. ¬

17/03 afternoon ¬ Sent Retail Round-up for a scatter. Image quality seems ok, although lots of the images are from PR companies and aren't always all that great. ¬ Tidying up layout tonight so that subs can work on it asap. ¬ Still haven't had the Domus Design Centre images; they were meant to send low-res today. ¬ We have a pile of colour to do. ¬

19/03 morning ¬ Have had to cancel the illustration for Satellite. Have asked Nigel Robinson to do it; he'll do it brilliantly I think – should have asked him from the start really. ¬

At over 50 metres (164 ft) long, 3 metres (9.5 ft) wide and 10 metres (33 ft) high, these web printing-presses are large and impressive machines. They require constant monitoring and four machine-minders watch them all the time. One is responsible for registration and folding, two are responsible for control checking the colour and the other for the stacking of sections. Sections can be bound as soon as they are printed, but there tends to be a gap due to other work. There are two methods of web offset printing, known as heatset and coldset. »Wallpaper*« prints heatset. In the heatset process, the ink is dried rapidly by forced-air heating. In the coldset process, the ink dries more slowly by ordinary evaporation and absorption. The cover takes between 15–30 hours to print, so somewhere in the region of 2–3 seconds per cover. The main body takes roughly 55 hours to print, with the presses running 24 hours a day. ¬

When all the sections have been printed and the cover delivered, the magazine is perfect bound and trimmed on a Ferag binding and finishing machine, which can reach speeds of 30,000 copies per hour. Inserts can be added in-line without any reduction in speed. ¬

Printing processes and finishing ¬ At its most basic »Wallpaper*« prints in cmyk throughout and generally employs at least one spot colour in addition on the cover. However, Meirion and his team are always looking for opportunities to exploit more unusual printing processes and finishing methods to ensure that their magazine is unique. These range from kiss and die cuts, embossing and debossing to UV varnish, foil blocking and double hit colours. This issue included a bound-in gatefold insert and a separate promotional publication supplied with the magazine in a bellyband. ¬ **Binding** ¬ Once printed, the sheets are folded, bound and trimmed. The magazine's format and binding are fairly typical for such a publication. Its size (width 220 mm – 8.5 in, height 300 mm – 11.8 in) is determined as much by paper sizes as ergonomics and leaves very little waste from the sheet size. Most books, particularly hardbacks, are section-sewn at the spine so that they will withstand constant opening and still remain intact, but the shelf life of paperbacks and magazines is anticipated to be far shorter than a hardback book, and so most are perfect bound (the sections are collated together in the correct order and rough-cut at the back to help absorb the strong, flexible glue used to bind them. The cover is then glued in place before the magazine is trimmed to size). As a collectible magazine which readers tend to keep, the binding process must also make for easy stacking of back issues. ¬

19/03 afternoon ¬ Sent a sample of the folded Swiss poster to St Ives so that they can factor it into the binding and spine width. ¬ Sarah is going to go down to the printers to pass the issue. Starts printing next Friday. ¬
25/03 ¬ Lee has styled up Satellite, Nigel should be sending us over his illustration tomorrow morning.
I'll be on a shoot at the grocery for a bit, for next issue's Nice Basket. ¬

Design Diaries

The simplicity of the finished
cover and spreads belie the
many hours of scrutinizing and
adjusting design details and
reprographic work that have
gone into their production.
From planning, designing
and art directing through to
printing, binding and ultimately
distribution, the scale of the
creative process of each issue
is of an unusual magnitude.
As this issue hits the shelves,
Meirion and his team are well
underway on the next issue.
»It's relentless!« ¬

Circulation ¬ The magazine's 113,000+ readers span 93 countries with 30 per cent of these in the UK, 30 per cent in the rest of Europe, 30 per cent in the USA and 10 per cent in the rest of the world. ¬ **Distribution** ¬ Once »Wallpaper*« has been designed, printed and bound the final task is to get the copies of the magazine from the printer to the outlets around the world which sell it. »Wallpaper*«'s distributor in the UK is Marketforce, who are owned by IPC, and who also manage the international distribution of the magazine by overseas distributors. Distribution involves more than the physical carriage and delivery of the magazine. Distributors allocate supplies to wholesalers and overseas shipping agents, collate and compare data from retail groups and analyze current sales trends. Ensuring distribution plans and sales schedules are met is essential for the circulation of any magazine. In this highly competitive sector circulation relates directly to the amount and type of advertising – and therefore revenue – that a title attracts Monthly sales figures for UK consumer magazines are provided by the Audit Bureau of Circulation and are scrutinized by advertisers and media agencies to monitor sales trends and help in planning their marketing spend. ¬ **Local/ Global** ¬ It takes two weeks from printing »Wallpaper*« for it to reach the shops in the UK, with some holding time usually involved to ensure the magazine arrives on the second Thursday of each month, the set UK on-sale date. While the bulk of overseas deliveries are sent by sea – taking 28 days to reach the USA and seven weeks to reach Australia – a section of the supply is air freighted. These advance copies go on sale a couple of days after the UK on-sale date in the USA and roughly a week later in Australia. ¬

26/03 ¬ Got final imagery from Nigel. Although he went a bit off message, looks good now though. ¬
27/03 ¬ Loads of signing off and tweaking pages; Vignettes has finally gone, but is quite simple – we ran out of time basically. ¬

When design practice is discussed, all too often it is clothed in mystique, with only superlatives used to describe designers and their work. It may make the whole process sound less glamorous, but a dispassionate investigation reveals that compromise is often a prerequisite to success, even for designers who are flourishing. A little »give and take« between designer and client sounds like a fair trade, but client persuasion is a repetitive activity and it can leave practitioners jaded. ¬ As a champion of do-it-yourself graphics, designer Emmi Salonen (born 1977) has found that one way to avoid frustration is to balance commissioned work with personal projects. Like many designers, she dreamt of making her self-initiated work money-making too. She has done just that, managing to turn her badge-making cottage industry into a viable enterprise through hard graft coupled with an open-hearted and positive temperament. ¬ Milton Glaser (famed for the I heart NY logo, often seen on a badge, of course) once said that one of art's many functions is to remind us of what we have in common. Emmi has been politically active since she was a teenager and recognizes that badges are a way of making small connections with like-minded people. Although a T-shirt is a much bolder statement than a badge, Emmi delights in the potential for badge-wearers to play discreetly with identity, hopefully raise the odd smile and sometimes pose the odd question too. ¬ Impressed by her admirable and optimistic lightness of touch when it comes to politically-aware and ethical design practice, we followed Emmi as she developed her latest set of badges. How does she find the time to labour over badge making while running a successful studio, we wondered, and how has she mustered the necessary fearlessness to persuade retailers to sell her wares? ¬

A badge seems a very small item to design, but it is its scale as an object, allied to its limitless reach, that gives it such appeal. From a fellow commuter, whose nose almost touches a badge-pinned lapel, to a dinner party host who spies a badge as they hang a guest's coat up on arrival, the opportunities for the wearer to connect subtly with the rest of the world are many and varied. So, does Emmi's delight in this knowledge inform her overall approach to design? From what does she draw inspiration and what are her long-term career plans? ¬

Broadening minds ¬ The idea that there is some correlation between artistic genius and personal trauma is entrenched, but Emmi talks openly about her happy early years and how this experience has informed her approach to work. She left home at nineteen to study in the UK, subsequently working in Treviso, Italy and New York before moving to London and setting up her studio. Emmi is an optimistic citizen of the world who is confident taking risks: »It is because of my solid upbringing, I think. I feel there is a safety net that allows me to explore. I am willing to learn, to see new things and I'm not afraid of changing everything around me.« ¬

Give me the child till the age of seven ¬ Emmi is from Finland, where all children are taught how to use a sewing-machine and a lathe, regardless of gender. Her father built the family's wooden house and her mother »paints and does crafty things«. For her first seven years Emmi was an only child. Her parents encouraged her to make things, entering her often humble efforts into competitions: »I still have a newspaper cutting mentioning me as the youngest one to take part; I was three.« Since neither of Emmi's parents applied their artistic talents in their careers, it took a leap of imagination and faith for Emmi to decide that she could harness her creativity in earning her living. ¬

Making a difference ¬ Emmi describes growing up in Finland as politically informing: »When I was growing up there were no rich and poor kids, we were all the same. There were no private schools for example.« Security and stability didn't rob Emmi of political verve, however. Instead she had time and energy to ponder on the state of the rest of the world; allying herself with the left, going on anti-fur marches and on demonstrations to raise awareness of racial discrimination. She felt empowered: »One human being can change a lot.« She has remained aware of individual and collective responsibility ever since, but it was only later that she reflected on the leaflets, badges and other campaign materials she had seen. She is amused now to remember that at the time she gave little thought to how they were produced, or by whom. ¬

Start as you mean to go on ¬ Aware of her ignorance, aged nineteen, Emmi bought a book about the history of graphic design and enrolled on an art foundation course. Four years later, as her subsequent degree in graphic design drew to a close, she felt troubled that her career would always necessitate conveying other people's messages: »I realized I could make something more personal – and more ethical and political.« For one of her final degree projects Emmi made 60 badges, each carrying an icon pertinent to a contemporaneous news story. Each badge was packaged with its relevant press cutting: »I wanted to raise awareness and provoke debate among young people. The badges covered lots of issues – from foot-and-mouth disease to human trafficking and violence in schools.« ¬

Message in a bottle ¬ It takes courage to send work out into the world with little or no idea how it will be received, but designers know that success relies upon this strange amalgam of control and chance. Emmi sent her student badge project, along with her application to undertake practice-based study, to Benetton's communication research centre in Italy. She was accepted – largely because of her badges. Fabrica is a unique hybrid of educational body and commercial studio, where young designers from around the world explore new directions in their work: »The lesson I learned was that there is no real wrong and right way in design. Fabrica broke down my preconceptions from university. It felt liberating, but was mainly about self-expression and so I had to move on. I knew that I wanted to work for various causes.« ¬

Do-it-yourself ¬ Emmi says that she likes to be aware of current graphic-design practice but that it is the output, rather than the philosophy, of any particular designer that moves her. Her inspiration, in a pure and conceptual sense, comes from »the underground music scene«. The appeal for Emmi is that it's unpretentious; it is a form of creative endeavour that is divorced from the world of commerce and which engenders a sense of community in its followers: »The people who play are also the people who organize the gigs, make the T-shirts, the flyers – they make everything. They make things happen and are truly independent.« Emmi doesn't consider prevalence to be a mark of success, and would like to think that a stripped-down approach is possible in graphic design too. She argues that designers can make small things that »prompt a feeling of discovery, contentment and surprise and can provoke thought and open up new worlds« – and that this is surely enough. ¬

Being a designer ¬ Emmi set up her studio in London in 2005. Since then she has combined her more commercial work with various self-initiated projects and is happy continuing in this vein. As befits a designer with her political inclinations, Emmi's clients range from cultural bodies and arts publishers to charities and non-governmental organizations: »I hope that there's just a lot of goodness in it – I believe this is possible, which I suppose comes back to being positive and taking the initiative.« Emmi prides herself on running a professional, well-organized studio. She makes sure that she gives time to researching new materials and production techniques while keeping an eye on current design trends but says, »The real reason for getting up in the morning is the feeling of fulfilment if the end product serves the client and the target audience – that what you make is useful and at the same time surprising because it looks so lovely or is so nice.« ¬

Emmi acknowledges that the process of developing self-initiated projects and answering commercial briefs is different: »When I start on a badge I never think whether it will sell or not, I just focus on what intrigues me. With the commercial work, I think about the end result straight away. I consider what it's meant to communicate, and to whom.« ¬

Emmi's choice of notebook papers for each badge was fairly arbitrary, reflecting the peculiarity of people's choices of notebook: »People choose different types of ruled page for their different needs and sometimes they just want their usual notebook. It's as simple as that.« ¬

Emmi's collection of notebooks is lovingly stored away. They are from all over the world – South Africa, America, Canada, Russia. Whenever Emmi travels she checks out a local stationer, examining the paper types, rule weights and spacing to see what is missing from her collection: »Look at this one. I just love everything about it. This top bit looks a bit like wood and then they've done this bit in gold – lovely little details. The blue lines all back-up perfectly on both sides of the paper and then look at what happens when you tear the page out. These lovely half-circles are left from the perforation.« ¬

Self-expression ¬ Graphic design is, generally, a response to a problem posed by a fee-paying client for use by a predetermined audience. Designers channel their talents and passions in response to a brief and must embrace constraints and compromises as a determining part of the process. Emmi's badges may seem self-indulgent within this context, but she is quick to point out that this work »serves a specific purpose and still makes me money«. For Emmi, personal interests and graphic design are not mutually exclusive – instead, one feeds the other. ¬ **First design ideas** ¬ Emmi describes nostalgically her childhood delight in cutting out forms from newspapers and filling them in. An interest in low-tech interactive bits of print has informed her work ever since. She has an extensive collection of ruled notebooks and these were her inspiration for her most recent set of badges. From school rough books to jotters, these utilitarian objects fascinate her with their thin paper, pale colours and fine rules: »I make my business cards resemble notebooks so this has become my identity in a way. I thought it interesting to create a pin [badge] that doesn't talk about music or politics – that's almost empty and yet acts subliminally as self-promotion.« ¬ **The self-directed brief** ¬ Emmi's overall intention was to celebrate the loveliness of these everyday objects – her notebooks – in a series of badges. She established some basic parameters first – the badge size and how many types of badge she would design. A 2.5 cm (1 in) diameter is popular commercially as it's a fairly unobtrusive size, so Emmi decided to stick with this. Emmi needed several badges to display her collection adequately. She wanted to discourage false pairings, so considered an odd – rather than even-numbered set. Three badges wasn't enough, seven too many, so Emmi decided to go with five. ¬

Weeks 1/2 ¬ Initial badge idea starts to develop, I put some time aside to think of it when work allows. ¬ »Thinking Objects« book – get a go-ahead on the visuals. ¬ My friend Pekka visits for a couple of days, only time we have to see each other is at 8am in the morning. Rough! ¬ Met up with my monthly »advice session« – time set aside to see a student/recent graduate to help them with their portfolios – part of the studio ethics of donating time/skills to the community/charities. ¬ Making Christmas invite badges for the Finnish Institute. ¬ Went to see some gigs at Concrete and Glass that my friends designed a lovely leaflet for. ¬

mini badge note book

When compared with the eventual outcome, Emmi's first sketches show that she had a pretty clear idea of what she wanted to produce from the beginning. Not only the badges, but also the detail of the packaging, are all clearly identified in these three rough jottings. ¬

try different cover lines w/ correspon... badges

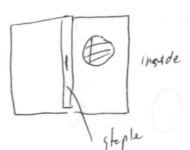

inside

staple

»This is the most simple notebook cover that you could have – there's just a couple of lines for you to fill in, printed in black on coloured paper stock.« It was this notebook cover that inspired Emmi's final packaging solution. Her badges are pinned inside a mini version of this cover, complete with a redundant mini staple on the spine that adds to its quirky charm. ¬

Working up ideas ¬ Ironically for someone so fascinated by ruled notebooks, Emmi makes all her design jottings in blank sketchbooks. She considers herself to be »a sketchbook person«, in that she carries one with her at all times; it is generally filled with notes and rough scribbles that act mainly as a form of aide-mémoire. Emmi moves quickly from sketches to testing out her ideas. In this case, ten sample badge designs were rejected before Emmi arrived at her final set of five. ¬ **Developing the packaging** ¬ Emmi named this current set of badges »take note« and started experimenting with various packaging solutions while concurrently designing the badges themselves. Emmi wants her badges to be cherished. Although some have been sold loose, she has come to realize that the way they are housed and presented is as important as the badge itself. Her best-selling badge carries the slogan »home is where the record player is«, and comes pinned to a pre-printed piece of card showing a record player, in a clear plastic bag. Her heart-shaped envelope badge comes in a tiny brown envelope, stamped »with love«. She understands that people may buy a badge and leave it unworn – if anything Emmi sees this as a mark of how complete and alluring the whole ensemble is. Emmi identified one type of notebook cover that could act as a starting point for the packaging of the »take note« badges, and developed a miniature version in five different colours. ¬

An old adage is that simple solutions are often the best. Emmi decided that covering her badges in various notebook papers was sufficient, but then had a crisis of confidence, thinking she should experiment with other ideas. She tried punching holes in the paper to reveal some of the silver badge mould behind: »It didn't look very good«, she comments. She then tried a variety of papers; some of the rejects are shown below. ¬

Week 3 ¬ Spent a few hours sketching and trying out materials for my badges. ¬ Designing a new identity for the Finnish Institute, with Klaus Haapaniemi ¬ Blanka took my Studio Brochure #2 on sale, great news. ¬ This month's »volunteer time« went towards designing Christmas cards for the Prince's Foundation for Children & the Arts. ¬

Weeks 4/5 ¬ Spent a full day testing things out for the badges. Ordered paper samples. ¬ A friend had a little bike accident outside the studio. Trucks are the cyclist's nightmare in London. ¬ Met up with Tate Britain about exhibition graphics for a William Blake exhibition. ¬

DIY ¬ The last few years have seen an increased interest in the relationship between craft and design. There is an authenticity in hand-rendered images that is missing from computer-generated depictions of our world. How much more delightful, for example, to see the cut paper in Dan McPharlin's cover image for »Wallpaper*« magazine featured on page 088 than a »perfect« rendering of his machine. Emmi's badge-making production line is nothing if not hands-on and »real«. She sits in front of the evening television, first cutting out round pieces of jotter paper, then wrapping them around the badge mould before adding the backs with their pins. All this is a precursor to folding the notebook cover packaging, pinning the badge inside and adding the single staple to the spine. ¬ Emmi sells on average 1,000 badges a year. Work experience students at the studio often get involved in the process: »It is such a big part of my studio that badges are made here.« The margins on production are tight – Emmi knows that she may have to succumb and have her badges made elsewhere as it makes little sense to turn away paid work that could end up subsidizing less financially fruitful projects. ¬ To date, Emmi has made 6,000 »home is where the record player is« badges, her best-selling design. She recently relented and had a new batch of 5,000 printed. These arrived die-cut as circles, with holes pre-cut in the card support where the badge would be pinned: »I think when I'm selling more than 100 badges a month, then it's time to rethink more generally. But for the time being I like the way that people can order just three or four, or ten, or twenty, and that I can make them on demand.« ¬

If not watching television as she works, Emmi's soundtrack to making badges includes: Israel Vibrations/»What's the Use«, Tiken Jah Fakoly/ »Justice«, The Gladiators/ »Rise and Shine«, Mikey Dread/ »Roots and Culture«, Pablo Gad/ »Hard Times« and U Roy/ »Natty Rebel/Soul Rebel«. ¬

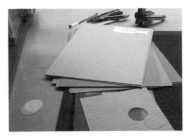

Emmi chose 285gsm Fedrigoni Woodstock as the stock for the display cards – a coloured, uncoated, recycled pulp board that is utilitarian in feel and reminiscent of school rough book covers. The mid-tone colours are insipid, but this is part of their charm. Emmi chose these colours from the range: Giallo, Rosa, Celeste, Verde and Noce. ¬

Emmi used a hand-held circle cutter to cut out the examples of each notebook paper that she wanted to test, trying out far more papers than she eventually used. The notebook paper was often pre-coloured and then printed with rules in a variety of colours and formations. The badges were eventually gloss laminated. ¬

The display cards were printed on one side only in black with three rules on the front and the series title and a web address on the back. Cut and fold guides were also printed to indicate the trimmed size and spine width so that Emmi could make them up more quickly. ¬

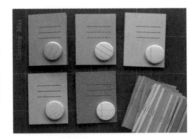

Emmi had to go to a local community centre to make her first badges until she could save up to get this badge-making machine: »It paid itself back quite quickly so that's good.« ¬

Emmi wanted to maximize the richness of her notebook collection. She tested twelve different types of badge against her five display cards, gradually eliminating them until she got down to her final set. ¬

Lastly Emmi adds the single staple in the spine: »It's totally useless«, she acknowledges, »but it's the detail that I wanted to reinforce the idea of a notebook«. ¬

Week 6 ¬ Finalized the badge design. ¬ There's a leak in the studio! Damn bricks. ¬ Had to pull out from doing a poster for a charity client (on volunteer basis). They didn't like my illustrations. ¬ Busy filling the Christmas badge orders. ¬ Attended a discussion about book design at Café Oto. ¬ Met up with usual friend at a usual café to talk about the usual frustrations. ¬

When Emmi was a child
a family friend gave her kilos
and kilos of old buttons to
play with. She set about sorting
them by colour and type into
containers from a local
sweetshop. Then one June she
set up a shop to sell the buttons
from her parents' garden. No
one visited, so she made signs
saying: »Emmi's buttons this
way«, with a directional arrow,
which she positioned at nearby
road junctions, but still nobody
came. Emmi recalls that her
grandmother Kiikka tried to
console her by buying some
buttons but Emmi didn't feel
any real disappointment
because she had so enjoyed
organizing the whole thing.
Perhaps this experience has
made her a more resilient
salesperson in later life. That
said, Emmi is delighted when
she sees someone wearing
one of her badges: »I saw
a guy on the bus the other
day wearing my pin and I just
looked at him so many times
that I think he thought I was
flirting with him!« ¬

Each one of the set of final
»take note« badges has
a different coloured card cover
with staple, and each type of
badge carries a different kind
of jotter. The cover board was
chosen to complement the
jotter paper. The papers were
chosen to maximize contrast –
from a green jotter with green
graph paper rules to a yellow
paper with two pink vertical
rules and blue horizontals. ¬

Being a sales rep ¬ For lots of designers, telling people what they design and why they should be commissioned is utterly daunting. With the advent of email and the web, the agony of cold-calling has all but disappeared – but there is still nothing as effective as word of mouth and eye-to-eye contact in establishing whether client and designer have a real rapport. Selling something to a retailer takes the art of persuasion to a different stratosphere altogether, particularly when the item being sold is the result of your own personal passion and ingenuity and crafted by your own hand. ¬ Emmi seems to have taken all this in her stride. She remembers with a smile that it took two years for one shop to come back to her and agree to take some badges, but now her badges are sold via ten different outlets – art and design bookshops, record shops and galleries in Finland and the UK. ¬ Whenever Emmi has a new type of badge to sell she starts by making about 50, which she sends out as samples to her stockists. She might follow this up with a visit or take the dummies in personally to secure an order. Upon receiving the tests, Present & Correct in London and Galleria B in Finland immediately agreed to stock Emmi's »take note« badges. ¬

Weeks 7/8 ¬ Spent a day making first sample sets of badges to send to stockists. ¬ Met a Finnish illustrator, Jesse Auersalo, who's moved to London. Had an interesting, unplanned, conversation about women in the design industry. ¬ Agreed to do a lecture at Nottingham Trent University early in the New Year. ¬ Met up with Lucie about her and Becky's book in a café. She left first and I offered to pay for her. But then bumped into an old employer, got distracted, and forgot to pay! Truly embarrassed, had to call Lucie from the studio to ask her to go back to pay! ¬

Making connections ¬ Since her first set of 60 in 2000, Emmi has designed 150 different types of badge. These have undoubtedly raised client awareness of Emmi, even if in subliminal ways. A few small illustration commissions can be traced back to her badge designs, as can an approach from Nike, who asked her to design an icon for a football shirt for them – a commission that she chose to turn down. ¬ Emmi explains that there are important benefits in showing potential clients self-directed projects. She always presents a mixture of personal and commissioned work: »The latter involves compromise and inevitably has some of the client's personality in it, so I do like to show who I am and the way I do that is to show self-initiated work.« Having some kind of personal project on the go is a creative lifeline for Emmi: »It's very important for me to have an outlet, to do something without any censoring. So definitely if somebody stole my badge-making machine today I would be very upset but then I would have to do things in another way. Maybe I could finally get through my endless to-do list of dreams!« ¬

Emmi made her first set of 60 badges when she was a student. She is still constantly thinking of new badge designs and related packaging ideas. All her badge designs, so far, are shown on this spread. Although describing it as »almost like a hobby«, she approaches badge-making professionally: »I like to do it and I want to do it, but I make sure that there's enough stock to cover orders so I never feel stressed by it.« ¬

Emmi's best-selling badge, »home is where the record player is«. ¬

As a direct result of her self-initiated work Emmi was asked to take part in the group exhibition »Helvetica 50«, which celebrated the font's birthday. All the participants were given a year to illustrate. Emmi's was 1990 and so she chose Nelson Mandela's release from prison as her theme. Her motif – a cloud combined with abstract bars metamorphosing into a symbol for the rainbow nation – was so successful that she ended up producing mugs and badges featuring the design. ¬

Emmi was approached by the Finnish Institute and asked to design an invitation to their Christmas party, accompanied by a special celebratory badge. She was delighted to be invited and find all the guests proudly sporting her design. ¬

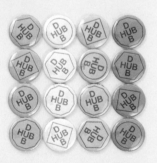

Week 9 onwards ¬ From here on I send the samples out when I send new orders of other badges. So it remains an ongoing project. ¬

The graphic design equivalent of trainspotters
they may be, but type designers are an exclusive
bunch. Necessarily rigorous, passionate and
highly knowledgeable about their subject, they
often engender a cult following within the design
community. Although the occupation is below
the public radar, the results are ubiquitous. Users
may not be aware of the components that give
a design its unique identity, but designers know
that in selecting a typeface they are setting
the tone for a whole project. ¬ This is nowhere
more obvious than in the area of bespoke font
design for public transport networks, where
the letterforms become redolent of a whole city
or even country. The UK-based company
Dalton Maag, with offices in Switzerland and
Brazil, was commissioned to develop the font
to be used on signs for wayfinding in Dubai's
Roads and Transport Authority's public transport
systems – a challenging assignment that
interested us all the more once we knew that
designers Bruno Maag (born 1962), Ron Carpenter
(born 1950), Marc Weymann (born 1978) and
Jérémie Hornus (born 1980) had to design
an Arabic typeface with a matching Latin. ¬
We assumed that the brief was to develop
a face that had a distinct character, but was
neutral enough to be simultaneously authoritative
and accessible. However, we were ignorant of
the process, particularly in designing two versions
for alphabets with utterly different roots. We
were intrigued and wanted to know more of this
mysterious but essential art. ¬

Designing fonts is exacting. It's the kind of multifarious activity that could drive a designer a little mad. How is it possible to consider simultaneously the minute details of each letterform and the effect of several characters in combination? Isn't trying to achieve optically-even letterspacing, for all possible letter combinations, enough to reduce the most consummate professional to tears? What strategies does the team at Dalton Maag employ to keep their love of typography alive, and how do they each evaluate their craft? ¬

Universal appeal ¬ Bruno and his team would be redundant had the more ardent modernists had their way. Many were advocates of the notion of the »universal« font – one that is so generic it is appropriate for all design jobs. Although examples include radical all-lower-case fonts, such as Herbert Bayer's 1925 design Universal, most designers looking for one font that they can work with repeatedly choose a »grot«: a sans serif that is slightly oval in shape and has several variants within one family. Bruno understands the theory but says, »I think there could be as many fonts as there are people on the planet. It's like ice cream; everyone wants their own flavour of vanilla. Think about the merits of Helvetica, Akzidenz Grotesque and Univers – most people couldn't tell the difference, but each has a slightly different texture.« ¬

Watch this space ¬ Bruno co-founded Dalton Maag in 1991. He is quick to divest us of any romantic illusions about his initial motivation for designing bespoke fonts. »I wanted to design fonts, but I needed to be paid straight away«, he admits, explaining that large type foundries operate entirely differently, selling usage rights in fonts from their libraries and designing new fonts or modifying the old as more of a sideline. Bruno hopes to shift the focus in Dalton Maag a little, so that alongside working on bespoke designs the team will design fonts in-house as self-initiated projects that can be sold online. ¬

Lost in translation ¬ The team at Dalton Maag acknowledge with some sadness that deadlines and budgets are constraining factors when designers select a font for a new project: »They get the brief today, tomorrow they have to show the first sketches, so they use what they know to have worked before, or what their mates have used, or Helvetica because of the movie!« That said, typography has its own language and a comprehensive knowledge of this terminology, including type classifications, helps in making informed choices. Bruno isn't convinced that graduates leave college with a comprehensive typographic vocabulary. »How do they know where to look and what to look for in a font, if they have hardly ever been shown?« ¬

Perfect isn't perfect ¬ Type designers strive to achieve versions of perfection that are impossible to enumerate. Contrary to expectation, it doesn't necessitate imposing rules that are derived purely from geometry or maths. Theirs is in part an intuitive process that requires enormous attention to detail and concentration: »We're compulsive obsessives«, admits Bruno. Font designers apply both a theoretical and emotional knowledge of how typefaces are used and responded to, as they consider each form singly and in combination with others. Bruno cites Adobe's Garamond as a font that is only successful in one area: »In my opinion every single letter is a piece of art, but you can't assume that this makes beautiful words or sentences. In text it's lifeless.« Ron agrees, explaining that what might give a font its authority is actually the imperfections, »being rough around the edges«. ¬

Reverting to type ¬ Sixteen years apart in age, Marc and Bruno »were the last typographers educated the Swiss way«, says Marc, a legacy that both embrace. Bruno reflects on the Bauhaus principle of »form follows function« that underpinned his education at Basel School of Design and still holds good for him today: »Aesthetics are only part of the process. You need to be able to rationalize your decisions, why a line of text stands here and not there.« He is proud to »have a job to do«, and is uncompromising in his belief that typography is as much a craft as an art: »You can have a good idea but if you can't execute it, it falls flat on its face. Craft skills are absolutely paramount if you want to achieve a creative goal.« ¬

The heavy weights ¬ Unsurprisingly, Bruno and Marc cite fellow Swiss Adrian Frutiger, responsible for the revered font Univers, as their type-design guru. Ron and Jérémie bring different, but no less nationally-derived, design sensibilities to the team. »It's the Romantics versus the Swiss!«, quips Ron, as he and Jérémie muse fondly on the joys of Hermann Zapf's serif font Palatino: »It's a marvellously sensitive coming together of type and calligraphy. The first time I saw it, I thought, ›I want to do that.‹ I still haven't.« Jérémie goes on to explain that his education at the Scriptorium in France emphasized an appreciation of lettering rather than typography. »Your work is organic, you can see the flow of the pen«, says Bruno, explaining Jérémie's approach. »Marc and I come from a hardcore typographic background; our work is harder, and Ron's is more humanistic.« Ron nods, referring to his formative years at the illustrious type foundry, Monotype. Monotype was responsible for developing and releasing the sans serif Gill Sans in 1928. A quintessentially English design, Ron cites seeing the original drawings as a decisive moment in his appreciation of organic, humanistic sans serif forms. ¬

Mutual respect ¬ Dalton Maag's clients are often graphic designers with whom they have established long-standing relationships. The London-based design group North, for example, has commissioned Dalton Maag repeatedly since 1998 and Bruno now commissions them to design some of Dalton Maag's publicity. »It's interesting for us«, says Ron. »Ours is such detailed work and we get a bit cocooned, we don't see the bigger picture. So it's quite useful to see how things fit together and to work with designers who are constantly in a highly creative mode. They work on a different level. They think on a different level. That's quite useful for us to tap into.« Bruno agrees: »With North, it's evolved into a good relationship. We respect them and we learn from one another. Quite often our first reaction is ›Ooh, no you can't do that!‹, but then they push us and that can be stimulating.« ¬

Designers as clients ¬ Dalton Maag specialize in designing bespoke fonts. Their designs range from the exceedingly noticeable to the less perceptible, but highly purposeful. All are unique to a company, a brand or an information system. Their immediate clients tend to be design companies, who understand the value of an exclusive font in making the voice of their clients visible and distinct. Dalton Maag has developed ongoing relationships with many of these clients and is often also commissioned to turn their logo concepts into finely-crafted marques. Their work can be seen every time you go to the Ministry of Sound in London, book a holiday through Thomson or go into an Ulster Bank in Dublin. ¬ Bruno and his team arrive at a full brief by posing various incisive questions. These range from asking whether the font will be used primarily for text, at large display sizes, or both, to how it will be reproduced and via what system. Bruno explains that they are often brought to projects after the designers' client has approved the initial design concept: »The parameters will have been established. The designers will use an off-the-shelf font to demonstrate the intended typographical direction and then we will be briefed to design a typeface that encapsulates this look and feel, while considering the nuances that will make it unique.« ¬ **Copyright and fees** ¬ Unless specifically requested by the client, Dalton Maag retain the intellectual property rights of their designs. The fonts are licensed to the client for exclusive use for a predetermined number of years and number of users. The design and production of a four-style font family consisting of Regular, Italic, Bold and Bold Italic takes about three months. The fees are calculated on the estimated time it takes to create the fonts but Bruno also budgets for potential user support after the fonts are delivered. »If we're working for a global corporation there may be half a million users. Having this information helps us gauge the extent of any future support they might need.« ¬

A glyph is the graphic representation of a character. For example, the letter »A« can have different variants – glyphs – such as lower-case, small cap, swash and more. The graphic representation changes but the character does not. Each character is assigned a standardized code (Unicode) that is recognized by operating systems and programs. If the key »A« is pressed, the character code for »A« is activated, calling the glyph occupying this code to be displayed on the screen or printed. The latest font specifications allow for 65,535 characters to be encoded, covering most script systems currently in use in the world. ¬

Every new font that Bruno and his team design includes all the letters and marks of the universally agreed character set called Latin A Extended. This includes upper- and lower-case letters, numerals and all punctuation, plus all the accents and accented characters for Eastern and Western European languages. The characters shown here in black are the basic Latin A Extended character set, those in grey are added by Dalton Maag to form their standard character set. Dalton Maag's »typographic character set«, designed for more professional use, also includes the characters shown here in blue. »We've extended our standard set to include superior and inferior numerals, fractions and the extended f ligatures.« Small capitals and non-ranging figures would be additional to this standard set. Bruno explains that it is important to know if either is required before starting their process: »It affects the way you design and how you compose the character sets.« ¬

ABCDEFGHIJKLMNOPQRSTUVWXYZÆŒ&

abcdefghijklmnopqrstuvwxyzæœøfiflffffiffflß

$¢ƒ£¥€0123456789%‰0123456789 0123456789 0123456789

½ ⅓ ⅔ ¼ ¾ ⅕ ⅖ ⅗ ⅘ ⅙ ⅚ ⅐ 2/7 3/7 4/7 5/7 6/7 ⅛ ⅜ ⅝ ⅞ ⅑ 2/9 4/9 5/9 7/9 8/9

{[(_)]}*,.:;-/|¦\□!@^~†‡§•·¶®©™ªº¿¡«»‹›…—"""',„#"'°ℓ℮

¬+<=>≠≤≥±÷−×/∞∑√◊∏π∫∂∆≈µΩ

ÁÀÂÄÃÅĀĄĂÇĆČĈĊĐĎÉÈÊËĒĚĖĘĔĜĠĢĞĦĤÍÌÎÏĨĪ

ĬĮĪĴĶĻĿĹŁĽÑŃŇŅŊÓÒÔÖÕŌŐØŎŔŘŖŠŚŞŜŤŢŦ

ÚÙÛÜŪŲŮŰŬŨŴẂẄẀŸÝŶỲŹŽŻÞĲ

áàâäãåāąăçćčĉċďđðéèêëēěėęĕĝġģğħĥíìîïıĩīįĭĵķĺļŀłľŋñńňņŉó

òôöõōőøŏŕřŗšśşŝťţŧúùûüūųůűŭũŵẃẅẁÿýŷỳźžżþſĸĳ

ABCDEFGHIJKLMNOPQRSTUVWXYZÆŒØFIFLFFFFIFFLSS

{[()]}&!?*@ªº''""$¢ƒ£¥€0123456789%‰123456789

ÁÀÂÄÃÅĀĄĂÇĆČĈĊĎĐÉÈÊËĒĚĖĘĔĜĠĢĞĦĤÍÌÎÏĬĨĪĮĬĴĶĻĿĹŁĽ

ŊÑŃŇŅŉÓÒÔÖÕŌŐØŎŔŘŖŠŚŞŜŤŢŦ

ÚÙÛÜŪŲŮŰŬŨŴẂẄẀŸÝŶỲŹŽŻÞKIJ ` ´ ¨ ^ ¯ ˜ ˘ ˙ ˚ ¸ ˝ ˛ ˇ

Lining figures are numerals that sit on the baseline and have a similar height as the upper-case letters, like those shown in black and grey here. They are normally designed always to occupy the same width so that they form neat columns for tabular work. This means that a number 1, for example, will have more space around it than a number 9. Non-lining figures, or old style or non-ranging figures, are designed rather more like lower-case letters. Examples in blue are pointed out below. Some have descenders that fall below the baseline, others have ascenders that sit proud of the x-height. Examples of use include postcodes and continuous text. Non-lining figures are normally proportionally spaced for use in text. Most fonts contain lining figures, with non-lining available as part of what is called the Expert Character Set, or OpenType feature. Non-lining figures are not available for all fonts. Designers often kern lining figures in text to make the letterspacing visually even. ¬

Small capitals, generally referred to as small caps, are versions of the upper-case letters of a font redrawn to have a similar appearing height as the x-height of the lower-case characters. The proportions and weight of small caps are adjusted so that they sit alongside the lower-case – using a smaller type size is not a substitute as the overall weight of the letterform is scaled and therefore looks too thin against the other characters. Examples of common usage are postcodes and acronyms that represent qualifications after someone's name. In both cases the standard upper-case can be obtrusive. ¬

Superior and inferior figures are normally used for referencing, indexing or mathematical purposes. The top of superior figures sits slightly above the cap height of the upper-case letters, while inferior figures sit below the baseline. Some fonts also contain superior lower-case characters, again mostly used in mathematics. ¬

Ligatures replace two characters that overlap or sit uncomfortably next to each other. A ligature is a single glyph that is not normally accessible directly via the keyboard but is automatically substituted by the program. The most common are fi and fl. ¬

12/11/07 ¬ Great excitement in the studio. We just sent off some Latin design concepts to the client and are now starting to think about Arabic. ¬

As part of their briefing TDC had been given signage specifications from architects Aedas with designers Atelier Pacific, so the size and positioning of the panels was largely established and agreed with their client, Dubai's Roads and Transport Authority (RTA), when Dalton Maag became involved. Although used to divorcing themselves from how their fonts will ultimately be used, Bruno's team did feel constrained by some of these predetermined factors. Jérémie explains that the team drew some inspiration from the architects' plans and drawings of the proposed Metro stations: »They looked very futuristic«.

Being economic with space is always a consideration when designing a font for signage. In this case the panels were designed to be expandable in 300mm (11.8 in) width units should an extra long description require it, but nevertheless Bruno's team were briefed to consider fitting all lettering comfortably into as short a space as possible. Bruno explains that this is why typefaces developed for these purposes often have a fairly narrow fit. ¬

Early on in their process Bruno's team were told that the signs would be backlit: »This was crucial information. We had to consider the halo that this bright white lettering would have as it makes the characters look stronger than they actually are.« Along with making sure that their font was as accessible as possible, the team at Dalton Maag had to bear in mind that lettering at large sizes behaves quite differently to small type. The spaces between and inside the letters appear to be disproportionately bigger, which generally needs to be compensated for. However, in this case these considerations had to be weighed against the resultant luminosity because of the way the signs were being made: »We always come back to functionality.« ¬

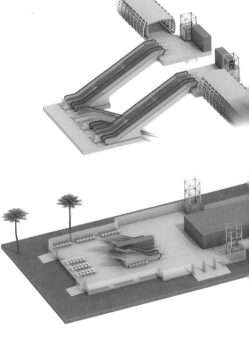

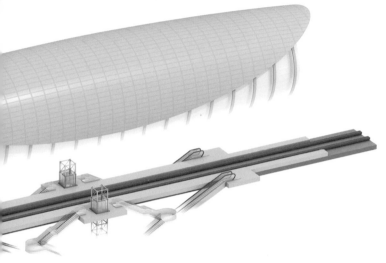

Wayfinding ¬ It is generally agreed that, alongside spatial planning, consistently used sensory prompts are the best way to help people orientate themselves in public spaces. Alongside signage these might include announcements or strategically positioned tactile surfaces. Analysis of the user experience of navigating spaces, combined with the development of various architectural and graphic design devices to make this effective, are within the realm of »wayfinding«. There are experts in this field, and graphic designers who work regularly alongside them, but the Dubai project did not arrive at Dalton Maag's door via this route. Instead, they were approached by Transport Design Consultancy (TDC), a UK-based agency that specializes in design consultancy for the transport industry and had developed the brand strategy for this new transport network. ¬ **Transport Dubai** ¬ The Dubai Metro system, in the United Arab Emirates city of Dubai, has been under construction since 2006. Bruno and his team were delighted by the challenge of designing sister Latin and Arabic fonts for its signs, but describe their initial brief as »fairly restricted«. TDC presented Dalton Maag with their approved concepts for the interiors of the Dubai Metro network. They envisioned that the whole network would be given its visual identity via a bespoke font and comprehensive signage system. Their first proposal for the signage used off-the-shelf Arabic and Latin fonts that Bruno explained were unsuitable for the task and had no visual relationship. He was also concerned that these fonts would be inappropriate for other possible applications in the future, such as maps and road signs. However, the Dalton Maag team concentrated on the brief at hand with the clear stipulation that the fonts had to be reconsidered for other usages. ¬

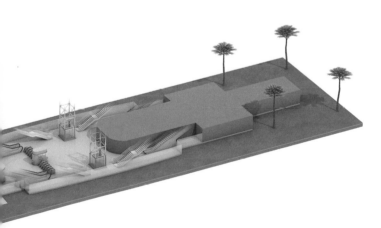

28/11/07 ¬ Sent off some Arabic trials following the design concept decision. We need to start again as our trials are rubbish. ¬

Burj Dubai Station

Burj Dubai Station

Burj Dubai Station

Burj Dubai Station

Burj Dubai Station

Burj Dubai Station

Burj Dubai Station

Burj Dubai Station

Burj Dubai Station

The team initially presented these nine Latin options to TDC. →
All were slightly narrow in fit and all were heavier than the average roman. Most were sans serif, although some introduced slab serifs. Research has shown that the irregular shape of words in upper- and lower-case makes them easier to read, particularly from a distance. These options all had relatively large x-heights in relation to ascenders and descenders. This was to compensate for any loss of legibility because of the overall narrowness of the font. ¬

Starting points ¬ Dalton Maag applies a standard method to developing a new font: »Sometimes the client first wants to see a specific word set in the new font, but to do this we have to start with an ›o‹ and an ›i‹ at least – a round shape and a stem give us the basics«, explains Jérémie. Ron says that he would generally pick up to 12 characters to experiment with first. These are not chosen randomly. Collectively, the set displays all the main variables. A lower-case »g«, for example, not only acts as a model for an »o« but also has a descender, while a lower-case »h« is the basis for a letter »n« and has an ascender too. »After looking at a few letters you start to get a look and a feel«, adds Bruno. Most of the team work straight away on the computer, albeit roughly. Marc occasionally uses his sketchbook too, although this is rare. Depending on the project, and everyone's availability, Bruno might draw on the whole company to present initial ideas: »On the Toyota project, pretty much everyone contributed sketches, so we ended up with something like 27 different design ideas!« ¬ Given that none of the team had any experience of Arabic, they decided to experiment with the Latin version of Transport Dubai first and identified three key words as their starting point: »Noho« and »Burj Dubai«. It took an intense week to be ready for the first presentation: »We could have spent months to get to this stage«, says Marc. Bruno chips in, »which makes personal projects a real bummer, because we have an endless amount of time and no restrictions so we're faffing about forever!« »Yes, sometimes the restriction of time does make the brain tick over a bit better«, acknowledges Ron. ¬

Marc says that the nine options comprised of four approaches, each developed and refined in subtly different ways. As experienced professionals, the team knew that the option selected would change enormously once fully developed. They are pragmatic about this process: »All of these needed many changes to become successful.« ¬

The proportions of these options are similar, but even a cursory glance reveals a number of differences between them. Take a look at the arm of the lower-case »t« or the terminals of the lower-case »j«, for example, or the ear of the lower-case »r«. The versions with the least variance look contemporary, those with curving terminals are flamboyant but also more conservative in feel. ¬

11/12/07 ¬ Working with Rayan Abdullah pays off. Arabic nailed down and we're making great progress with both script systems. Basic glyph sets are to be drawn up now for evaluation by client. ¬

Presentations ¬ For all the talk of the joys of working remotely, designers generally like to present their work to clients face-to-face. The odd wistful glance, or overly firm handshake, can reveal as much about the response to a design proposal as any lengthy discussion. Dalton Maag's designer clients generally handle the client presentations, so Bruno can't observe these subtle exchanges at first hand. He has to rely upon his immediate client to act as intermediary but does all he can to avoid falling prey to misinformation. »This is why the initial briefing stage is so important – to gauge from the commissioning designer how much everyone understands about typography and to ensure that they ask the right questions of their client.« ¬ **The second stage** ¬ TDC presented Dalton Maag's nine roughs to their client and one direction was selected for development. Bruno explains that this second stage is generally still conceptual and so it is important that their designer client doesn't commit Dalton Maag to working in only one direction: »The way you treat a stem terminal, for example, can have a major effect on the overall texture of the type. At this stage we experiment more fully with these kinds of details. So, it's still development work but within a fairly tight framework.« It was at this point that Bruno's team started to consider the Arabic cut of the font. Ron explains that until the general approach to the Latin was agreed it was impossible to consider the Arabic. Redolent of the font Frutiger, the Latin version of Transport Dubai is based on an oval, rather than a circle, but is still very open in feel: »We were all in agreement that a sans serif was most suitable, and one that was humanistic in feel. For signage purposes it makes sense to design something that is friendly and approachable.« ¬

DubaiMetro1c

Burj Dubai Station Union Square Trains to Rashidiya to Nakheel Station

bdhkltijumnprat

Only ascender charmses are with a rounded stroke. Also a trial with different dot shape.

2007-11-26 DubaiMetro1c

Even when x-height to ascender/descender ratios, line weights and the characteristics of each stroke are agreed there is a variety of subtle adjustments that can significantly alter the overall feel of a font, as these three versions of the second stage of Transport Dubai demonstrate. ¬

This version has rounded stem terminals on some characters, the second in the row shows a diamond-shaped dot on the lower-case »i« and »j« (an admiring nod towards Edward Johnston's famous 1916 font for London Transport) while the third has rounded stems on all strokes. These adjustments are surprisingly perceptible, making each font distinctly different in character. The unusually-shaped terminals also help make the font more accessible. Ron explains: »The overall word shapes and the relationship between x-height and ascenders are very significant in aiding legibility from a distance. As you draw closer you see the details. These are also important as they make the font identifiable.« ¬

DubaiMetro1d

Burj Dubai Station
Union Square
Trains to Rashidiya
to Nakheel Station

bdhkltijumnpr

A trial with all the strokes rounded. It
might changes the font now to much and
looks a bit quirky for a signage font.

2007-11-08 DubaiMetro1d

DubaiMetro1a

Burj Dubai Station
Union Square
Trains to Rashidiya
to Nakheel Station

bdhkltijumnprat

Font as in the original version.
Ascender letters as well as t l j have a
cut stroke which is in contrast to m n p r
and also endings like in a or t for example. In t or j are mixtures of both, the cut
at the top and the almost rectangle end-
ing of the letter.

2007-11-08 DubaiMetro1a

DubaiMetro1b

Burj Dubai Station
Union Square
Trains to Rashidiya
to Nakheel Station

bdhkltijumnprat

Similar to the DubaiMetro1a font but with
a change in the cut, which is rounded off
and fits very well to dynamic shapes like
in b, d etc.

2007-11-08 DubaiMetro1b

31/01/08 ¬ Latin more or less finished and sent for design approval. We expect only some minor comments.
Arabic with basic character set supplied for comments. Also sent to Rayan Abdullah and Fiona Ross for critique. ¬

Latin and Arabic forms ¬ The Latin alphabet started to be standardized in the mid-fifteenth century when the German printer Johannes Gutenberg cast the first characters as movable metal type. Prior to this all texts were produced as manuscripts, laboriously handwritten with all the quirks and idiosyncrasies that you would expect from copies penned by individual scribes. With print came mass production and the rationalization and simplification of typographic forms. The history of Arabic letterforms is entirely different. The Quran prohibits figurative imagery and so lettering is recognized as abstract and ornamental decoration as well as a means of conveying information. Calligraphy is a revered component of Islamic culture and so the printed Arabic alphabet is still deeply rooted in the handwritten form. To design one font for both the Latin and Arabic alphabets, with visually sympathetic characters, is therefore a difficult task. ¬ **Starting the Arabic version** ¬ Once the approach to the Latin font was agreed the team at Dalton Maag turned their attention to the Arabic version, with the intention of developing them in tandem. Initially they experimented with a variety of Arabic scripts, unsure of what constituted a text or a display font in Arabic. Ron explains: »They're two distinct styles. It's almost like comparing a handwritten script in Latin with Helvetica. They're quite different in structure. One of the mistakes we initially made was not appreciating this. We analyzed our Latin alphabet and assumed that we needed to produce an Arabic version with a similar overall texture for the two to be consistent. These sorts of misunderstandings are a real problem dealing with foreign scripts – even with Greek or Cyrillic there are national differences in the way that the letterforms are perceived. It's our job to understand these parameters and work within them.« ¬

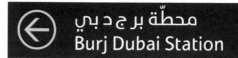

The team started by experimenting with the translation of »Burj Dubai Station« in Arabic. Even to non-Arabic readers it's clear from these tests that they were struggling to understand the structure. Although the process was conceptually interesting, Bruno soon realized that they were working in the dark, unable to develop a cohesive set of characters because they couldn't arrive at a set of rules to underpin them. Bruno decided to approach typographer and designer Rayan Abdullah to ask if he would act as consultant. Rayan was born in Iraq, but studied design in Germany and is currently Professor of Typography at the Hochschule für Grafik und Buchkunst Leipzig. He is fluent in Arabic and German, with good English which, coupled with his expertise in typography, made him the perfect advisor for the design team. ¬

Rayan agreed to act as consultant to Dalton Maag but was unimpressed by their first attempts. Ron explains: »He spent a couple of days here and gave us a presentation on the development of Arabic type. Then we saw that we were going in the wrong direction. We understood that we needed to use a Kufi script as a starting point and not a script used for Arabic text. It's arrogant to assume that we can create fonts in different scripts without a more thorough understanding.« ¬

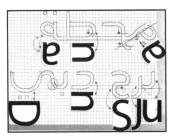

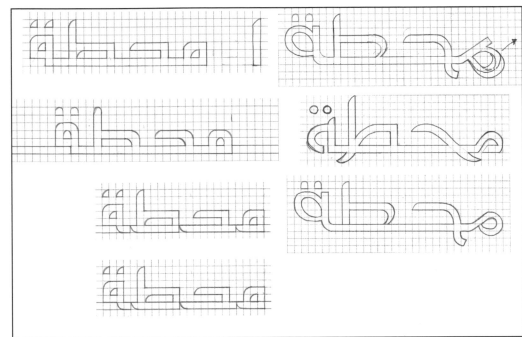

Here, Rayan takes some Latin forms and explores which elements could be appropriated in the Arabic version of the font. The shape and scale of the dots and the curves on the terminals are obviously transferable, but by turning the forms on their sides or upside down he identifies other parallels that the team went on to explore. ¬

In these drawings Rayan demonstrates that the Kufi script is more angular and square in construction than the equivalents used for Arabic text. It has specific proportional measurements – its verticals are low but it is extended horizontally. This means that the forms are wider than they are high, which gives it a directional momentum suitable for signage. ¬

The geometric construction of Kufi script makes it highly adaptable, while its visual simplicity means it is suited to display purposes. »In essence, the letter shapes are relatively simple to construct«, says Ron. »The problem for us was understanding why we were doing what we were doing. We needed that information from a native reader to be quite sure that we were doing the right thing.« ¬

04/03/08 ¬ Some unexpected changes to the »k« and »y« in the Latin. Arabic is progressing well and we're expecting to send the font for design sign off. Sign off is crucial so we can proceed with the engineering of the font. ¬

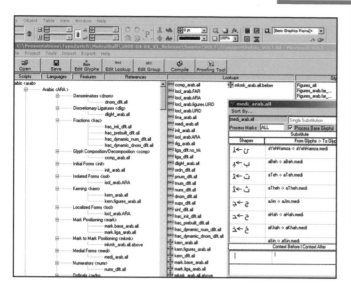

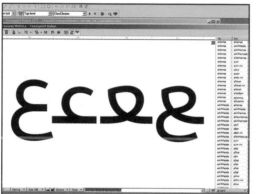

Arabic is a joining script, although not all letterforms are designed to join. The alphabet has 32 characters, including Farsi and Urdu. All but five characters have four variants, the use of which is determined by where they fall in a word. The variants are stand-alone, initial, medial and terminal. Some characters have less design variation than the one displayed here. The initial form isn't the equivalent of a capital in a Latin alphabet – in Arabic the initial is used after every word space, acting as a break in the continuous joining forms. All intermediate characters in a word are medials, and each finishes with a final form. Isolated forms are stand-alone characters. »The same thing applies in Latin script fonts, of course«, says Ron. »You have initials, medials and finals. The effect isn't quite as dramatic but you can see the relationship with the original calligraphic forms.« ¬

The Arabic keyboard has one key per character. In order to use the correct glyph variation the font has to be programmed accordingly. The system and program that use the font know what character needs to be placed. The programming in the font ensures that the »stand-alone« glyph is replaced with one of its variants depending on its position in the word. Specialized font specific software allows these substitution tables to be built. ¬

Bruno asked author, lecturer and type designer Fiona Ross to work on the basic spacing and kerning of the Arabic version of Transport Dubai. While at the type foundry Linotype, Fiona was responsible for the design of non-Latin fonts and typesetting systems and so brought considerable expertise to this task. Usually the design of the letterforms and their spacing and kerning precede the technical production process, when both are brought together and turned into a usable font. Arabic is a joining script that reads from right to left, so it's important that users work with software that supports the change of reading direction. This meant that it couldn't be kerned by Dalton Maag as a standard Latin would be. ¬

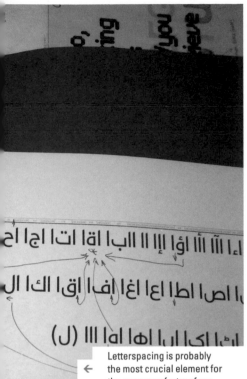

Letterspacing is probably the most crucial element for the success of a typeface. This goes for Latin as much as for Arabic. The relation of each character to another has to be carefully considered to give an even texture when set. Critical character pairs, such as »TA«, are treated individually by applying a kerning value. Whilst the work is carried out on screen, the Dalton Maag team know that only in print can the spacing and kerning be judged accurately. ¬

It's rare for Dalton Maag to design a text and display version of the same font, but if budgets allow they will happily do so. »We had one commission to create a text version of a font optimized for 9pt and a display version that had an adjusted design and different spacing and kerning.« Theoretically it is possible to produce one font that has differing designs and spacing for use at different sizes. »It's a little bit frustrating for us as type designers«, explains Bruno. »We could make a font sing and dance because an OpenType font is, in essence, a program. We could build intelligence into it, but the problem is that application and system developers want to keep the control over how fonts behave and so won't support these kinds of fonts.« »It would be very nice for the tracking to change according to the size at which a font is set – and the x-height, the weight, the width, the spacing. Optical-scaling – that's our passion«, says Ron. ¬

Testing ¬ Font design is a continuous process, explains Ron: »Present, comment, refine, present, comment, refine«. For Transport Dubai tests included simulating how the fonts behaved once backlit: »We had to make them a bit thinner so that the counters were bigger, to compensate for the halo effect«, explains Marc. ¬ Once the characters of a new font are complete, the team turns its attention to the exacting task of letterspacing. Both versions of Transport Dubai were created in the program FontLab Studio – including the basic spacing and kerning. Text fonts tend to be looser set than display, which means that the spacing of individual pairs of letters is less noticeable. But, to maintain an even visual texture, the spacing of various critical pairs in display fonts requires more attention. »We look at every character against every other character«, says Ron. »That's 26 squared for lower-case, same for caps and 26 squared again for caps and lower-case – plus the punctuation of course.« »It's foolish, I know, but it's satisfying when you test it out and it works«, adds Jérémie. Bruno comments: »The better the basic spacing, the less you have to do with individual pairs.« ¬ The team follows a procedure for testing letter spacing and kerning, clicking through a list of all possible character combinations. The designer judges how character pairs behave in context and where necessary applies a kerning value to optimize the balance of white and black space. Bruno explains that the goal is to achieve an even texture: »Obviously if I have a cap ›T‹ followed by a cap ›A‹ there's a big gap between them but I can't do much about this, bearing in mind that I am trying to get an even texture between this and a combination like ›T‹ and ›H‹.« »The tighter you make everything, the more those holes shine through«, adds Ron. »At the end of the day, it's a compromise. After all, even spacing depends on the whole word that you happen to be setting and in what language.« At Dalton Maag all spacing and kerning is done manually. Bruno believes that so far no-one has created a suitable algorithm that creates good spacing. Spacing is a methodical process for which the basic combinations »straight/straight«, »straight/round« and »round/round« are established before going any further. That allows the designer to be in full control of the spacing and to easily apply any corrections if necessary. ¬

01/04/08 ¬ No, not an April joke. The fonts are going into engineering. All design work is completed. Our production guys now have the task of making the fonts actually work in programs and systems. This is going to take a few days. ¬

Technical work ¬ Once a type design is finalized, Jérémie is responsible for turning it into a usable font. He programs the glyph substitution for each character so that the correct version is used depending upon where the character falls within a word. With FontLab Studio, several thousand characters can be generated for one font. Bruno explains the process more fully: »These guys do the basic kerning, the basic character set – caps, lower-case and so on. In production we extend this to include all the accented characters and the ligatures. So, we have to double-check the kerning and amend some of it for accented characters.« ¬ Jérémie's work is more extensive if the team has designed a whole font family. Then, he has to work on all the alternatives simultaneously, checking that the roman and bold of the same font, for example, sit on the same baseline when used at the same size. He also tests the basic behaviour of every new font within different operating systems and applications: »It's a very important part of the process, making sure a font conforms to the laws laid down by Adobe and Microsoft«, explains Bruno. ¬ Once ready, the final typeface is exported as an OpenType font – a small file that contains various tables; the glyphs are one, the kerning another, along with tables that improve the rendering on screen. ¬

Transport Dubai is also used in the wayfinding for the Marine Agency Services (waterbuses, ferries and water taxis). In addition to these and the Metro signs a further 2,500 street markers for the Metro also use the typeface. TDC produced a comprehensive manual to show how the font should be used in the sign layouts. The »Dubai Signing Manual« covers sizing, spacing, leading and the relationship of type to all pictograms. ¬

The Metro signs have been made in the United Arab Emirates by two companies. The directional signs are all illuminated using specially-made vinyl applied to acrylic panels mounted on LED lighting in stainless steel cases. Approximately 11,000 signs have been made so far. ¬

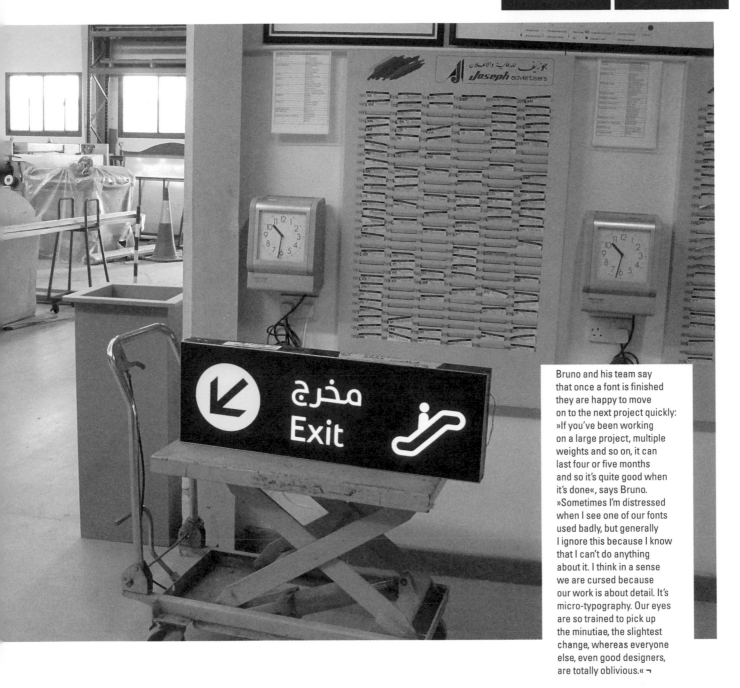

Bruno and his team say that once a font is finished they are happy to move on to the next project quickly: »If you've been working on a large project, multiple weights and so on, it can last four or five months and so it's quite good when it's done«, says Bruno. »Sometimes I'm distressed when I see one of our fonts used badly, but generally I ignore this because I know that I can't do anything about it. I think in a sense we are cursed because our work is about detail. It's micro-typography. Our eyes are so trained to pick up the minutiae, the slightest change, whereas everyone else, even good designers, are totally oblivious.« ¬

04/04/08 ¬ Engineering went smoother than anticipated. The fonts are ready to be released to the client. After extensive testing we're happy that this is it. ¬

29/07/09 ¬ We haven't had any complaints from the client a year after delivery. I guess we did a great job. The fonts will go live in September, when the Metro is finally open to the public. ¬

We were interested in following Namibian designer Frauke Stegmann (born 1973) because of the distinctive approach to craft and materials that characterizes her work. Unhampered by the commonly recognized boundaries between disciplines, Frauke's practice includes ceramics, film, illustration, design and fashion – a world to which her experimental and sensitive appropriation of unexpected materials is well suited. The prospect of this project – developing the graphic identity for South African knitwear designer Richard de Jager's fledgling fashion label PWHOA – was intriguing, not least because it entailed the merging of the worlds of fashion and graphic design. We were also curious about the open-ended nature of the project: the apparent creative freedom, lack of specific brief, scarcity of fixed deadlines and absence of any budget. What kind of creative process and outcome would this generate? ¬ Irreverent and avant-garde, Richard de Jager describes PWHOA as »a new nightmare in craft«. A creator of individual and one-off pieces, his inventive and at times outlandish designs have attracted international attention. ¬ Frauke's clients and collaborators include fashion brands Prada, Miu Miu and Eley Kishimoto, Peter Saville, Treader records and Pulp frontman Jarvis Cocker, whose wedding invitation she designed. ¬ This new collaboration, between two designers keen to push possibilities and with similar scepticism about the commercial ends of their disciplines, was also interesting as both are African designers working in South Africa. How would this geographical, political and social context shape the project and would this context be apparent? ¬

Graphic design allied to fashion often nods towards the experimental and yet employs high-end production values with results that are refined and slick. Frauke is a broad-based designer, however, whose education and experience straddles two very different continents – Africa and Europe. Both inform her approach. So what is it that really matters to Frauke and where do the foundations of her low-tech, craft-based practice lie? ¬

The Himba ¬ Frauke talks excitedly about the joy she finds in creating something »incredible« out of nothing. She finds inspiration in the country where she grew up: »In the north of Namibia there's a tribe called the Himba. They manage to create the most incredible lifestyle with very, very little. They create an environment out of straw and mud and animal fat, but it is so beautiful and overwhelming in its simplicity.« Despite Frauke's work being dominantly European in aesthetic, her sensitivities, tenacity and resourcefulness seem more African in influence. Her interest in overlooked materials is an example of this: »I like using certain papers in printing processes that bring out something really special in them – seeing opportunities where you think there's not an opportunity.« ¬

Out of Africa ¬ »I'm definitely an African.« Although Frauke studied in Germany and the UK and is now based in Cape Town, South Africa, she was born and brought up in Namibia, a small and sparsely populated desert country in southern Africa – and these roots run deep. Her great-great grandparents emigrated to Namibia from Germany and she is the fifth generation to be born outside Europe: »I would say absolutely, I'm totally informed by the place that I come from. Namibia has no industrial development; it's all about landscape. It is completely unspoiled and very African – there's not much trace of Europe. You get the sense of a completely different world. It's really about nature; that's what I was informed by.« ¬

On idealism ¬ Frauke confides that working on paid graphic design projects can feel like being in a confined space. She is happiest working on more exploratory projects and challenging conventional modes of graphic design. This may sound naïve but her quiet and fierce determination to pursue her own path in graphic design involves compromises not all designers would be willing to make: »I've always had to do these odd jobs in order to do the graphic design that I need to do. This might sound depressing, but for me it's a necessity. In order to do the graphic design that I believe in, I would sweep floors.« ¬

Honesty and craft ¬ »Graphic design is a less self-conscious activity in Namibia but I always had this feeling that I wanted to be a graphic designer.« This might have something to do with her father's job as what she calls an »old-school artisan in letterpress« and growing up surrounded by ink and paper: »I'm very interested in printing processes and in trying to create the best possible work that utilizes the finest craftsmanship.« For her album covers for British jazz label Treader she commissioned two of the last surviving traditional block engravers to translate her detailed bird drawings into dies, from which they were foil blocked in gold on to coloured stationery paper. ¬

Beyond the logo ¬ Frauke explains her rationale for the identity of Birds Café, run by her mother and sister in Cape Town: »We didn't want to have the logo outside as the sign and on letterheads and menus. It's just so boring and limited. Instead, we wanted to create an identity through the crockery. Crockery forms such a relationship between the space and the customer and the kitchen. It made perfect sense to create the identity through the ceramics.« Using a kiln in the workshop beneath the café, everything was made on-site and the home-made Namibian food served on Frauke's bespoke hand-made crockery has garnered attention locally and internationally. She says it was wonderful to discover that Birds Café didn't need a logo, she says with satisfaction, but is insistent this does not make her a ceramicist: »I'm a graphic designer interested in how materials can be utilized within a graphic design context.« ¬

Finding freedom ¬ Frauke studied graphic design in Mainz, Germany, where her design training was formal and therefore fairly restrictive. »I couldn't entirely recognize this thing that I wanted graphic design to be. There was great work and great typography but…« Her decision to move to London and study for her postgraduate degree at the Royal College of Art proved to be the right one. The experience was exhilarating: »When I studied at the RCA, it was everything that I was looking for.« Freed by the discovery that it was possible to create her own graphic design and work independently, she describes the experience as a kind of epiphany: »I could just be myself because I could understand this thing that I wanted to do within graphic design. I think perhaps some people find things through travelling, but for me it was through studying and coming to that place.« ¬

Extreme clients ¬ »I am at a stage where I want the client to be challenging. I want the client to be extreme – in the way of being unconventional.« Frauke's hunger for this kind of client is more difficult to feed now that she is based in Cape Town. In London she found more acceptance of difference and the possibility to make projects that would be uncalled for in Cape Town. »I think living in Cape Town has been very educational because there is less acceptance of this free way of working. I have to find niches, I have to really look out for where I can practise this approach.« ¬

```
Hi Frauke

Its all so exciting. I must say i think i make clothes because i
cant express myself in words properly everything seems funny but
here follows some:

power
kotz
ha-ii
organic tech
techno hobo
wont u please run over me
soldiers
camping fetish
loser
strange flora
fox
violence
smell
eyes
climbing
bad
sunshine on t.v
army
protection to the wearer
taking a yarn for a walk
chaos
future
the nothing


/

richie
```

The conversations between Frauke and Richard, which to all intents and purposes constituted the brief, took place initially by email but developed into meetings over coffee. »It was a verbal process; it was about the person and about chance and the possibilities of conversation.« This organic approach reflected Richard's working process and gave Frauke an understanding of »how he thinks, what he wants, how long his process is«. They quickly discovered their attitude was simpatico. Each employs an esoteric approach to their practice, neither being interested in conventional commercial work. Their conversations also revealed »that there was so much going on that the challenge was going to be how to embody that in the logo«, she recalls. ¬

Frauke first saw Richard's clothing being worn by friends – »a real way of getting to know the clothes« – before they started collaborating, but she was clear about not wanting to be too influenced by the visual aspect of his work. She enjoys the creative challenge of taking inspiration from the way people think, so she asked Richard to send her a list of words. »We had this very loose, open-endedness to how we wanted the project to come about, and instead of him sending me pictures I thought it would be much cleaner, much more unspoilt to just get a list of words.« ¬

Richard's list of seemingly disparate words and phrases encompasses nonsense and nihilism, the organic, the man-made and the mundane. From this and their conversations it was clear to Frauke that the graphic identity for PWHOA would need to reflect the flexible aspirations of the label. They both felt that a single graphic identity would be limiting: »Because PWHOA needs to stay open-ended at all times it needs to be able to change logo, change identity and not be fixed to a certain stature or a fixed, finished stamp.« ¬

It became clear early on that this would be an ongoing, evolving collaboration with very few defined deadlines. Indeed, Frauke tells us that this is »a lifelong project«. The only fixed deadline Frauke had to work to was the date of Design Indaba, an annual design showcase, international conference and expo of African design held in Cape Town, where Richard was launching his new collection with a catwalk show. ¬

An open brief ¬ Most graphic design projects start with some kind of formal briefing and a written brief that sets out deadlines and deliverables. In contrast, this project was notable for its informality and openness, both evident even in how it came about. Both Frauke and Richard are based in Cape Town, where the art and design scene is growing but still relatively small. They were aware of each other's work and knew people in common, despite not having met. Richard knew of Frauke's work at Birds Café and was interested by her approach. Frauke recalls, »It was in the Fall that I started hearing that PWHOA wanted me to develop the identity but it was a while before I got to speak to Richard de Jager and really understand what it was about.« Subsequently introduced by friends, it was through conversations by phone, email and in person that their collaboration took shape. ¬

Creative collaboration ¬ Many designers hope for and indeed seek out projects for sympathetic and like-minded practitioners from other creative fields. These are attractive generally not for their financial rewards (budgets are often small or projects self-funded, as is the case here) but because of the kind of creative collaboration they involve. Based on respect, trust and equality, it makes a huge difference creatively to avoid the more hierarchical client/designer relationship common to most commissions. »The working relationship is very important«, Frauke explains. »I've often seen that the job is only as good as the client or as good as the client allows it to be. Of course, you can always persuade your client to do certain things but it is also up to the client to decide how far he or she wants to go.« ¬

12/07 ¬ Meet with Richard for the first time. ¬
20/07 ¬ Richard sends through his email of words. ¬

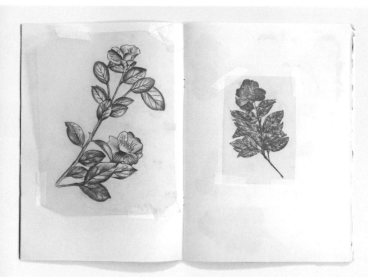

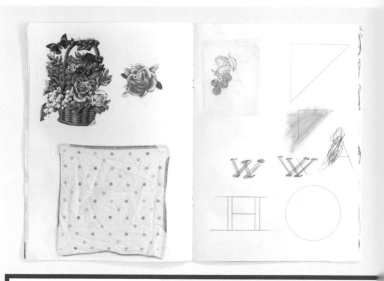

Frauke decided very quickly on what she calls »the charming use of very low-key materials«, an approach which although forced upon the project because costs had to be kept to a minimum, also »gave the possibility of making and integrating lots of different feelings in the identity«. ¬

Frauke's studio is in an area of Cape Town where there are lots of businesses moving in and out, providing her with rich pickings for her work. She uses her local area to source materials and finds a surprising range of things, especially when offices move and leave their unwanted items on the street. She also trails stationery shops looking for old and discounted stock, delighting in requisitioning such items, which many people would consider of little value and eminently disposable. She used found papers for this project. »It's wonderful to refresh discarded material that would otherwise be wasted.« ¬

Frauke is interested in using personal references in her work. She asked Richard for memorabilia from his childhood and was also inspired by the flora and fauna of the region of southern Africa where he was born. Starting with the sketches of plant life she then incorporated these drawings with individual letterforms. Drawing has always been important in Frauke's working process and she finds the connection between the pencil and her thoughts liberating. ¬

Instinctive responses ¬ With many graphic design projects, research is a natural starting point. This might be into the subject, content or context of the brief. It will inform choices, direction and prompt ideas. Frauke's approach is more intuitive and less about sourcing information than sparking her imagination. She finds that initial conversations with a new client are often revealing and that exploring her instinctive responses to these can be fruitful: »That first fresh idea is always quite important. Maybe like a vision. That might sound funny but when you have these conversations with your client, the thing that you envision in that initial stage can be quite, quite important.« This process does not necessarily manifest itself in images on a page. »I'm not sure whether this is good or bad, but I guess often the first thing is a picture in my mind. Then it is about finding things that connect to that picture or vision, or whatever it is.« Writing and note taking are important to Frauke and it is usually from these that she makes sketches: »It just builds up from there.« ¬ **Materials** ¬ With self-funded or very low budget projects there are inevitably constraints on materials and production options. In this case a resourceful approach necessitated by lack of budget tied into the philosophy of both designers. Richard uses an old knitting-machine to create his one-off pieces and Frauke says that his aspirations to be self-sufficient and »go back to the source« extend as far as wanting to have his own flock of sheep from which to obtain wool. Frauke explains: »If it's not about money, it's about passion and you can be true to the integrity of what the project needs as a visual answer.« ¬

The meanings of words have become increasingly relevant in Frauke's work as they spark links and create contexts. She asked Richard for lists throughout the project and continues to do so, transposing his emails into her sketchbooks as she has here. She finds lists peculiarly suited to the nature of their project and to the discipline of fashion: »It fits very well – this chance and indirectness and finding things that are suitable at a given time. In much the same way as with trends and fashion, things change from season to season.« ¬

Over the long course of their ongoing collaboration, the lists that Richard sends become points of reference for the design process, »like a constellation of stars or something, it helps me find direction.« ¬

10/09 ¬ Working on birds for the overhead projection at the fashion show, making the male birds colourful and females dull in colour. ¬
21/09 ¬ Development of official logo and PWHOA floral type. ¬
01/10 morning ¬ Begin rescuing paper, envelopes, card and fabric from skips and old stock in shops. ¬

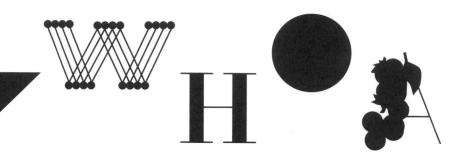

Richard's designs
for PWHOA are influenced
by the styles of the 1980s,
a decade associated with
geometric shapes, fluorescent
colours andextreme angles.
Frauke took inspiration
from this, most visibly in the
triangular »P« and circular
»O«. She drew the »W« as
a kind of wire construction
to introduce playfulness
and openness. She included
the »strong« typeface Bodoni
for the letter »H«, »to add
the seriousness and starkness
of Richard's approach«. ¬

Designed in 1798
by Giambattista Bodoni,
Bodoni is a Modern typeface,
characterized by extreme
contrast between thick and
thin strokes. This exaggeration
and its flat serifs give Bodoni
a contemporary feel while
still alluding to the past. The
»H« binds the logo, as Frauke
elaborates: »You're probably
not sure whether the ›P‹
is a ›P‹ but then you read
the ›H‹ and you can feel your
way through to the left and the
right. It's about not identifying
the letters immediately, but
trying to figure out what it
says. We didn't want to be too
direct. We wanted this slight
barrier of information.« ¬

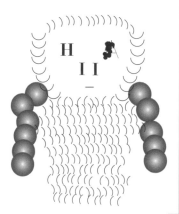

Richard's intention is
to develop a companion
menswear line named
HAII. PWHOA and HAII are
made-up words, which found
animal incarnation as an owl
and gorilla retrospectively,
through Frauke's hand. These
playful digital drawings are
constructed from typographic
and geometric elements,
informed by the spontaneous
and intuitive approach that
typifies PWHOA. »It's about
that animal instinct kind
of thing«, Frauke explains. ¬

She observes that placing
the name within the face
of each animal to provide
its facial features »softened
the logo. We thought it was
nice just to keep things light.«
Neither of these characters
has yet been used, and may
never be: »It's just that we
thought it was very important
not to be driven by one logo.
The great thing is that we've
created possibilities that
can continue.« ¬

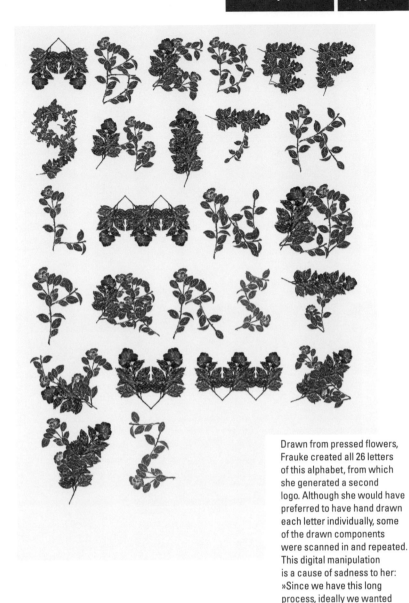

Drawn from pressed flowers, Frauke created all 26 letters of this alphabet, from which she generated a second logo. Although she would have preferred to have hand drawn each letter individually, some of the drawn components were scanned in and repeated. This digital manipulation is a cause of sadness to her: »Since we have this long process, ideally we wanted each letter to be specially drawn. We both love the luxury of creating something specific for one use only.« The two logos were designed simultaneously and were »different expressions of the same thing«. ¬

Designing for fashion ¬ Both graphic design and fashion involve the construction and projection of image and identity. However, where inclusivity (designing from a premise of access for all) is desirable – if not essential – in graphic design, the worlds of avant-garde or haute couture fashion are built around exclusivity and the individual, so the one-off and bespoke is highly prized. While a logo or identity for a fashion label still needs to be distinctive and recognizable, there is more latitude to play with legibility, suggestion and the unconventional. Frauke and Richard share a desire to operate at the edges of their disciplines and enjoy the unfettered exploration this involves. »Neither of us like that fixed finality or visibility of ›there's a fashion designer and there's a label and there's a certain identity‹. We both want it to be unclear. Maybe it will scare people off but it is because it is experimental and there's the opportunity to keep it indirect that we both like it.« ¬ **Serendipity** ¬ Frauke's initial conversations with Richard were, she says, inspirational. She started by exploring the typographic potential of the name, PWHOA, trying to embrace Richard's eclectic and energetic approach. »There was a lot going on, on lots of different levels, so in each letter it was good to try and embody a different feeling«, she explains. »This idea just made so much sense to us both. Accidentally it was perfect, so it was quite a quick process. It was ready when the right shape was found and when that happened it was good.« But she is clear, too, about the unfinished nature of the project and identity: »We have the name PWHOA but it can come in all shapes and sizes.« ¬

01/10 afternoon ¬ Development of PWHOA's sewn-in label and swing-ticket with washing instructions. Sourcing and collecting paper for posters. ¬

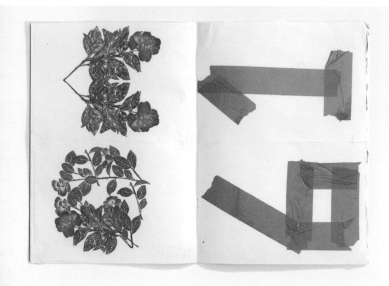

The poster system that Frauke designed meant that each letter could be photocopied on to an A4 sheet of paper and then tiled together to form a large poster to whatever scale and proportions needed. She made a simple alphabet for Richard out of tape, so each time he had a show he could photocopy the letters and construct the posters himself. The poster shown above right was displayed around Cape Town International Convention Centre. Frauke put them up outside the venue herself but she is relaxed about handing this responsibility over to others and letting the posters »have their own life«. ¬

Frauke wanted to keep a feeling of movement and dynamism in this alphabet, to keep the essence of the language of tape. »If you try to be too perfect with a thing like that then it kind of kills it. It's always important for me to look at the general function of the material I'm working with. That's why I kept it very instinctive – sticking the pieces down as if I was taping closed a box or whatever, to catch that feeling of speed and spontaneity.« ¬

Creative recycling ¬ South Africa's great cultural diversity and richness is reflected in the range of art and craft it continues to produce. Alongside more traditional media, such as beads, glass and leather, there is inventiveness in the appropriation of found materials, such as petrol cans, telephone wire and food labels. This adaptive and innovative approach to materials is driven largely by economic necessity. After a troubled history and 42 years of apartheid, South Africa held its first democratic elections in 1994; yet despite political progress, daunting social and economic issues remain. Against this backdrop, resourcefulness and invention are significant survival strategies, evident in the creative consciousness of a range of contemporary art and craft makers, including Frauke and Richard. ¬ **Economies of scale** ¬ The nature of craft production generally involves low volumes and a close relationship between designer and production and between customer and manufacturer. Both Frauke and Richard identify with this approach and were keen from the start that the identity of PWHOA should reflect these values. Frauke's choice of materials and simple production methods, which include using stamps and stencils, allow Richard to be self-sufficient and in control of this process himself – he can make the labels and posters as and when demand dictates. »Everything can be crafted very carefully, we don't need huge quantities… It's a very low-budget, low-key approach to making things.« ¬

Cut from clothes that had been sterilized and vacuum packed, the garment labels were made from recycled rags, which can be bought cheaply from the recycling depot. Using a stencil that Frauke made of the logo, each label can be individually sprayed and branded before being sewn into the garment. She wanted to avoid making the label look too commercial. »PWHOA needed something very raw. It was so wonderful to develop this extreme rawness for Richard. To have a stencil is much better for PWHOA at the moment. That way you are in control of how you do it.« ¬

The envelopes for the washing instructions were also found or second-hand. Frauke used Richard's childhood memorabilia to develop a form of decorative iconography. These illustrations were then made into ink stamps to be hand-stamped on to the envelope as needed. This hand-made method of production and use of personal stationery accentuates the bespoke and hand-crafted nature of the garment and creates a more intimate dialogue between the designer and the owner of the item. ¬

13/02 ¬ Richard has been developing his collection over the past months. Preparations now begin for his show at Design Indaba. ¬

Design Indaba ¬ The only fixed deadline during the time we followed this project was the PWHOA fashion show at Design Indaba. Supported by the South African Department of Trade and Industry, Design Indaba has become a significant annual event, raising national and international awareness of the diversity of South African design and, through Design Indaba Expo, promoting and encouraging its economic potential and attracting buyers from around the world. In 2008, Design Indaba launched a dedicated fashion arena hosting an all-day fashion festival in which PWHOA was invited to participate. Eschewing the conventional formula of what Design Indaba calls »the pedestal-like catwalk«, fashion designers are asked to present their work in an original format that »communicates their ›story‹ or brand«. ¬ **The fashion show** ¬ Initially Richard conceived this PWHOA collection along two distinct colour lines, with his womenswear in grey and the menswear in bright colours: »Like in the bird world, where the female is always a dull colour and the male is very bright«, clarifies Frauke. The ornithological relationship is extended through the folds and features of his garments, which exaggerate and emphasize areas of the body such as the neck and shoulders, transforming the models into something resembling birds attracting mates. Although Frauke had seen some pieces from the collection, once again her designs were interpretations of verbal rather than visual influences: »A lot came through conversations.« The PWHOA show was eagerly anticipated and well received, attracting national press and television coverage. »Now that everything is set, PWHOA can launch and start selling properly«, Frauke says happily. »Now everything has come together he can start putting it in the shops again…« ¬

In designing the fashion show, Frauke and Richard wanted to keep the simple, manual feeling they had developed. They decided to use an overhead projector and black and white photocopies on acetate to make a feature of their low-tech approach. The minimal light provided by the overhead projector accentuated the theatrical atmosphere and was offset by a strong directional spotlight from one side, which cast exaggerated shadows of the models. The length of the show was determined by the piece of music Richard had chosen. The discordant soundtrack reinforced the unsettling ambience of the performance. ¬

↑
Frauke made photocopies of her reference photographs of birds, to achieve grainy and more distressed images. She acknowledges that birds are commonly associated with beauty and goodness but wanted to suggest that the reality is more brutal. »Richard's approach has a dark side to it as well, and making photocopies took away a little bit of that perfection and made it just that little bit darker.« ¬

At the time of writing Frauke and Richard are busy developing the PWHOA website. She admits that this is taking a long time, but feels speedy solutions are not appropriate for the philosophy or specific demands of this project: »I think what's interesting is that it is ongoing. There's not a final PWHOA design – it will change throughout. As things are done they can be thrown out of the window completely or used in a new context.« ¬

19/02 ¬ Finalize sequence of images for overhead projection for show. ¬
15/03 ¬ Dress rehearsal. ¬
16–19/03 ¬ Design Indaba fashion shows. ¬
10/07 ¬ DIY kit with stencils for sprayed labels and stamps for washing instructions ready – PWHOA is ready to DIY! Website development is ongoing… ¬

This project for the charity War on Want by graphic communication consultancy Bond and Coyne particularly interested us because it made unusual demands of the designers. The brief was to design a temporary exhibition in a small public arts space, and unusually gave the lead to the graphic designers rather than the more conventional practice of assigning it to 3D designers. Constraints on budget and time were extremely tight, in contrast to the freedom given over the presentation and content of the exhibition. In exhibition design, and design for arts and cultural bodies in general, there is often latitude for designers to be experimental, whereas the charity sector tends to be more conservative and mindful of the need for mass appeal. So we wanted to know how this combination of constraint and freedom would work. How would graphic designers approach a spatial design project, what imperatives would shape their creative process and what would working for a charity as a client entail? ¬ War on Want is a British-based charity fighting inequality, injustice and poverty in developing countries and campaigning for workers' rights in partnership with local organizations around the world. This exhibition project continued a relationship between Bond and Coyne and War on Want that began in 2005 when, seeking to capitalize on the interest in fighting poverty that had been generated by Make Poverty History, they were commissioned to work on an advertising campaign for the London Underground. ¬ Mike Bond (born 1977) and Martin Coyne (born 1978) founded Bond and Coyne Associates in 2001. Committed to applying design thinking to solve problems beyond the realm of graphic design, their work ranges from branding projects to communications analysis for clients including the Design Council and the British Heart Foundation. ¬

Designers who work in the charity or voluntary sectors often do so because the ethos of their clients chimes with their own. As designers who work in some of the less obviously commercial areas of graphic design, we were interested in discovering if Mike and Martin's inspirations and aspirations would be in any way different to those of their peers. We asked them to tell us about the experiences and influences that lie behind their approach to work and the business of design, and how they define their design philosophy. ¬

What's in a name? ¬ Mike and Martin redden as they recall how they used to be referred to as »the boys«, and it's easy to see why this might sit uncomfortably with them. Calmly spoken and quietly composed, it would be hard to find two graphic designers less laddish in temperament. They met at Central St Martins College of Art and Design and worked on joint projects throughout their degrees. Mike reflects that, »We kind of knew from that point we wanted to launch together in some form.« Working on their first external projects as a partnership marked the start of a new formality: »We were calling ourselves Mike and Martin but we thought we'd grow up and say Bond and Coyne instead.« ¬

Materials and making ¬ While studying together for their masters degrees at the Royal College of Art, Bond and Coyne worked on a project that illustrates their enterprising approach to materials. Using security tape found around the windows of abandoned shops, they created what Mike calls a »physical typeface«. Through a series of folds – to avoid breaking the electrical circuit running through the tape – they created an alphabet of continuous letterforms. This process resulted in a final piece that simultaneously functioned as security tape and communicated information. Mike and Martin take real pleasure in the tactile nature of materials, and this is reflected in their sources of creative stimulation – architectural books and journals are a rich source of reference to which they regularly return. Mike admits that although they look at graphic design magazines, this is »really just to keep tabs on the industry rather than to get inspiration«. ¬

Beyond graphic design ¬ »We don't want just to create beautiful, frivolous stuff; we want design to do some good as well«, Mike tells us. As research associates at the RCA's Helen Hamlyn Centre – where the remit is to investigate design initiatives aimed at improving quality of life for people of all ages and abilities – they gained valuable insight into the possibilities of inclusive and user-led design. They worked alongside influential research-based design group IDEO and the Design Council on an 18-month project looking at the impact of school design on learning. This involved running workshops with pupils, talking to head teachers and caretakers, writing and designing the project report and creating the launch workshop, which won a substantial budget to take the project's recommendations forward. One of the results was the design of a new school desk and chair. »That's what inspires me most«, says Mike, »solving problems that reach beyond the design world«. ¬

Something out of nothing ¬
Most designers enjoy working within constraints, and for Mike and Martin this includes working with the restrictions of the budget. »The budget is an unexpected source of inspiration for us – it is a bit of a thrill, I suppose, to be able to create something out of nothing.« Although this necessarily involves a degree of compromise, they delight in the fecundity this demands. Martin tells us that one of their inspirations in this is design group Graphic Thought Facility, whose versatility and inventiveness they admire, particularly in relation to materials and production methods. Mike tells us their enterprising approach is »perfect« for the charitable sector but is welcomed by their commercial clients too; »They appreciate that we are able to deliver more than is asked of us.« ¬

Teaching matters ¬
»I'm passionate about education«, says Mike. »It's good for keeping your brain alive, it's good to be in a different space, it's good to go from meeting two or three clients in a day to dealing with 75 students. It's very rewarding.« Mike and Martin have lectured in graphic design since graduating and each teach one day a week at Kingston University and the Arts University College Bournemouth, respectively. Many designers find teaching a useful way to supplement their income when starting out, but Bond and Coyne found teaching quickly became an integral part of their practice and they enthuse about the symbiotic nature of this relationship. They are proud to tell clients that they teach, and feel it demonstrates their commitment to looking at design problems from a fresh perspective as well as actively contributing to and questioning the future of the industry. »In terms of our philosophy, design education plays a big part.« ¬

Divisions of labour ¬
»I know how Martin would put it«, laughs Mike of their working relationship. »He does it and I talk about it.« Their long-founded trust in each other makes negotiating roles and responsibilities easy. Mike is generally the front man in client dealings and presentations, while Martin drives what they call the »nitty-gritty of getting stuff sorted«. With the addition of Mark, a graphic designer, Riaz, a screen-based designer and an intern, Beth, there is rich dialogue in the studio and an opportunity to draw upon a range of ideas, perspectives and reference points. They all discuss project aims, concepts and general directions but most of the hands-on, creative and design side of things has shifted to Martin and Mark. »I tend to play the role of devil's advocate a bit more«, Mike says with a mischievous smile. »I try to challenge from a client's perspective. I'm the killjoy.« ¬

The wrong haircuts ¬ Saved from running their business from their bedrooms when IDEO invited them to share their London offices, Mike and Martin later moved to a space within a business incubation centre connected to the Arts University College Bournemouth, where Martin teaches. The discovery that being based outside of the capital did not mean they were out of the industry loop influenced their move to Winchester. »It's about work-life balance«, says Mike of the decision to move studio to the historic cathedral city south-west of London, equidistant from where he and Martin each live. »It's a beautiful place. It's a city but it's a very small city, there's culture here, we can walk around the block to blow away the cobwebs. And it definitely gives you a relaxing place to work without the pressure of trying to fit in or be too cool or anything like that… Our hair isn't trendy enough to be based in Shoreditch.« ¬

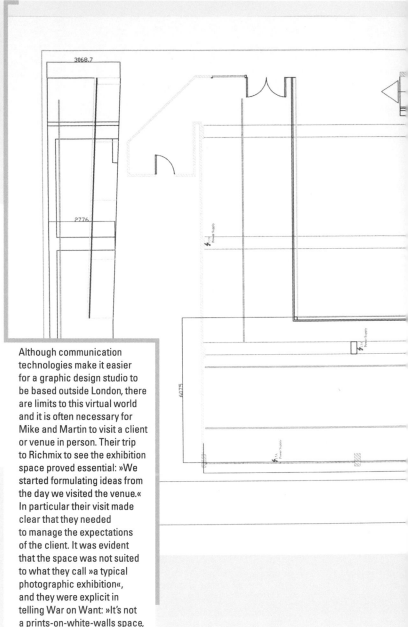

Each year War on Want commissions a photographer to go to a part of the world in which the organization operates to document the work it does and any surrounding stories. Mike and Martin describe the established pattern of the briefing for this annual short-turnaround and tight-deadline photographic exhibition as »a kind of ›help‹ situation«. Their relationship with War on Want means that rather than receive a specific brief, they are given the photographs and a framework of budget, space and deadline. Within these parameters, War on Want trust them with the ultimate authorship and control of the interpretation and organization of both the exhibition content and design. This exhibition was of photographer Julio Etchart's trip to Guatemala where, with partner organization Conrado de la Cruz, War on Want runs a project empowering Mayan child labourers – whose human rights are commonly ignored – by providing essential services and training. ¬

Richmix is an arts centre in the East End of London, which incorporates cinemas, an events space, café and bar and is home to BBC Radio London. Promoted as a drop-in cultural and creative community hub, the venue attracts the sort of demographic that War on Want sees as a target audience – aged between 20 and 40, culturally aware, knowledgeable about world issues and willing to be involved in positive action. ¬

Although communication technologies make it easier for a graphic design studio to be based outside London, there are limits to this virtual world and it is often necessary for Mike and Martin to visit a client or venue in person. Their trip to Richmix to see the exhibition space proved essential: »We started formulating ideas from the day we visited the venue.« In particular their visit made clear that they needed to manage the expectations of the client. It was evident that the space was not suited to what they call »a typical photographic exhibition«, and they were explicit in telling War on Want: »It's not a prints-on-white-walls space, and if that's what you want, change the venue. If you want to stick with this venue then we have to look at it in a different way.« ¬

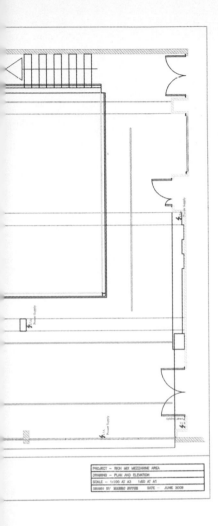

← A plan and an elevation, which map out the floor area of the exhibition space and show windows, doors, fire exits and power supplies, are usually supplied to the designers of an exhibition by the venue. These enable designers to check that their design fits and functions. The plan of the site for this exhibition revealed both the positive and problematic features of the mezzanine space. Of three possible walls, one had a number of prominent features, including fire exits, a cupboard and a ledge. The second wall was filled almost entirely by a long window, which provided decent light but limited hanging opportunities, and the third wall was sloped and painted bright red. »We came out of the venue realizing we needed to build a gallery within a gallery, and literally construct a space within a space. That's when we got the 3D designer involved.« ¬

Budgets ¬ Designing an exhibition for a charity is different to other forms of exhibition design. In the first instance this is because the aim is usually to communicate an issue rather than primarily to display artefacts, but no less significant is the budget, which is invariably small. For large gallery or museum exhibitions, budgets can extend to tens or even hundreds of thousands of pounds. In this project Mike and Martin had a modest budget for which they were wholly responsible. Many designers prefer to be budget holders due to the level of control this affords. In this case it enabled Mike and Martin to manage the process of commissioning and contracting other collaborators and companies such as their 3D designer and printing firm. ¬ **Content** ¬ The subject and content of exhibitions vary enormously and devising apposite, illuminating and engaging ways to display and communicate this is the core challenge of exhibition design. For a charity, an exhibition is a way of publicizing a cause, raising its profile and demonstrating the effective action that fund-raising has achieved. Unlike an exhibition with an entry charge, this free exhibition needed to attract and inform visitors who happened to be passing through the venue. ¬ **Space** ¬ Whether large or small, grand or lowly, the space in which an exhibition is held is clearly a critical part of the brief. From fundamentals such as structural dimensions and access, to considerations of audience, tone and atmosphere, the exhibition space is a determining feature of any design. War on Want had found a new venue for this exhibition and, with no formal briefing, it was only when Mike and Martin visited the space that they fully understood the challenge of the project. ¬ **Deadline** ¬ Large museum exhibition design projects can take six months to a year from commissioning to the exhibition opening. This project was extremely short in comparison, with just three weeks between receiving the budget and the private view. ¬

05/08 ¬ Independent site visit to Richmix with the full team and chance to look around Brick Lane, etc. ¬
19/08 ¬ Discussion with War on Want about concerns regarding the non-traditional nature of the space. ¬

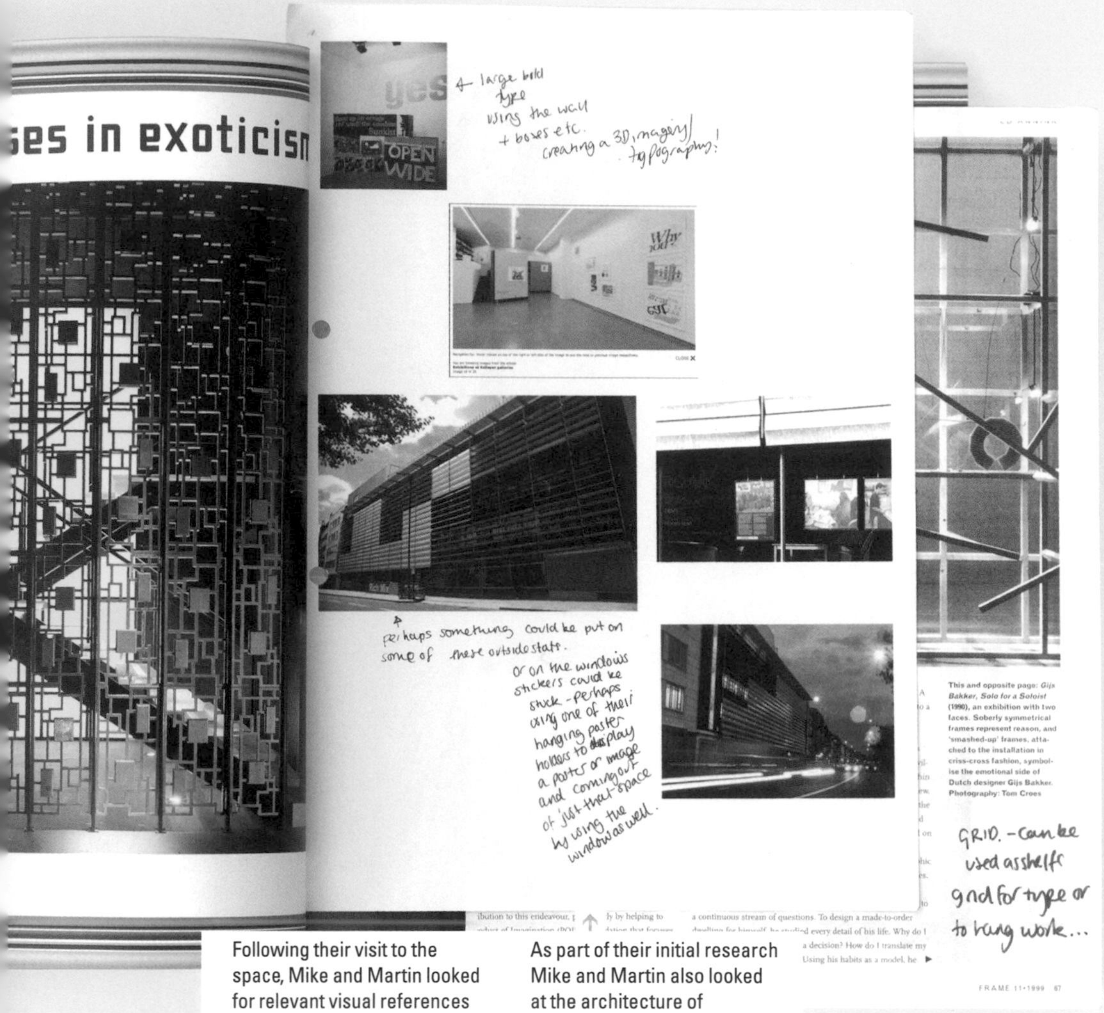
large bold type using the wall + boxes etc. creating a 3D imagery/typography!
OPEN WIDE
perhaps something could be put on some of these outside slats.
or on the windows stickers could be stuck - perhaps using one of their hanging poster holders to display a poster or image and coming out of 'just that space' by using the window as well.
This and opposite page: Gijs Bakker, Solo for a Soloist (1990), an exhibition with two faces. Soberly symmetrical frames represent reason, and 'smashed-up' frames, attached to the installation in criss-cross fashion, symbolise the emotional side of Dutch designer Gijs Bakker. Photography: Tom Croes
GRID. - can be used as shelfs grid for type or to hang work...
FRAME 11•1999 97

Mike calls this spread featuring the exhibition space from international interiors magazine »Frame« a »key image« in their research. Drawn to the basic construction and raw aesthetic of the design by Gijs Bakker, Mike remarks on the possibilities of this type of structure, identifying the potential of an open grid to be used »as shelves, for type or to hang work«. The open construction had immediate resonance, as Mike explains, because »to some extent it suggested a blank canvas, which was the sort of structure we knew we needed«. ¬

Following their visit to the space, Mike and Martin looked for relevant visual references for inspiration. Browsing their collection of architectural books and magazines, which span a range of spatial design disciplines, including retail, commercial and exhibition design, they looked closely for appropriate construction methods and building materials to spark ideas. ¬

As part of their initial research Mike and Martin also looked at the architecture of the building, searching for any existing structural devices to inform their design and that could be utilized to advertise the exhibition to passers-by. These annotated digital printouts show that they considered how to use the outside slats, adhere stickers to the windows and hang posters from the fixed holders. ¬

Designing for charities ¬ It has become common for charities to use graphic design to help promote their message, but this was not always so. Before this became widespread, the charities that used design saw it as a way to make themselves different and were often willing to allow designers creative freedom to produce experimental work. Now that the use of graphic design has become commonplace in this sector, the design briefs tend towards the conventional and the opportunities for designers to push projects have become more limited. ¬ **Tone of voice** ¬ An important aspect of most design is finding and projecting an appropriate tone of voice, but this takes on particular significance when the client is a charity. Graphic design plays a valuable role in the charity sector and is mostly harnessed enthusiastically and effectively to communicate issues, publicize campaigns and galvanize support. However, while recognizing this positive potential, some charities are mindful of the negative connotations they consider an overt use of graphic design to carry. A perception still lingers that graphic design can be an extravagance for a not-for-profit fund-raising organization, and might send out a misleading message about their bank balance and priorities. While wanting the authority and trust that good design can engender, charities can be cautious not to project an image that could be interpreted as too corporate or slick – or removed from the reality of the cause they represent. This can be a delicate balance to strike. Bond and Coyne have created a distinct visual identity for War on Want, which Mike describes as »relatively gritty«, using bold type and punchy brand colours of red and black. While well suited to the campaigning nature of the charity, their public image must be considered with sensitivity. »We need to ensure that we do not make them appear militant in any sense.« ¬

Mike and Martin are mindful that their design for War on Want reflects the hands-on involvement of the charity and does not look too sophisticated or sleek. For this reason they have evolved a low-tech utilitarian aesthetic across their work for them: »We know when we see a use of material that fits their brand.« ¬

The bold use of distressed woodblock typography and stark colour combinations in this annual report and newsletter, both jobs which Bond and Coyne previously designed, have a striking visual impact in keeping with the hard-hitting message they carry. It is important that War on Want's visual language remains coherent across the range of events and items that they design. ¬

10/09 ¬ Meet with War on Want to discuss ideas. ¬

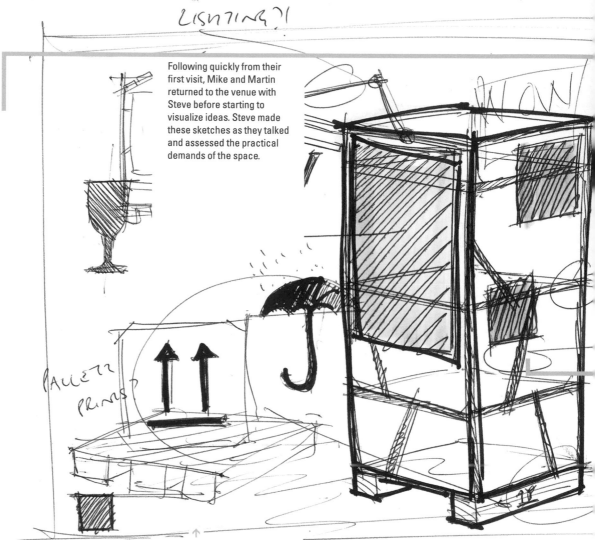

LIGHTING?!

Following quickly from their first visit, Mike and Martin returned to the venue with Steve before starting to visualize ideas. Steve made these sketches as they talked and assessed the practical demands of the space.

PALLETS PRINTS?

»We knew we probably wanted something modular that could also stand together to make one wall, and that was it«, says Mike of these early discussions. Their approach to the design was more that of product designers than architects. »We needed something we could build off-site to some degree and then finish constructing in the space in a day. Creating one massive structure would be a great deal less flexible.« Having agreed on the basic principle of building a modular system, discussions turned to the sorts of materials they might use. Mike and Martin shared their visual references with the product designer Steve Mosley and considered the practicalities and broader issues of the message of the exhibition. From an aesthetic and budgetary perspective, »It was quite clear we'd have to use wood in one form or another and that got us thinking about what sort of structure we might create. We talked about the themes of childhood and work, and thought that as the photos depict childhood, the structure should reflect work and could be a bit industrial.« ¬

They considered using wooden pallets as the bases of the freestanding structures. »We had hoped to use found ready-made pallets but they just weren't good enough quality.« Instead, Steve designed and built his own base modelled on this idea. This brainstorm sheet also shows sketches of the graphics found printed on to industrial pallets and packing, an embellishment that was quickly discarded as unnecessary, in favour of using untreated timber to convey the raw industrial feel they were after. ¬

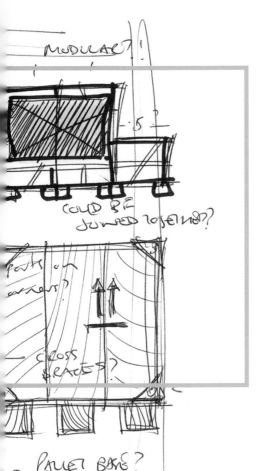

Steve intended that the cross-braces would be positioned randomly, but this ended up placing too many restrictions on the placement of the images. In the final design the angles and positioning of the cross-braces on each stand were the same, creating a more consistent grid on which to place the images. The photographs varied in size so, once attached, an impression of randomness was retained. The large photographs always crossed two brackets and so it was easy to hang them securely but for smaller images the designers had to consider the precise contact points between images and brackets. ¬

Having drawn up his sketches, Steve emailed PDFs to Mike and Martin the following day. »From the start we had to give Steve an indication of the scale and the quantity of photographs we were using so that we could begin thinking about how these would fit.« As these initial sketches show, the design of the structures included horizontal cross-braces, which not only strengthened the structure but also provided fixing points for the photographs. ¬

Designing exhibitions ¬ Exhibitions fall loosely into three main categories: permanent, temporary and touring, each having different design requirements and specifications. For permanent and long-running displays the design and construction must be durable. For a touring exhibition the design needs to be a kit of parts that can be reassembled in different venues and must take into consideration the logistics and price of transportation. With a short, temporary exhibition such as this, Mike and Martin were working with a small budget and a tight deadline that determined the design be economically and logistically efficient. With only one day to install the exhibition, they needed to make the most of the three-week lead-in period for design and construction. They had to ensure their design would allow for easy dismantling in a single day too. ¬ **3D design** ¬ It is more usual for the graphic design – and graphic designers – to be supplementary in an exhibition design project and for the 3D design to take the lead. This is especially the case for exhibitions in large galleries or museums where the specialist skills of the 3D designer can be fully stretched and their wide-ranging responsibilities might include not only the design and construction of the build but the organization and display of artefacts, essential conservation considerations and implementation of health and safety regulations. Many 3D designers are architects and their work can involve complex structural builds. Aware of the small scale and nature of the Richmix exhibition space, Mike and Martin commissioned 3D and product designer Steve Mosley. Mike was upfront about the budget from the start. »We had to say, ›This is not going to be a money-making project for you, are you still interested in it?‹« ¬

26/09 ¬ Meeting with Steve at Richmix. ¬
02/10 ¬ Presentation of wooden stands to War on Want. Approved – production can start straight away. Let Steve know he could order the wood and start building. The aim is to have these built a week before the exhibition. ¬

Selecting the images ¬ It is very unusual for graphic designers to choose the images or objects for inclusion in an exhibition and have a curatorial role as Mike and Martin did here. For them to be given this level of involvement in the content was a reflection of the trust they have built with War on Want. Mike is pragmatic about the rationale behind this. »It's the only way it could work. They know they're up against it with budgets, time and human resources and in terms of creative decision making, they feel confident in knowing they can relax and leave it to us.« Although both the photographer and War on Want made an initial edit of the photographs, Mike and Martin were sent digital files of every image from which to make their own selection. They were given freedom not only to choose which images to include, but also to decide at what size they should be printed. ¬ **Layout** ¬ In most exhibition design projects, the curators and 3D designers work closely on the arrangement and sequence of the exhibits, which can be eclectic and include everything from static pictures or objects to films or interactive experiences. This was a purely photographic exhibition and allowed Mike and Martin to approach the layout of the pictures in a way that was similar to laying out spreads in a book or magazine. ¬ **Choosing a title** ¬ At this point the exhibition was still without a title. Mike and Martin felt this was necessary before they could begin to select images: »For us it was all about the fact that childhood is taken away. So we suggested that this could be the theme – removing childhood or blocking childhood. After a meeting War on Want had with Julio, they let us know the title was going to be Childhood, Interrupted.« ¬

It was primarily Martin's role to select and design the layout of the images. Looking first to identify a story, thread or point of view to inform his selection and design concept, he printed out thumbnails of every image to give him an overview. The process of editing the original 200 images down to 28 took three days. Rather than choose by theme or story, Martin's final selection was informed largely by the aesthetic relationships and rhythms of colour and composition he could establish between photographs. ¬

Establishing the configuration of the stands was essential before the layout of the photographs could begin. Having used the plan as an »early demo« for this, these InDesign sketches mapped out the final position and configurations of each bank of stands. Each bank comprised a number of stands. Mike explains that these »became a bit like spreads« as they considered which images should sit next to one another. A thumbnail of the plan that details where the stands were situated ensured that Martin maintained an overview of how the exhibition worked as a whole while designing. The photos were printed at A1, A2 and A3, as the margin notes record. ¬

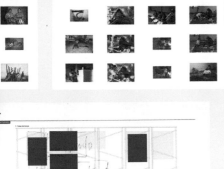
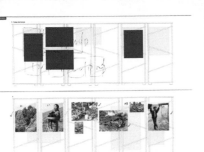

Because of the way the stands were constructed, there were restrictions on where the images could be placed. Each had to be securely attached to the cross-braces while the »see-through« nature of the design made it necessary to consider the positioning of images from both front and back. This layout shows how seeing the reverse of the images created useful quiet areas that helped pace the overall exhibition. The offset alignment of fronts and backs created an asymmetric and dynamic layout, which encouraged the viewer to move through the space and discover what was shown on the other side of the stand. ¬

Through a process of cutting, pasting and rescaling, Martin tested different sequences and combinations of photographs, looking for stories and graphic relationships. »We went through quite a number of stages of this«, says Mike. Each photograph was positioned carefully to take into consideration the effect of the angle of the cross-braces. The alignment of horizon lines, the tension between the angle of an arm or washing-line and the angles of the braces running behind, were subtle but significant details in creating a coherent and convincing hang. ¬

There were tight deadlines for getting the images printed, mounted and delivered in time. On previous projects Mike and Martin have had to get involved in the time-consuming business of checking the accuracy of the colours of photographic prints, but in this case, »We didn't have the luxury of time – there was just no way«. Instead, the photographer supplied colour-balanced files at high resolution. ¬

Perhaps surprisingly, the photographer was happy for Mike and Martin to determine the selection, sequence and scale of his work. »I think he'd done exhibitions before where they'd pretty much taken his prints and stuck them on the wall. He seemed excited we were treating his photographs differently.« ¬

13/10 ¬ Editing of the running order of the images – main edits need to be made over next three days. ¬

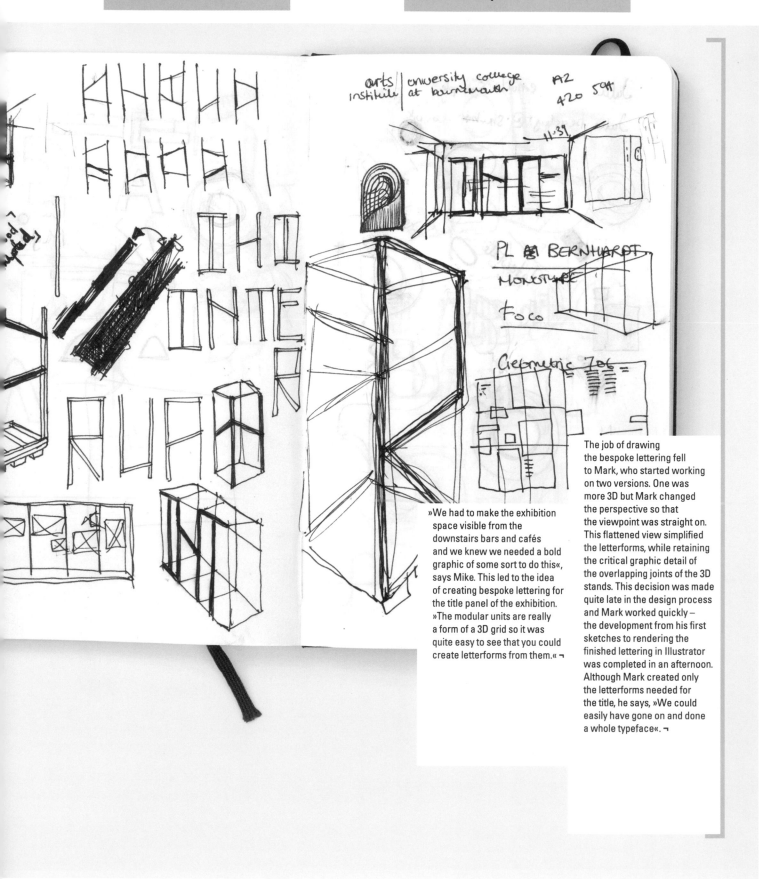

»We had to make the exhibition space visible from the downstairs bars and cafés and we knew we needed a bold graphic of some sort to do this«, says Mike. This led to the idea of creating bespoke lettering for the title panel of the exhibition. »The modular units are really a form of a 3D grid so it was quite easy to see that you could create letterforms from them.« ¬

The job of drawing the bespoke lettering fell to Mark, who started working on two versions. One was more 3D but Mark changed the perspective so that the viewpoint was straight on. This flattened view simplified the letterforms, while retaining the critical graphic detail of the overlapping joints of the 3D stands. This decision was made quite late in the design process and Mark worked quickly – the development from his first sketches to rendering the finished lettering in Illustrator was completed in an afternoon. Although Mark created only the letterforms needed for the title, he says, »We could easily have gone on and done a whole typeface«. ¬

Exhibition graphics ¬ In most exhibition design projects the role of the graphic designer is to develop the graphic language and visual identity of the show, working in dialogue with the 3D designer and the curators. This can include all exhibition graphics from information display panels, object labels and signage, to associated printed materials, catalogues and gallery handouts. Creating a striking visual identity for this exhibition was important to attract attention and draw visitors into the upstairs space, which could easily be circumnavigated or overlooked. ¬ **Access and inclusivity** ¬ Designers must also take into account issues of access and inclusivity. In the UK the Disability Discrimination Act (DDA) sets out a clear objective that spaces and information in the public domain should be accessible to all. Within graphic design for exhibitions this means considering fonts, type sizes and spacing, colour and hanging heights of all text matter. It might also mean considering alternative formats for delivering information, including moving image and sound. For instance, on object labels a sans serif typeface with a generous x-height is regarded as easy to read. Black on white is the most legible colour combination and any move away from this decreases legibility, for which the design will need to compensate in other ways. One of the challenges that the DDA raises for graphic designers is how to avoid outcomes that look or feel too similar. Although inclusive design is necessarily about ensuring access for all, not all people are the same and graphic designers are highly conscious of ensuring that they do not patronize the viewer or make assumptions of this kind. Other considerations that affect accessibility include the height and visibility of objects and the lighting. The responsibility of meeting DDA requirements is shared between the 3D designers, graphic designers and curators. ¬

It was chance that the painted wall in the mezzanine area was red, a colour that is easy to match through the cmyk process. It was »pure fluke« that this red was also so close to Pantone 485, the War on Want red. By choosing to reverse the bespoke lettering out of red, they exploited this coincidence and used the repetition of colour to punctuate the space and draw viewers through the exhibition. »We wanted something relatively close to the edge of the mezzanine and we knew we had to have something facing people at the top of the stairs to draw them round.« ¬

Mike and Martin were in the enviable position of being able to make the decision not to include image captions for the photographs in the exhibition. They felt these were not needed as the direct nature of the photographs rendered supplementary information unnecessary. From a graphic design perspective Mike concedes this was »a bit of a bonus – we could locate the text in one area rather than have it interspersed throughout the exhibition«, thus avoiding excess visual clutter. This also allowed them to concentrate on creating the introduction and title panels. ¬

16/10 ¬ Present final exhibition panels. ¬
17/10 morning ¬ Sign off exhibition panels. We need them printed by next Thursday… ¬

Steve and his associate finished constructing the partially-built panels in the space. Mark and Martin laid the photographic prints – pre-mounted on Foamex – against their corresponding stand. Some last minute changes in the running order of images were made during the hang. Sometimes »things don't quite match up«, and the best-laid plans can feel in need of alteration once the hang begins in the space. To maximize their design time Mike and Martin decided to use a local London-based printer. Working with a new printer inevitably involves an element of risk and Mike made time to visit and meet the printers and look at their work. »They were really, really helpful – good on cost and understood the needs of the client. The printer promised to jump in the van and make the delivery himself rather than send a courier, which was great. We needed someone in London who could print in a particular way and we felt we could trust him.« Their pre-planning and careful organization were pivotal in ensuring the installation went to schedule and was finished ahead of time. ¬

The tight deadline meant avoiding any features that would have involved time-consuming health and safety measures: »We did consider how we might light the space differently, but that would have been a whole other ball game. If we'd fixed lighting on to these modules or brought in extra lighting there would have been the heat, the fire risk and the electricity to consider. Without these the build is actually pretty inert stuff from a health and safety point of view.« Mike and Martin kept the venue informed of their plans but knew from experience that there were unlikely to be any major issues and that their design allowed enough space for access. ¬

Exhibition installation ¬ Project managing the design of an exhibition requires careful planning and co-ordination. Once the concept has been developed and the design mapped on to the plans, the build must take into consideration deadlines for different stages of the project. The design and build have to come together in order to be completed within a specific time frame, usually dictated by the date of the private view. Most decisions relating to the hang and installation, such as the placement of the objects, are made beforehand. In a gallery situation, objects are often on loan and come with requirements and specifications, for example the distance they must be from the viewer. Installation can be a lengthy process and handling precious objects demands precision and care – and frequently white gloves. Large galleries or institutions have an in-house installation team but in this case it was down to Steve and his associate, with Martin and Mark working alongside. ¬ **Preparing the pictures** ¬ The photographs were delivered to the exhibition space on the day of the hang and Mike's biggest worry during the final stages of the project was that they would arrive on time and be good enough in quality. They chose to output the photographs as Lambda prints, which use laser technology to produce photographic prints from digital files, giving greater sharpness and accuracy of colour than many other print processes. Photographic prints can be mounted on rigid Foamex, or printed directly on to board, MDF or aluminium, for example. Prints can be sealed or laminated, wrap-mounted or printed flush to the edges. ¬

Mike and Martin were responsible for organizing and budgeting for all aspects of the exhibition, including printing the photographs. »The budget had to cover absolutely everything, the printing, mounting and delivery of the photographs, all materials, the construction, paying for Steve's time, oh and the Velcro to put it all up with as well!« ¬

17/10 afternoon ¬ One of us to jump on a train to take high res files to printer in London, to avoid any issues with file transfer. ¬
20/10 ¬ Exhibition panels printed. Agree that the printer will drive them to the venue himself! ¬
22/10 8.30am ¬ Prints arrive at venue. ¬ **9am** ¬ Build starts. ¬ **10am** ¬ Graphics etc… ¬

The exhibition opening ¬ The private view is often the first time that designers see their exhibition functioning and filled with an audience. Graphic designers are not always privy to comments from the end-users of their work, and so the public judgement of a private view can be nerve-racking. Mike is casual about this vulnerability, however, enjoying seeing a space animated by visitors. He is also a little sheepish as he explains that he was the only studio member able to attend the private view: »It's the natural point where people congratulate you, and although they all built it, I was there for the glory.« ¬ For their client a private view provides valuable press and publicity opportunities and a direct way of communicating the positive change the charity achieves. For this event War on Want had brought one of the Guatemalan girls who had been a beneficiary of the project to London. This was a powerful way to make real the people and lives the project has changed and increase understanding and awareness of the work that War on Want does. This was important for their supporters and also the politicians and policymakers who were invited guests and whom War on Want seeks to influence and lobby for change. ¬

The exhibition came in on budget and on time but then, as Mike says, »it had to«. Although such limitations add pressure, Bond and Coyne enjoy this kind of work, both for its value to War on Want and the opportunity it presents to try things out. »If there's a sort of project we're prepared to invest in, it is this. In fact we'd have wanted to invest more in it and take less money for ourselves, but in reality we set aside an amount that covered our time, to a certain extent, and the rest was spent on production – you want to get the best results you can.« ¬

Mike admits with satisfaction, »We're really pleased with the results and the client was too – I think they were fairly blown away by what we managed to do with the space and budget they'd given us. The venue said it was the most successful use of that space that they'd seen. We also got to develop our collaborative relationship with Steve. We're going to continue and together push for more of this sort of work, probably on a larger scale.« ¬

In their ongoing role as designers for War on Want, Mike and Martin are alert to the potential for this event to live on beyond the exhibition dates: »We made sure we recorded everything photographically so that we've got material should further opportunities to use it present themselves«. ¬

23/10 evening ¬ Private view. Mike attends. ¬
07/11 ¬ Show comes down. ¬

When we first met Experimental Jetset
to discuss their identity design for 104
(Le Cent Quatre), a new 39,000 square metres
(128,000 square feet) arts complex in Paris,
the project was underway and we predicted
an impressive outcome. The commissioning
process had been unusual, and the design
development was taking some curious turns,
but the results already seemed exceptional.
So, we were surprised when designers
Danny van den Dungen (born 1971), Marieke
Stolk (born 1967) and Erwin Brinkers (born 1973)
subsequently felt it best to walk away. We knew
that the decision would not have been taken
lightly; but this new turn of events afforded
us the opportunity to explore the more subtle
and sometimes turbulent aspects of the design
process. ¬ Danny, Marieke and Erwin bring
maturity, objectivity and kindness to their
assessment of the project. They tell us with
delight about the unpredictable nature of the
initial contact: 104's team had seen their work
featured in a design book they had assumed
would only be looked at by other designers. They
quip that they were expected to bring a »Dutch
sensibility« to this design task, commenting:
»One of our proposals was rejected because
it was considered too French!«. As we monitor
Danny, Marieke and Erwin's creative process
and invite them to reflect on the eventual
outcome, we ask whether the enormity and
timescale of the project was a cause of anxiety,
and if politics became a distraction from
the design job in hand. ¬

Designing the identity for a new and multi-discipline arts organization sounds like a dream job, but it requires design dexterity as well as enormous commitment and well-honed organizational and diplomatic skills. Experimental Jetset are self-styled modernists who are culturally eclectic. So, from what do they draw inspiration and how do they remain calm and collected when design passions start to rise? ¬

The magical centre ¬ Experimental Jetset find working and living in a design-conscious and politically-charged city like Amsterdam, an important influence on their work. They talk excitedly of how underground movements, from the anarchist groups of the 1960s through to the squatters of the 1980s, are all part of the city's subconscious. (Incidentally, Marieke's father Rob Stolk was a founder member of the 1960s anarchist group Provo.) Although their graphic language has been shaped most obviously by the work of the later modernists such as Wim Crouwel, Experimental Jetset say that their roots really lie »in the Fluxus-like anarchy of our home city«. ¬

The one true path ¬ Danny, Marieke and Erwin don't remember what careers they had in mind as children – it's irrelevant, so certain are they that they have found their vocations – »Since graduating, we never considered anything other than being graphic designers. We simply couldn't do anything else.« They met as students at the Gerrit Rietveld Academy, Amsterdam, in the early 1990s. »College shaped us immensely«, they say, acknowledging their debt to teachers Linda van Deursen and Gerald van der Kaap, who employed an unlikely amalgam of pragmatism and anarchy in their work. »We are a bit more timid than they, but their ›can-do‹ attitude informed us greatly.« Despite recognizing that they are defined through graphic design, they cite advertising as one area of design practice that they wouldn't feel comfortable working in: »If that were the only option, we'd feel forced to do something else – deliver newspapers, be a nightwatch at an abandoned building – something unrelated to design.« ¬

Total Design/total football ¬ Even though they proudly describe themselves as »not football fans at all«, Experimental Jetset cite the legendary Dutch player Johan Cruijff's concept of »totaal voetbal« as inspirational. In total football the role of each player isn't fixed, so any player can be an attacker, defender or midfielder. »It's a very modernist, modular system; it's also very egalitarian, very Dutch in a way.« Having been influenced greatly by the work of one of the first multi-disciplinary design groups in Holland, Total Design, Experimental Jetset delight in the conceptual parallels between total football and Total Design: »Cruijff meets Crouwel«. The system of total football acts as a model for Danny, Marieke and Erwin's studio. Although deadlines sometimes necessitate fixed roles for each of them, on the whole Experimental Jetset try to avoid this. They aim to share roles and responsibilities, doing everything together as colleagues and friends: »The stress can cause irritation, but we never take it out on each other.« ¬

A culture clash ¬ Danny, Marieke and Erwin talk passionately about the relationship of punk to modernism. They acknowledge that theirs is an arguable position: »The whole DIY model of punk; for us, that's modernism in its purest form.« The echoes of punk still redolent in the mid-1980s were Experimental Jetset's shared teen inspiration: »They were our beginning point. Punk was of mythical proportions, affecting everything that came after it. Think about things like the fold-out record sleeves of Crass, the ›dripping blood‹ logo of The Cramps, the propaganda-like sleeves made by Foetus and the brilliant English new wave comic magazine called ›Escape‹, that explained in detail how to Xerox your own mini comics«. In their independence of spirit, their demarcation-free approach to culture and their celebration of the small, these influences are right at the centre of Experimental Jetset's work. ¬

Being modernists ¬ Modernism is lazily misunderstood to be a style rather than a way of thinking. So, as Experimental Jetset use ranged-left Helvetica, they are idly passed off as modernists. They are, but not for that reason. Admittedly, modernism is hard to define but Danny, Marieke and Erwin's starting point is this deductive reasoning by Karl Marx: »If man is shaped by his surroundings, his surroundings must be made human.« A belief in the positive value of human intervention is a cornerstone of modernist thinking, and it is this principle by which Experimental Jetset live and work: »For us, it means creating an environment that is clearly made by humans. This doesn't necessarily mean it is warm, cosy, friendly. We would define it as one that reminds us that everything is shapeable, changeable and breakable.« This philosophy is manifest in all of Experimental Jetset's work. »Clients that come to us because they have seen our previous work usually understand our ideas, because the ideas and the work are one and the same.« ¬

Sweet and sour ¬ Although purporting to be objective criticism, design comment can swing wildly between adulation and ridicule, something that even established designers find difficult to handle. Experimental Jetset have been shocked by some of the unfavourable attention they have received: »It came as a total surprise. We always thought we were designing in an honest, sincere way, but many critics described (and still describe) our work as cynical, ironic, postmodern drivel. We have decided to try and remain humble and open, as our way to deal with the sometimes very hostile industry that surrounds graphic design. We know that the moment we become bitter, we are lost and we won't let that happen.« ¬

In all things ¬ For all three designers, graphic design is so all-encompassing that it can easily relate to all their other interests. In this sense, they never stop thinking about graphic design. Music and music theory are two of their greatest influences. So when, for example, they read an article about a »motorik beat«, a 4/4 rhythm used by Krautrock bands, they immediately start thinking how this could be translated into a graphic design grid. »We spent hours thinking about how Phil Spector's ›Wall of Sound‹ technique could translate into graphic design; thinking about the way the Beatles, four white kids from the UK, could transform American black music from decades earlier into something truly revolutionary; thinking about the transformative power of music in general. When we are stuck, we always look to rock music, because for us, it is the mirror of design.« ¬

Danny, Marieke and Erwin's first meeting with the 104 directors took place here. At this stage still a very large construction site, the directors explained their plans for the space. »It all sounded very interesting, and we listened with attention, all wearing protective helmets and nodding politely, but we still weren't sure to what extent they were actually interested in working with us. We didn't have to show any of our work and were convinced that this meeting would not lead to an actual assignment.« ¬

Once the project was under way, Experimental Jetset visited Paris every few weeks for two or three days: »We had meetings with lots of people from 104: the directors, the financial people, the technical staff, the publicity people, the people responsible for maintaining the website. Sometimes meetings were really exhausting, but always laid-back. The 104 team were very respectful, very friendly and warm.« ¬

Perhaps unsurprisingly, given France's rich fine art heritage, the expectation was that Experimental Jetset would be more interested in the pictorial aspects of their design. »In France, star designers are seen as artists and an anonymous set of people apply their images to websites, printed matter, etc. The idea that the application is a creative act is not recognized. In the Netherlands, we are much more interested in how creativity can be applied in an integral, systematic way. The French designer Pierre Bernard explained it perfectly with the analogy that in France there are beautiful flowers, but in the Netherlands there are beautiful gardens.« ¬

Being commissioned ¬ All three designers delight in the unpredictable way that projects arrive at their door: »In 1999, we were asked to design a catalogue for an exhibition at the Pompidou Centre, with a signage system and large mural, all because the curators had seen an A6 invitation we designed – carrying one sentence in Helvetica!« In this case, 104's directors had seen Danny, Marieke and Erwin's work for the Stedelijk Museum, Amsterdam, featured in a design book. They invited the designers to Paris, confident that they had the experience to develop the visual identity for 104 – although it wasn't immediately clear to Experimental Jetset that this was a preliminary briefing meeting for the job: »We were under the impression that they were testing the water and were convinced that the project's scale would necessitate a pitch.« Danny, Marieke and Erwin left the meeting with various papers, all in French. That night, some French-speaking friends looked at the documents and assured them that it was a contract for them to sign! ¬ **Pitching** ¬ In France, when a project is publicly-funded, the law dictates that it has to be announced openly so that any company can compete for the work. From the outset, Experimental Jetset made it clear they would not participate in a design competition and so, as a way to avoid this process, the contract referred to them as »artists-in-residence« and specified that their work was »to create artworks that would be the basis for the graphic identity«. This was clever, but did lead to misunderstandings: »We were expected to come up with expressive, creative gestures, and not be bothered about specifics. But we want to design the small type under a logo as well as the logo itself, and we want to think about where and how it should be used.« ¬

06/02/07 ¬ Mails received from, and/or mails sent to: Park Jungyeon, Monica Eulitz, Guus Beumer, Noëlle Kemmerling, Debra Solomon, Gary Hustwit, Vanessa Beecroft, Peter Jeffs, Casco Projects, Cécile Renault, Bruna Roccasalva, André Viljoen, Constance de Corbière, Stéphanie Hussonnois, Fritz Haeg, Raoul Teulings, Christian Larsen, Jorrit Hermans, Thomas Smit, Celine Bosman, Pascalle Gense, students of the Rietveld Academy, Raoul Teulings, Linda van Deursen, Floor Koomen; etc. ¬

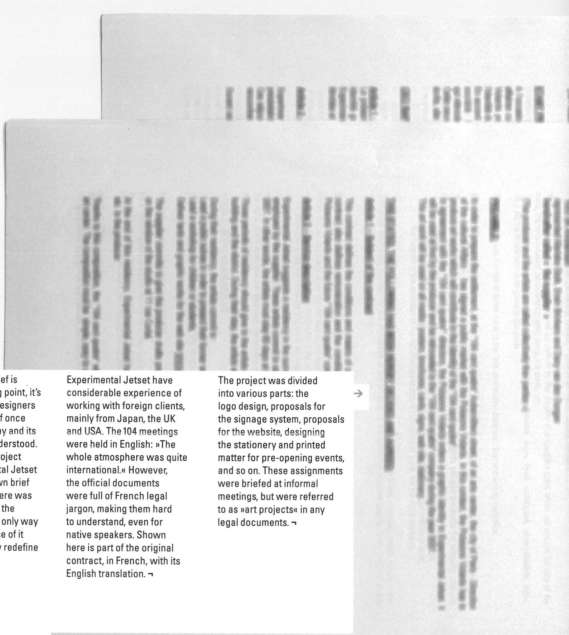

Although a client brief is a necessary starting point, it's not uncommon for designers to devise a new brief once a project is underway and its parameters truly understood. Unusually, the 104 project required Experimental Jetset to formulate their own brief from the outset: »There was the official brief and the ›unofficial‹ brief; the only way we could make sense of it all was to constantly redefine the demands.« ¬

Experimental Jetset have considerable experience of working with foreign clients, mainly from Japan, the UK and USA. The 104 meetings were held in English: »The whole atmosphere was quite international.« However, the official documents were full of French legal jargon, making them hard to understand, even for native speakers. Shown here is part of the original contract, in French, with its English translation. ¬

The project was divided into various parts: the logo design, proposals for the signage system, proposals for the website, designing the stationery and printed matter for pre-opening events, and so on. These assignments were briefed at informal meetings, but were referred to as »art projects« in any legal documents. ¬

Contracts ¬ Designers are generally required to sign legally-binding contracts for large projects, but for medium and small-sized projects this is rare. Although professional organizations would caution against it, most briefs and budgets are agreed verbally or via an exchange of emails. Experimental Jetset did have a contract for the 104 project, but it didn't accurately outline the work expectations, time frames or budgets as this would have triggered a tendering process. ¬ The first design meeting was in February 2007 and from this Experimental Jetset understood that they had 20 months to develop the identity, implement it and produce various promotional items before the opening. There were fixed budgets for some parts of this work, and others were quoted for: »It took a lot of puzzling to fit the right activity to the right portion of money, but the financial people at 104 were really helpful with this.« ¬ **Funding** ¬ The project was primarily funded by the municipality of Paris, which led to a slightly skewed client/designer relationship. Although Danny, Marieke and Erwin saw themselves as answerable to 104's directors, it became apparent that there were »higher powers«, inaccessible to the designers. »One of our first proposals, approved by the directors, was later rejected because ›the mayor doesn't like yellow‹ – now a sort of depressing catchphrase in our studio!« ¬ **Audience** ¬ Experimental Jetset resist the perceived wisdom that the audience need to be categorized for design work to communicate effectively: »It's all too manipulative for us.« Danny, Marieke and Erwin assumed that 104's audience would be as culturally inquisitive as they are themselves: »We try to produce design that makes sense to us. We don't think we are so unique or exotic that what seems logical to us will be nonsensical to others. We are part of society, and society is part of us. We sometimes use subtle references, but only in the way that a chef might use ingredients that are hard to identify, but still influence the meal.« ¬

03/04/07 ¬ Mails received from, and/or mails sent to: Park Jungyeon, Joel Priestland, MacGregor Harp, Jorrit Hermans, Sander Donkers, Lara Suarez-Neves, Agnes Paulissen, Karen Borrelli, Alex deValence, Antonio Carusone, Claus Eggers Sorensen, Christian Larsen, etc. ¬

Starting points ¬ Danny, Marieke and Erwin's curiosity is nourished by extensive research. This is often far-reaching, but nevertheless germane to each project, and usually entails an enormous amount of reading. Their design proposals are always presented alongside this documentation. Unafraid of intellectual discourse, their French clients particularly appreciated this: »They enjoyed discussing ideas, philosophy, politics – the meetings were always intellectually stimulating.« ¬ Already familiar with the work of literary critic, essayist and philosopher Walter Benjamin, all three designers became engrossed in Benjamin's critique of the bourgeois experience, »Das Passagen-Werk« (»The Arcades Project«). Unfinished at the time of his death in 1940, Benjamin cited the nineteenth-century shopping arcades of Paris as a metaphor for the broader commodification of many aspects of modern life. Alongside chapters entitled »Boredom«, »Prostitution« and »Dream City«, is one dedicated to the history and ideology of metal constructions, especially the use of iron in passages and arcades. Effectively a street with a roof, 104 occupies just such an arcade. »We knew Benjamin wrote a lot about this subject, so when we got involved in the project one of the first things we did was study his book, looking for clues and starting points.« ¬ Concurrently with this research Danny, Marieke and Erwin identified the notion of »a work in progress« as a key curatorial vision for 104. Benjamin's writings about iron constructions, coupled with this idea of a constantly evolving work, became their focus for the early stages of the design process. ¬

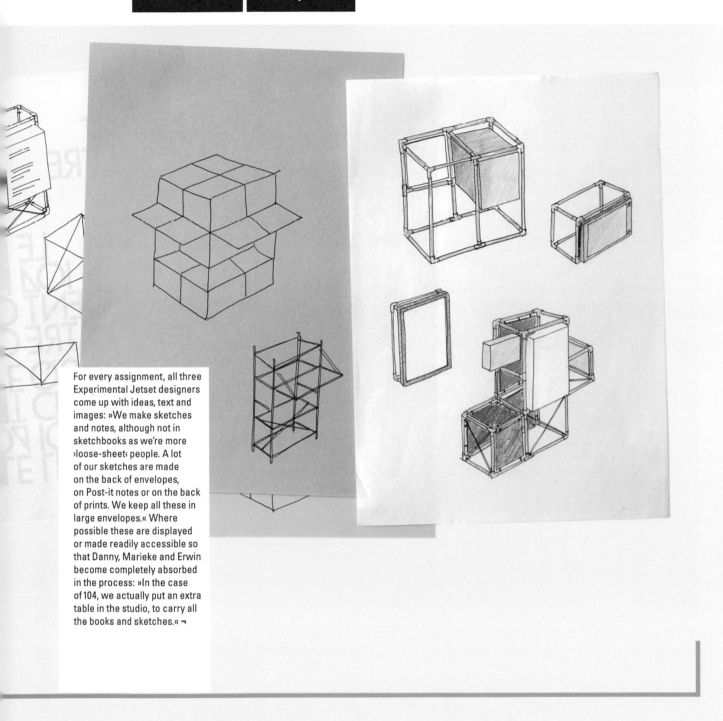

For every assignment, all three Experimental Jetset designers come up with ideas, text and images: »We make sketches and notes, although not in sketchbooks as we're more ›loose-sheet‹ people. A lot of our sketches are made on the back of envelopes, on Post-it notes or on the back of prints. We keep all these in large envelopes.« Where possible these are displayed or made readily accessible so that Danny, Marieke and Erwin become completely absorbed in the process: »In the case of 104, we actually put an extra table in the studio, to carry all the books and sketches.« ¬

22/05/07 ¬ Mails received from, and/or mails sent to: Femke Dekker, Liang Lu, Monica Eulitz, Ryutaro Uchiyama, Shipmate Screenprinting, Cécile Renault, Agnes Paulissen, Dennis Bouws, Jeroen Klaver, Rafael Roozendaal, Brita Lindvall, San Yin Kan, Tomoko Sakamoto, Vanessa Beecroft, Celine Bosman, Christian Larsen, Andrew Howard, e-Toy, Ayumi Higuchi, Claudia Germaine Marie Doms, Revolver Books, Raina Kumra, Jas Rewkiewicz, David Keshavjee, Sebastian Tola, students of the Rietveld Academy, Gary Hustwit, Jan Dietvorst, Zak Kyes, Vanessa Norwood, Mark Blamire, etc. ¬

Corporate identity ¬ Since the 1950s, the perceived wisdom has been that the mainstay of a visual identity is its logo. Within corporate design, all graphic design roads usually lead back to it. The logo is generally the focus of the initial design work. With the intention of reinforcing, emphasizing and supporting the logo, the overall visual identity is developed to reflect it or to contrast with it. Although commissioned to design the centre's identity, Experimental Jetset's clients at 104 were wary of the idea of a logo. »They were coming from a more French and postmodern way of thinking. They were very suspicious that logos were ›authoritarian‹ – too ›fixed‹, too ›centralized‹.« Experimental Jetset were therefore left with no choice but to start developing the identity from a different perspective and decided to begin with the interior signage for the space. ¬

The interior signs ¬ Having read the relevant sections of »The Arcades Project«, and mindful of their clients' brief, Experimental Jetset hit upon the idea of developing a signage system around walls of scaffolding. They explain: »A scaffold is a structure that automatically refers to ›work-in-progress‹. We realized that a sign system using scaffolding would be a constant reminder of the continuous cycle of building, demolishing and rebuilding, and that by using iron in its construction we would also emphasize the early industrial architecture of the space.« ¬ Danny, Marieke and Erwin are wary of overworked design solutions, but this seemed a very organic approach with an honest aesthetic: »It has the casualness of a ›ready-made‹ object.« ¬

Before Experimental Jetset were commissioned, 104's architects had submitted a design proposal for permanent signs that had been approved by the municipality. 104's directors hoped to reverse this decision and asked Experimental Jetset to consider these signs along with the rest of their system. Experimental Jetset's designs are shown here. Sadly, a compromise was reached that left Experimental Jetset disappointed. It was proposed that the architects would design the fixed signs according to Experimental Jetset's graphic manual. Although the manual describes how to apply the identity in some detail, Danny, Marieke and Erwin felt that it would have been more coherent to have a clear demarcation between the »architectural« voice applied in the permanent signs and the »institutional/ curatorial« voice evident in their own designs. ¬

The proposed use of scaffolding for the signage at 104 was as practical as it was conceptually rigorous. It was the core element in a highly-flexible system. Each scaffolding wall could be moved or reconfigured, the signs could be changed easily and the structures were high on visual impact. Overall, the signage was unusual for not being fixed to the building itself or painted on the walls. ¬

Many designers profess to have an interest in control, but they are delighted nevertheless when chance plays a role in the design process. Experimental Jetset describe the fact that a scaffolding company employee was living next door to 104 as a happy coincidence. »Some maquettes of the sign system were exhibited in the window of the 104 office. The woman dropped by, curious about what was going on. We happened to be there. She introduced herself and gave us some brochures. She also turned out to be originally from the UK, so she could speak English perfectly, making communication really easy. Just what are the odds of that happening?« ¬

Danny, Marieke and Erwin were able to test run their signage solutions at various events before 104 opened. The signs were silk-screen printed on large perspex sheets, so they were durable and had the most intense colour possible. They were then attached to the scaffold with large metal clips. ¬

→

Although not highlighted in the brief, the team at 104 was mindful of health and safety regulations and asked Experimental Jetset to make sure that the scaffolding structures were secured firmly to the ground and were not easy for children to climb. Their clients also considered the design proposals in terms of access for visually-impaired and other disabled visitors. Luckily the designs didn't raise any concerns. ¬

17/08/07 ¬ Mails received from, and/or mails sent to: Blake Sinclair, Mike Mills, Linda van Deursen, Vanessa Beecroft, Floor Krooi, Jérôme Saint-Loubert Bié, Christoph Seyferth, Niels Helleman, Devon Ress, Frank Noorland, Cindy Hoetmer, Jorinde ten Berge, Femke Dekker, Internationale Socialisten, UOVO, Gary Hustwit, Daniëlle van Ark, etc. ¬

The logo ¬ Clients often issue directives with great confidence, only to change the brief once a project is under way. Experimental Jetset was specifically asked not to design a logo for 104. Danny, Marieke and Erwin felt some unease about the client's rationale but decided to bide their time rather than countermand their brief in any way. »We see things the opposite way to them – the idea of a logo-less, non-authoritarian ›soft‹ graphic identity might sound very human, but in the end it's almost like a form of repressive tolerance, almost like being smothered by cushions. We prefer the ›hard‹, authoritarian graphic identity, because it seems somehow more honest.« ¬ As they were sketching their preliminary ideas for the signage system they couldn't help but play with logo ideas too – if only to generate material with which to fill their dummy signs. The resultant signage visuals were presented to 104's directors. »We expected the logos to be voted off, but to our surprise, the directors immediately loved them. So that's how the logos became part of the project.« ¬ Although Danny, Marieke and Erwin explored various logo ideas, once they hit upon the line/circle/triangle concept they knew that they »were on to something«. Logos that are solely typographic, or only use lettering, are often the strongest because they amalgamate the two essential requirements of a logo: they reinforce the organization name and are distinct and highly-recognizable, stand-alone marques. Experimental Jetset's logo uses a line, a circle and a triangle to represent the name. Its simplicity, both visually and conceptually, is striking. The marque alludes to the elemental forms of the square, circle and triangle, synonymous with the Bauhaus and as fundamental as the three primary colours. By playing with these forms, their design is distinct and intriguing. ¬

Danny, Marieke and Erwin used the three abstract shapes that make up the 104 logo as the building blocks for their signage system. These forms were used as a code: the line stood for »follow the line«; the circle for »you are here«; and the triangle was used as an arrow. The angle of the triangle was also reminiscent of the scaffolding structures seen from the side. ¬

Because repetition is considered to be key to recognition, most organizations only have one logo. But 104's identity called for a more flexible approach, so Experimental Jetset decided to develop the marque as though it were a font. The final logo was supplied in four weights: light, medium, bold and extra bold. They experimented with how each might be used on various items of printed matter, finding that the finer weights were more »pictorial« than the heavier weights. ¬

Having developed the treatment for the name 104, Experimental Jetset were asked to develop other logo variants, this time in response to political concerns. Although 104's directors were happy with a purely numerical logo, shown far right, the city council was worried that this would lead to diverse pronunciation of the name. The directors saw this as an appropriate reflection of the multicultural ambitions they had for the space, but the local dignitaries worried that Le Cent Quatre would not be understood to be a French institution paid for through local taxes. So Danny, Marieke and Erwin developed a new text-based version of the logo that read: Le 104 Cent Quatre, shown above. ¬

Politics played an even more direct role in the next set of logo variants. Mayoral elections were imminent and the incumbent mayor wanted to emphasize that 104 was a project developed by the city of Paris. So the line »Établissement Artistique de la Ville de Paris« was added to the logo. A few months later, Experimental Jetset were asked to implement another change, adding the logo of the Mairie de Paris to all printed matter, as shown above. »We became angry a couple of times, but there's really nothing you can do when faced with this level of bureaucracy. So we grudgingly complied.« ¬

11/11/07 ¬ Mails received from, and/or mails sent to: Ivanka Bakker, Femke Dekker, Emily Wraith, Chiellerie, Will Holder, Laura Snell, David Bennewith, Fed-Ex Newsletter, Licor de Mono, Noa Segal, Get Records, Erwin K Bauer, Naïa Sore, Linda van Deursen, Edwin van den Dungen, Katja Weitering, etc. ¬

Danny, Marieke and Erwin produced various badges for different events at 104, as shown here. For the »badge-making performance«, their plan was to make and distribute signed and numbered badges that carried the message »It's Alive«. However, Danny, Marieke and Erwin's badge machine broke en route to Paris and so they were left in front of an expectant crowd, unable to perform. They remain enthusiastic about the original idea though and are gratified to have worked with clients who were such »fluid thinkers«. »They came up with these kinds of ideas really easily. They were great to work with.« ¬

ΔBCDEF
GHIJKLM
NOPQRS
TUVWXYZ
123Δ56
7890

ΔBCDEF
GHIJKLM
NOPQRS
TUVWXYZ
123Δ56
7890

**ΔBCDEF
GHIJKLM
NOPQRS
TUVWXYZ
123Δ56
7890**

**ΔBCDEF
GHIJKLM
NOPQRS
TUVWXYZ
123Δ56
7890**

Danny, Marieke and Erwin chose Futura as the house font for 104. As with the logo, it comes in weights that range from light to extra bold. Loosely based on the simple forms of a circle, square and triangle it was obviously the most appropriate font to accompany their design. ¬

Corporate font ¬ Along with the logo, another key element of a graphic identity is a corporate font, chosen for its appropriateness in terms of feel as much as application. Although Danny, Marieke and Erwin tested various contenders for 104's house font, it was pretty clear to them that Paul Renner's sans serif Futura would be the best complement to their logo design. First released by the Bauer Type Foundry in 1928, Futura is a monoline typeface – which means that the strokes are of even thickness – and is derived from simple geometric forms. Experimental Jetset added two extra characters to the font. »We didn't mess with the actual Futura font«, they explain. »We just made a mini font, consisting of the triangle-A, the triangle-4, the line and the circle based on the capital I and O, all in four weights. This mini font is intended to be used alongside the original Futura.« ¬ **Artists-in-residence** ¬ While Danny, Marieke and Erwin were working on the signage, logo and early implementation they also kept an eye on their contractual obligations as supposed »artists-in-residence«. Although this was a faux-role, thought up to avoid tendering processes, the directors were keen for Experimental Jetset's work to go beyond that of more conventional designers. »At one meeting we presented our logos as a set of badges, and the directors proudly pinned them on their jackets. We explained how we made these badges, using expressive movements with our arms, demonstrating how a badge-making machine is operated. Two of the directors, from a theatre background, shouted: ›This is great, you should turn this into a performance‹. So for the next Nuit Blanche (a pre-opening event), they asked us to do a 15-minute badge-making performance!« ¬

03/01/08 ¬ Mails received from, and/or mails sent to: Christel Gouweleeuw, Hanneke Beukers, Simone Vergeat, Frank Noorland, Karina Bisch, Point Ephemere, Maaike van Rijn, Tanneke Janssen, Olivia Grandperrin, Ryder Seeler, Thomas Demand, Bisbald, Matucana 100, etc. ¬

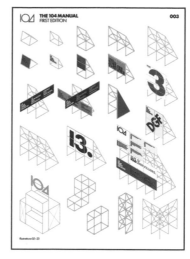

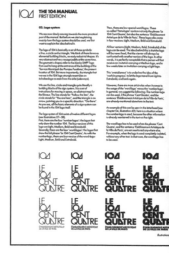

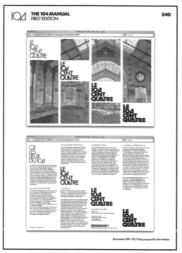

Experimental Jetset's graphic design manual for 104 runs to over 100 pages. Citing EM Forster, Walter Benjamin and Henry Ford to name but a few, it captivates, delights and saddens as it tells the tale of this particular graphic journey. ¬

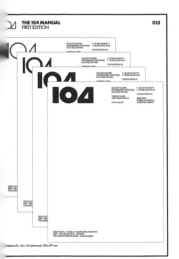

Implementation ¬ Most designers of a visual identity want to manage closely how their identity is applied, if not apply it themselves. Experimental Jetset planned to design as much of the initial printed material as possible, not only »to give 104 a good start« but also to demonstrate to any subsequent designers how the identity should be employed. Their client was very keen, however, that they develop a graphic design manual or »charte graphique«. »Instead of the actual printed items, the client was much more interested in templates and guidelines.« ¬ **The manual** ¬ Graphic design manuals vary greatly in terms of what they cover. The briefest of them are primarily simple logo usage guidelines. More extensive documents cover this and the use of fonts, images and colour. They outline core messages and tone of voice, as embodied in language and images, include templates and grids applicable to print, web pages and display materials, and outline production methods and techniques. ¬ Drafted in instalments, Experimental Jetset's manual for 104 is unusual. Rather than being objective and instructional in tone, it tells the story of the development of the identity in an honest and emotional way. »Our manual shows not only the ›winning‹ designs, but also the rejected proposals and the failures. Every time a design or template was approved, we added it to the manual. Sometimes the city council rejected something after the directors had approved it. In that case, we didn't remove the design from the manual, but just added another chapter, in which we made clear that the previous chapter was negated.« ¬

18/03/08 ¬ Mails received from, and/or mails sent to: Catherine Griffiths, Satoko Takahashi, Saskia Schoenmaker, Naïa Sore, Cécile Renault, Constance de Corbière, Leonhard Preschl, Matt Grady, Gary Hustwit, Jacqueline van As, Project Projects, Diana Bergquist, Cassandra Coblentz, Pae White, Buzzworks, Jean Bernard Koeman, Open Reading Group, David Reinfurt, Janine Ferguson, Lakshmi Bhaskaran, Oyvind Tendenes, Printed Matter, Herman Verkerk, Paul Kuipers, Sara Ludvigsson, etc. ¬

Printing ¬ Most of Experimental Jetset's work is print-based. Marieke's father was a printer and all three designers are acutely aware of the subtle sensory differences that are achievable through print and finishing. They consider all aspects of production carefully, both from an aesthetic and conceptual point of view – trying to avoid using cmyk, for example, because it is »a mere simulation of colour« when considered against the true colours of the Pantone range, and arguing in the 104 manual that paper weights should be chosen for maximum contrast to increase users' delight and surprise. ¬ The print buying for 104 was subject to the same tendering process as the graphic design, which posed obvious problems. Not only did it require print specifications to be fixed long before the designs were resolved, but it also meant that different printers could be selected for different parts of the job, with the obviously worrying implications for quality control and consistency across all items. Luckily, at 104 there was one person working full-time finding ways to avoid adhering to the tendering system and so it was with some relief that Experimental Jetset ended up working with one printer for the whole job. »These printers did a great job, but we do feel that in general, the expectations for printing are different in France than they are in the Netherlands. In the Netherlands, the print quality is seen as an integral part of the design, while in France, the focus in design is more on the creation of a ›beautiful image‹ – the application (including the printing) is seen as less important.« ¬

This umbrella was designed for a group of artists (Le Balto) who did a 15-minute performance during the Nuit Blanche, one of the pre-opening 104 events. Their piece required all the audience members to hold umbrellas with »Où est le jardin?« (Where is the garden?) printed on them. Experimental Jetset were asked to design an umbrella carrying this sentence and did so using the visual identity of 104. ¬

Danny, Marieke and Erwin cite badges and T-shirts as some of the items that attracted them to graphic design in the first place: »Our roots lie in post-punk subcultures. As teenagers, we were quite fascinated by movements such as garage punk, new wave, hardcore punk; not only by the music, but also by the way these movements manifested themselves in record sleeves, badges, T-shirts, fanzines.« ¬

The bag, T-shirts and badges were all Experimental Jetset's ideas, created for various pre-opening events. Danny, Marieke and Erwin don't draw a distinction between these objects and posters, brochures, cards and so on. »We regard a poster as a material object, an artefact that is just as 3D as a T-shirt or a badge. It's a physical sheet of paper with layers of ink on top of it. To see graphic design as the creation of objects (rather than the creation of images) has always been very important to us. To emphasize the material dimension of design is one of the main themes in our work. To us, images seem to float high above us, untouchable and removed. While images clearly tied to their material base are touchable, shapeable and changeable.« ¬

10/06/08 ¬ Mails received from, and/or mails sent to: Monica Eulitz, Min Choi, Valentina Bruschi, Bart Griffioen, Noëlle Kemmerling, Marie Guillemin, Sara de Bondt, Richard Rhys, Pedro Monteiro, Bella Erikson, The No, Ivano Salonia, Naïa Sore, Yoshi Kawasaki, etc. ¬

All possible colour combinations:

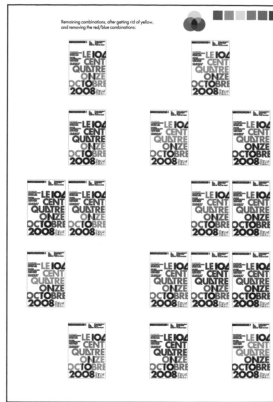

Remaining combinations, after getting rid of yellow, and removing the red/blue combinations:

The story of these posters perhaps best sums up the 104 design experience. Having redesigned the first 104 logo to incorporate »Le Cent Quatre«, Danny, Marieke and Erwin looked for ways to integrate text and numbers further. They experimented with overprinting effects – when two colours are printed on top of each other to make a third colour – and found they could play with secondary meanings this way. However, the process of choosing the actual colours became increasingly political. ¬

Colour always seems to provoke the most subjective of rejoinders but, having initially decided to work with the three primary colours, Experimental Jetset had to contend with the mayor who »doesn't like yellow« and directors who disliked blue and red! The three sheets above show the gradual process of elimination. They tried the secondary colours – purple, green and orange – next, convincing themselves that it was a rational solution to use the colours produced when primaries overprint. These colours were deemed to be open to misinterpretation: »Some people thought that green/red looked like the Italian flag«. The colours eventually chosen were green and blue, but shown above are what Danny, Marieke and Erwin describe as the posters that demonstrate »this absurd process of deductive reasoning«. ¬

Remaining combinations, after removing all double colour combinations:

Danny, Marieke and Erwin are unsure if they have learnt anything from the 104 experience that could stop it being repeated. They remain open and fatalistic: »It's so hard to predict how an assignment will develop. It's always such a gamble. Sometimes projects that started as dream assignments turn out to be nightmares, sometimes it's the other way round.« All three designers are keen to make clear that 104's directors and their immediate team were »great people to work with, who all really stuck their necks out for us«. They feel confident that even this last chapter in their design tale will be viewed as part of the 104 »work in progress«. »For us to be so open about the process is really just a continuation of that theme.« ¬

Walking away ¬ After a year and a half spent working on the project, when it was still incomplete, Experimental Jetset walked away from it – a bold gesture for any designer to make and a decision that was not made without heartache. The cumulative effect of negotiating with bureaucracy about unexpected but politically-sensitive amendments, coupled with witnessing the poor application of their identity by some other designers, made Experimental Jetset's job untenable. Their disillusion became all the more apparent when they reviewed what they had produced: »We actually only designed a handful of small items: a few badges, a shirt, a couple of brochures. Sure, we designed the logo system and the graphic manual, but that wasn't satisfying to us; we wanted to design beautiful printed matter.« ¬ Danny, Marieke and Erwin muse about their younger selves, admitting to being more cavalier then, albeit perhaps less humble: »It was certainly easier to walk away then. We were more stubborn, more self-assured. Getting older, we begin to doubt. We realize we don't know everything.« That said, they consider the exchange of services for money to be essentially a neutral one, based on equal need, and are therefore keen to retain some kind of meaningful freedom, despite the compromises that so much design seems to require: »Stopping an assignment is the ultimate freedom that a designer has. It's an existential issue. The possibility of quitting turns every assignment into a completely free assignment, no matter how restricted it is.« ¬ The aftermath of this experience is that Danny, Marieke and Erwin are toying with the idea of asking clients to sign a document that specifies how the approval process is to be managed and where print buying responsibilities lie. They muse on whether this might be the beginnings of a manifesto – a positive way to help other designers avoid some of the pitfalls currently inherent in the design process. ¬

04/08/08 ¬ Mails received from, and/or mails sent to: Mark Owens, EasyJet, Ruud van der Peijl, Angelique Spaninks, Mano Scherpbier, Linda van Deursen, Naïa Sore, Paul Elliman, Veronica Maljuf, Armando Andrade Tudela, Patta, Valentina Bruschi, The Wolfsonian, Colette Paris, Orpheu de Jong, etc. ¬

We leapt at the chance to follow this project.
First, because the designer was Paula Scher
(born 1948) of Pentagram New York, but also
because it was a commercial project with
two of America's biggest corporations as clients –
international producer and marketer of food,
agricultural, financial and industrial products
and services Cargill and soft drinks giant
The Coca-Cola Company. The project was to
design the brand identity and packaging for
a new zero calorie natural sweetener. Led by
Paula, it also involved Daniel Weil, a partner from
Pentagram London. We were extremely curious
about how a project of this kind would work –
what kind of relationship and constraints would
working on such a large-scale commercial project
entail and how would this shape the creative
process? ¬ Pentagram was set up in London
in 1972. Among its founding partners were
Alan Fletcher and Colin Forbes from whose
previous design company – Fletcher, Forbes, Gill –
Pentagram emerged. Pentagram's distinctive
ideas-based work proved enormously successful
and in 1979 Colin Forbes set up the New York office.
Pentagram has a pioneering structure involving
equal multidisciplinary partners who work largely
as individuals managing their own teams. ¬
Discovering more about the specialism of
packaging design intrigued us, incorporating
as it does such diverse considerations as physical
protection, regulatory criteria, health and safety,
transport and retail logistics, branding and
marketing, structural and graphic design. Despite
the obvious constraints of designing within
this commercial sphere, the combination of
ergonomics, information design and 3D graphics
is exciting for many designers. ¬

The design of packaging, particularly of mass-market food stuffs, has to have a broad – but nevertheless targeted – appeal. Many graphic designers would find this overtly commercial application of their work too compromising, but Paula embraces the challenge optimistically – happy that her work will be seen by so many. As a partner in a high-profile international company hers is a distinguished career, but has it met her expectations and how does she keeps her creative juices flowing? How does it feel to have earned a place among design's great and good – as a woman? ¬

Ordinary people ¬ On the AIGA website Paula is described as »unabashedly populist«, and she confirms that »I like ordinary people to like my work. I'm really happy when I make something that has massive popularity.« She describes her goal as elevating the expectation of what design can be among a mass audience. »I like to be able to do something that's at a very high level, which ordinary people who are not educated in design come to appreciate.« She sees this political aspect of her approach as fundamental to both her practice and the discipline at large: »That's the whole point of being a designer«, she states baldly. ¬

Freedom to fail ¬ Paula is frank in admitting that she didn't start her career with expectations or long-term plans. »I was very, very, very lucky to be in the record business and doing record covers in the 1970s«, she admits. As in-house art director at CBS Recordings, she found herself having to produce so many album cover designs that she had the opportunity to do some »really terrible ones«. She says that through her failures she was able to hone her craft, and stresses the importance of experimentation and failure as part of the design process. She sees this as something which few young designers are able to afford and rues this more restrictive climate. »It's very hard to push things or make discoveries when you have to be good. The act of making discoveries comes from the freedom to fail.« ¬

Counterbalance ¬ Alongside her prolific design work, Paula is a painter. Her detailed and »laborious« large-scale canvases, which can take up to six months to complete, depict intricate typographic maps of countries and regions of the world. She enjoys the freedom painting allows: »Design is very social, painting is very private. They balance me, and they both matter – I counterbalance one vocabulary with the other.« Paula's paintings have received critical and commercial acclaim, which has started to present her with something of a conundrum: »What's happened – and this is a problem for me – is the paintings began to sell and I started to get commissions. So now what I need is some really pure time to reinvent again…« ¬

Public canvas ¬ Paula began working with the New York Public Theatre in 1994 and it is clear that this long-standing relationship is enormously satisfying and rewarding for her. She is responsible for their identity and »every scrap of paper« they produce, from posters to tickets. She found the challenge to create what she has called the »visual voice of a place« liberating. The collaboration has allowed her to explore and express herself far beyond any limits she might have imagined: »Being able to pull off experiments has been fantastic«. The success and profile of this work helped establish her reputation, in particular her noisy and bold design for the production of »Noise/Funk« in the mid-1990s. It appeared on the Subway, buildings and hoardings of New York and was quickly subsumed into the graphic vernacular of the city, prompting her to declare with indignant pride: »New York City ate my identity!« ¬

Women in design ¬ »I'm getting to be this nice old lady«, says Paula self-deprecatingly, but the fact remains that she is one of only a handful of prominent and high-achieving women designers of her generation and this has required determination. She concedes that if she had had children this might have stalled or slowed her career but cites the example of her Pentagram colleague Lisa Strausfeld, who has a child and is »carrying right on«, as an indication that the culture of the design industry in the USA is changing. As a younger woman she admits, »I felt like an oddity. I felt very lonely for a while«, but reflects, »I feel less lonely now«. ¬

Pentagram ¬ Paula joined Pentagram in 1991 and is one of only two women among its 17 partners. She is effusive about the pleasures of Pentagram: »It's an organization for designers. It's run by designers, owned by designers, designers design.« She acknowledges their pride in their collective history and achievements; now into the fourth generation of designers, Pentagram continues to change, although the founding premise remains. With no account managers or other intermediaries, »We set up our lives to serve our ability to design«. She enjoys the »good company« of her colleagues although she admits that there is inevitable pressure to keep up with them too. Among her Pentagram partners is Daniel Weil, with whom Paula worked on this project. Daniel qualified as an architect. He joined Pentagram in 1992. His specialisms include interiors and product design and one of his major clients is United Airlines, for whom he has designed everything from cabin interiors to uniforms and tableware. ¬

Power couple ¬ Paula first married designer and illustrator Seymour Chwast in 1973 and then remarried him after a separation of more than a decade. While her work, identity and experiences are distinct and proudly her own, his impact is evident and celebrated by Paula, who calls him her greatest influence. At Push Pin Studios, which he co-founded in 1954, he helped forge a distinctive new visual language, which mixed historical styles and references from art and literature in striking and witty graphic images. His playful and inventive blending of type and image and embracing of popular graphic imagery ensured his influence over many generations of illustrators and designers, including Paula. In her bold and illustrative use of typography and hand-lettering, his mark is evident. ¬

The packaging of the three main brands of sweetener in the USA is visually busy, highly coloured and features gentle curves and swirls, reminiscent of the packaging of the 1950s and evocative of a reassuring homeliness. This sense of trustworthiness is reinforced by the use of descriptive pictures. Each box features a coffee cup somewhere in the image, making obvious the product and its uses. The packet contents are also illustrated, with each including a picture of an individual serving sachet. All sweeteners come in sachets, which equate to spoonfuls of sugar. All the sweetener boxes shown resemble food ingredients packets in both construction and appearance. ¬

A thorough brief ¬ Large organizations tend to take trouble over preparing a very thorough briefing document. The brief will often include contributions from marketing departments, product developers and legal teams, and is likely to have been vetted by a number of people at senior levels in the organization before being released. As Daniel explains, the brief for this project was »a good brief – a highly skilled package of research information and a wish list of things«, which rather than being too prescriptive and full of directions, was more concerned with indicating tone. Paula and Daniel, who flew to the USA to attend the first briefing, felt this opportunity to work with two corporations with such different experience of working with consumer brands was unique. ¬ **Brand competition** ¬ One of the key objectives for the Truvia™ identity was to make it distinctive and distinguishable from its brand competitors. In the USA the sweetener market is reportedly worth over one billion US dollars, with nearly one third of all households using sweetener. Historically, this has meant one of three household name brands. While these are all chemical sweeteners – Sweet'n Low is saccharin, Equal is aspartame and Splenda is sucralose – the Truvia™ brand is made using the leaf from the Stevia plant and can claim to be the first commercial scale natural sweetener. Released initially in the USA, Truvia™ natural sweetener is affirmed GRAS (Generally regarded as safe) by the Food and Drug Administration (FDA) and is manufactured by Cargill, an international producer and marketer of food, agricultural, financial and industrial products and services. ¬

As the first zero calorie natural sweetener, the Truvia™ brand needed to be clearly differentiated from the competition but also easily identifiable. Each brand has a predominant colour: Sweet'n Low is pink, Equal is blue and Splenda is yellow. This simple coding has become part of the shorthand for each product, making it possible to order »a coffee and pink« without causing confusion in much of the USA. These visually sweet colours – all on the pastel scale – may feel appropriate for artificial sweeteners, but the immediate colour choice for the Truvia™ brand, a natural alternative, was self-evident: it had to be green. ¬

There are no accompanying contemporaneous diary entries from Paula. As she explains: »it's not my process«. ¬

truvia

truvia

truvia

truvia

truvia

Both Paula and Daniel began their separate approaches by sketching their designs on paper. Paula favours the sensory experience of sketching over working on a computer, and has been frank in stating, »You don't type a design«. These sketches show how she familiarized herself with the rhythms of the letterforms and explored the font, weight and construction of the name. Her sketch using a script font shows her initial experiments with connecting letterforms, details that translated into her last geometric rough.¬

Progressing from sketches to these font samples, Paula set the name in a range of typefaces, observing the changes in visual impact on the page. Logos have to be unique marques. They are read as shapes rather than words and so their overall form has to be strong and easily recognizable. While using a light weight of letterform may be logical for a zero calorie product, the bolder versions have more presence. Paula initially experimented with scripts and italics. Both echo handwriting, optimistically moving forward in an intimate and accessible way. Although she rejected these versions, deciding they were too traditional, she retained some of the fluid characteristics in the final logo. ¬

truvia

Truvia

truvia

truvia

The tone of green that Paula chose is not pastel or overtly sugary, but is instead a fresh and natural shade. The obvious symbolism of this is enhanced by its translucency, which allows the colour density to build when overlapped, and visually reinforces the message of transparency and purity that the client wished to project. ¬

Set in lower-case, the round and friendly geometric font is sans serif with open circular forms. The choice of a single-bowled »a« highlights this, and the introduction of translucency accentuates the directional emphasis of the strokes, while adding colour interest and a more 3D feel. The dot of the »i« has been redrawn as a leaf. Looking for typographic details to elaborate or alter and redrawing letterforms are common in logo design where creating a stand-alone marque that becomes more than just a font is necessary. ¬

Naming ¬ A product name is intrinsic to the brand image and, of course, the logo or visual identity. Choosing a name for a product is considered a critical part of product development and branding. Considerations such as how memorable a name is, its originality, relationship to the product, pronunciation, international implications and associated meanings are important, and finding the right name can be complex and time-consuming. Many organizations employ specialist naming or branding companies to manage this process and it is not uncommon for products to go through name changes while in development, as happened here. The Truvia™ brand name alludes to the naturalness and authenticity of the product, while also including a reference to its organic origin, the Stevia plant. It is short, distinctive and easy to remember, and from a typographical perspective, is uncluttered as none of the letters have descenders. Product names are valuable and are usually trademarked to protect their copyright and usage. ¬ **Transatlantic tandem** ¬ When Paula and Daniel began working on this project, the name had not yet been finalized and at that stage the product was called something else. From the research and product information they had been given they worked together to establish their creative direction: »As a designer, what you want to do is get behind the client's mindset. You're trying to set the objectives. Having a point of view as a designer allows the client to respond.« Paula and Daniel identified aspiration and authenticity as two of the objectives they could use as inspiration to help establish a language for the 3D and graphic development. While Daniel concentrated on the paper engineering of the packet design, Paula was developing the brand identity and ways to treat the name – essentially a logo design. ¬

Overl
connote
and artis
tra

t

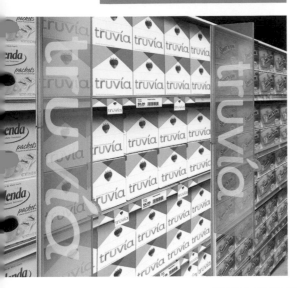

These examples from Paula's first presentation of the Truvia™ logo to Cargill and The Coca-Cola Company explain the rationale behind the details of the identity and illustrate the varied logo applications with simulations across a range of vehicles and scales. These include advertising on the sleeve of a take-away coffee cup and as a graphic in a swimming pool, an appropriate suggestion for a health food product with global aspirations. The size of marketing spend affects product visibility and brand recognition. The more prevalent the product, the less overt the design has to be, giving designers greater freedom to be abstract or adventurous. ¬

Paula's presentation included labelled analysis of the logo and visual elements of the packaging design, to make clear their significance. She placed emphasis on the openness – and by implication honesty – of the logo, from the font choice and leaf detail to the use of simple photography. As this annotated presentation made clear, her design »connotes naturalness« and the overlapping of colour on the name and triangular graphic »connotes naturalness and artisanal spirit«, with its allusion to the construction and folds of the carton structure and the act of making. ¬

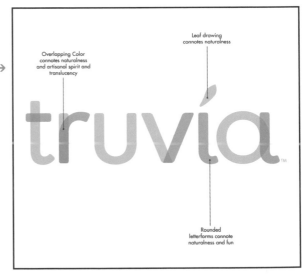

Overlapping Color connotes naturalness and artisanal spirit and translucency

Leaf drawing connotes naturalness

Rounded letterforms connote naturalness and fun

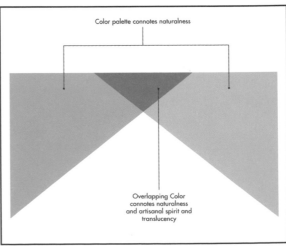

Color palette connotes naturalness

Overlapping Color connotes naturalness and artisanal spirit and translucency

Small team ¬ Throughout the project Paula
would present her design work to representatives
from Cargill and The Coca-Cola Company,
whose teams could include as many as 40 people.
In contrast, Paula works with a small team of
around forty people, including designer Lenny
Naar, who worked with her closely on this project.
This raised some eyebrows as she remembers:
»They would say, ›This is your team?‹« This is
not an uncommon experience and Paula says
she often finds herself up against larger design
firms and »a big pile of men in suits«. Unfazed,
she explains, »I'm not going to try and rustle
up a posse to go to a meeting. I'm myself and
they can wonder what all those other guys are
doing.« ¬ **Presenting ideas** ¬ The liaison between
Paula, Daniel, Cargill and The Coca-Cola Company
was made more complicated by the range of
geographical locations involved. As Daniel created
mock-ups they were sent to the client and to
Paula in New York. Video-conferencing and
conference calls allowed dialogue throughout
the process and Daniel travelled to New York
on a number of occasions so that he and Paula
could discuss things in person. Following
the name change, Paula and Daniel put together
a presentation that clarified the reasoning
behind the Truvia™ logo design and clearly
visualized the ambition of the brand. Every time
Paula presented ideas she made sure that the
competitor packets were on the table, to keep the
focus on the difference. »We just stuck the Truvia™
packaging on the table and said here's your
box and that's what it does in the grocery store.
You see it with the other stuff and you laugh.« ¬

The carton design is
remarkable for its white space
and restraint when compared
to the competitors' cluttered
designs. In contrast to their
curves, Paula and Daniel chose
to make a graphic feature of the
angles and triangles that related
to the construction of Daniel's
3D forms. The simulation
of the cartons stacked
on a supermarket shelf clearly
illustrated how different the
Truvia™ packaging looked and
its visual impact when viewed
alongside its competitors.
The logo incorporated the
product descriptor »Nature's
Calorie-Free Sweetener«, to
ensure that this key information
would not be overlooked. ¬

The choice of a strawberry
as the main image within
the design was the source
of some discussion. Using
a high-key photograph and the
complementary colours green
and red heightened visual
impact. Where the brand
competitors show a coffee
cup, the Truvia™ packaging
differentiated itself by showing
the sweetener sprinkled
on fruit as its primary serving
suggestion. Using fruit
reinforces the message
of naturalness and evokes
a sensory association with
summer and freshness.
Photographing the coffee
cup from above in the
sleeve design presents it as
a geometric form like the logo.
Clean and modern, it draws
attention to the coffee itself,
a powerful aromatic trigger. ¬

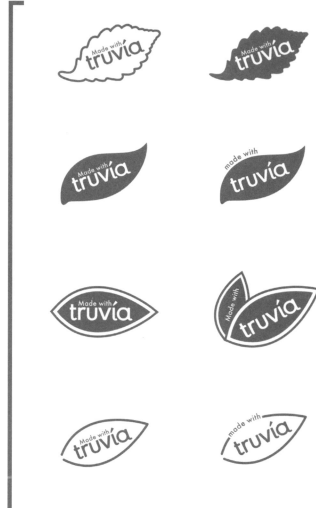

The decision was made that the »i« of the Truvia™ lettering should be an accent rather than a dot, and this evolved into the idea of using a leaf. »We drew the leaf about 50,000 times. We did the criss-cross and the logo almost instantaneously – the leaf went on forever.« These versions show Paula trying different shapes of leaf and various angles, outlines and structures. She explains that whether the leaf was shorter, longer, rounder or flatter, with more or fewer serrations, made little difference to the overall identity and packaging design. However, if it had had to be made a lot bigger, or changed in colour, »that would have been bad«, she admits. ¬

Paula explains that this kind of sticking point is fairly typical in a large job and that in general her response is to laugh. »I'm amused by it«, she says and explains that once she has the scale and proportions right – in this case the criss-cross of the green, the overlap of the letterforms and the positioning of the typography – she feels relaxed about the inevitable suggestions by the client, safe in the knowledge that the fundamentals of the design are secure. She expands: »If those things are in position and all we're going to do is goof around with the shape of the leaf, it doesn't matter. Because the package is already good it can't be screwed up. That makes me really happy, because it allows everybody to have ownership over the design by making a comment on this detail.« ¬

Focus group testing ¬ User testing and feedback are often considered an important part of the development process of a product, brand or packaging design. The Truvia™ packaging tested »brilliantly«, says Paula. »They tried everything, they practically gave the package a colonoscopy!« This kind of qualitative research can be greeted with suspicion by designers, who worry about the influence this gives to opinions shaped by taste, rather than a real understanding of the function of a design. However, from a client point of view user testing is seen as a valuable way of discovering consumer responses and developing their product to meet these expectations and demands. ¬ **Attitude to changes** ¬ Working with large corporations can be challenging for designers, as they are likely to want more control than smaller clients. Paula explains that because it involved two corporations, this was a complex project. Each company had a different methodology but Paula was impressed by how committed both companies seemed to be to her designs, from an early stage. »It could have been a disastrous process, but it wasn't.« Despite the inevitable quibbles over some aspects of production and budget, everyone was in agreement on the key issues. However, when changes are required, Paula's attitude tends to be optimistic. As an example she explains that if a design works in black and white, it will usually work in any colour, so changing the colour rarely destroys the design. She explains that she usually finds these exchanges with clients amusing, providing they are over details that won't ruin the design: »Say the client wants the design in red. You make it in red and they say they don't like that red; but it doesn't matter, as they can't mess it up. It is only if you have three colours and they want to change one colour against two others, then you've got a problem«. ¬

The Truvia™ name is pronounced tru-vee-ah, with the emphasis on the middle syllable, and the leaf above the »i« evolved into an accent, its eventual angle helping indicate where the stress should fall in pronunciation. It was also designed to be a stand-alone marque as an ingredient symbol. For this reason the shape had to work at various scales. Each shape also had to be carefully checked against a reference book of pre-trademarked leaves, to ensure that it was unique. The final design needed to be graphic but characterful and recognizable, even when separated from the Truvia™ packaging. ¬

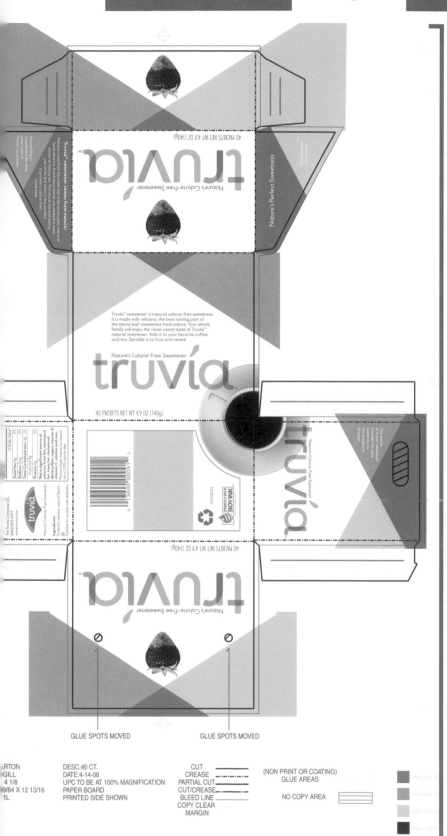

GLUE SPOTS MOVED   GLUE SPOTS MOVED

Every part of the manufacturing process of this packaging was automated, from the printing to the folding. This composite document was created by the printer and sent to Pentagram to check for accuracy. The net shows cut-and-fold guides, indicated by a solid line and dash-line respectively, neither of which print. Bleed area is indicated by a faint and fine key-line, and the position of glue spots and copy-free areas are marked too. The colour bars are used by the printers to check ink density. The packaging was printed, folded and assembled by Americraft printers in the USA. ¬

While one purpose of packaging design is to encourage buyers to purchase a product, it must also clearly convey certain product information, which is required by law. In the USA this includes a list of ingredients and nutritional facts, as well as the distributor's details and contents, specifications of weight and volume. Paula has contained this essential and statistical information within one side panel, together with a small Truvia™ ingredient symbol. The placing of information is designed with hierarchy in mind — the front of the box is largely reserved for the logo and images, to ensure clear communication from the shop shelf. Copy that provides informative descriptions of the product and serving suggestions, is applied to what will become the back panel of the box. The information pertaining to the carton itself, such as the barcode, and the recycling and soy ink symbols, have been placed on the base of the box. The Truvia™ logo appears on each face of the box except its base, ensuring that it is instantly recognizable, from any angle. ¬

RTON
GILL
4 1/8
9/64 X 12 13/16
1L

DESC:40 CT.
DATE:4-14-08
UPC TO BE AT 100% MAGNIFICATION
PAPER BOARD
PRINTED SIDE SHOWN

CUT
CREASE
PARTIAL CUT
CUT/CREASE
BLEED LINE
COPY CLEAR
MARGIN

(NON PRINT OR COATING)
GLUE AREAS

NO COPY AREA

Packaging design ¬ Packaging is sometimes perceived as a limited and low-brow specialism of design, largely because of the commercial imperatives that drive it. Daniel, who trained as an architect, takes a different view and calls packaging »an enormous topical subject for the world«. He says that his approach to designing a carton or box is no different to his approach to designing a chair or interior as they require the same investment of »intellectual commitment«. Nonetheless, it is true that packaging design involves very specific restraints, not least among them restrictions of format and the inclusion of compulsory legal and information copy. Designers who enjoy packaging design do so largely because of these many constraints and the creative challenges involved. ¬ **Production** ¬ Paula and Daniel had pitched their ideas in the first presentation not on the basis of a set unit cost, but rather, as Daniel explains, »setting an aspiration of where the product should live and compete«. They were determined to avoid simply supplying graphics applied to a very conventional box, and were convinced that the product necessitated a more original approach. Although the packaging designs they presented were »doable«, as Daniel explains, »Originality has a price and the price is the development cost, not in terms of design, but in terms of manufacture.« Manufacturers are configured to produce a particular range of boxes so changes to the set-up of the machines are expensive. Following the first presentation, Daniel started to look into the production and unit costs. Cargill was responsible for the production process and Daniel visited Cargill's printers, specialists in packaging, to familiarize himself with their process and set-up. »Manufacturers can do anything«, he says, but the critical factors are the quantity and speed of the processes involved – and the expense. ¬

Given that the product is natural, Paula and Daniel were keen to ensure that their design was as ecologically efficient as possible. This was debated at all stages of the project, but there were unavoidable restrictions. The moisture barrier required for each individual sachet is non-recyclable, for example. However, because each of the sachets is hermetic there was less need for external packaging to protect against humidity, so lightweight rather than heavy card could be used. This not only allowed extra malleability but reduced the resources used. As Daniel points out, at the volume at which the item is sold, this seemingly small measure constitutes a considerable saving. Food packaging must conform to food safety standards, which means that all materials including the inks, which are indicated here as environmentally friendly soy-based inks, had to be safety tested. ¬

The different experiences, methodologies and schedules of Cargill and The Coca-Cola Company inevitably extended the process of development and production. This involved a lot of back and forth, as Paula explains: »They had to do three sizes of box so that the base of the box could sit on a certain form of conveyor belt. Which meant that the graphics all had to refit, and the size of things was changing in terms of quantity too.« ¬

Mass market ¬ Paula and Daniel had begun the project by exploring what could be possible within this normally conservative area of sweetener packaging. From the start they had presented ambitious ideas that they hoped they might be able to convince Cargill and The Coca-Cola Company to adopt. It is evidently the source of great pleasure to them both that, with only minor exceptions, this happened. »We arrived at a very well-positioned, well-placed new product that competes in a different way and in a different category.« They succeeded in persuading their clients to take greater risks than they had imagined, although this was within reason, as Daniel explains: »They didn't want to make it difficult for people to understand.« ¬

Moving forward ¬ »I love it; I'm amazed it got made«, says Paula, as she describes the sense of achievement she feels in the final identity and packaging. She concedes that this is not necessarily an important design in terms of either her work as a graphic designer, or her personal development, but insists that in terms of moving the design of a commodity in a grocery store for a mass audience forward, »it's a phenomenal victory«. She explains: »If this can come out and be successful then it gives all the other packaging permission to improve. And the whole market goes up.« ¬

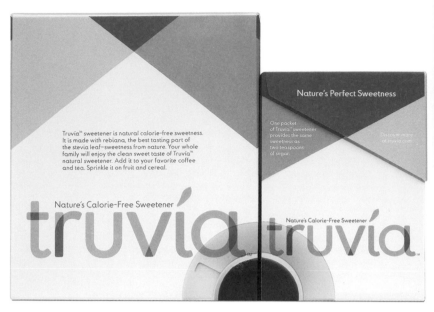

Packaging design for food products needs to balance the need for physical protection, which includes product safety and shelf life, with convenience. One of the distinguishing features of the Truvia™ packaging brief was that the box should be able to be placed on a table or counter and look and function appropriately. This meant not only making the box visually appealing but also designing a box that could withstand repeated opening and closing. In this regard Daniel's designs were more similar to confectionary packaging than the ingredient-style box of Truvia™ brand competitors. ¬

Daniel's hinged design ensured that the top of the box would open and close easily and, importantly, that it would stay closed when left on the counter, making the item more like a sugar dispenser than a storage carton. Good packaging design involves a marriage between structural and graphic design, and the relationship here between the architecture of different-sized boxes and their graphics shows an attention to detail that is characteristic of Paula and Pentagram. The completion of the coffee cup image is visually pleasing and suggests permeations for retail display. ¬

Ultimately, a successful piece of packaging design will help launch and sell a new product and as Cargill explain, the Truvia™ brand is »a success«. »We're really happy that the result is good, and it really is«, says Daniel. »It's professional and it looks good«. ¬

This packaging may not appear to be radical, but Paula and Daniel were delighted with the sophistication of the final design. When compared to the other brands and packaging conventions within this market it is perhaps the restraint of the design and its modern feel that contrast most. Paula's anecdotal evidence supports this: »What everybody tells me, which makes me supremely happy, is that it's shocking when you see it in the grocery store«, she says with evident satisfaction. ¬

We knew from the outset that we wanted to
follow a website design project. As yet an area
in relative infancy, the building and design
of websites is a constantly evolving field
that utilizes the skills of a wide and varied set
of creative professionals – including graphic
designers. This website redesign project
by Airside for international furniture company
Vitsœ excited us because of the pedigree and
reputation of both designer and client and
the creative potential this promised. How would
Airside, acclaimed for imaginative use of digital
media and quirky, characterful animations, tackle
this demanding brief? The scale of the project
was clearly ambitious and posed some fascinating
challenges: how would Airside manage and
contain the project and how would it balance the
demands of being responsible for both creative
content and implementation? ¬ Nat Hunter
(born 1966) co-founded creative agency Airside
with Fred Deakin (born 1964) and Alex Maclean
(born 1968) in 1998. Working across graphic design,
illustration, digital, interactive and moving image
the small studio currently comprises 12 full-time
employees, including Chris Rain (born 1972),
who has worked at Airside since 2005, having
started as an intern. Airside's idiosyncratic
and distinctive work has included creating mobile
content, idents and title sequences, exhibitions,
branding and toys, for clients including Coca-Cola,
Greenpeace, Live Earth, MTV, Nike, Nokia and
Sony. ¬ Vitsœ was founded in Germany in 1959
by Niels Vitsœ, to realize and sell the products
and furniture of designer Dieter Rams. Perhaps
best known for Rams' 606 Universal Shelving
System, widely considered to be a design classic,
Vitsœ is also celebrated for its sustainable ethos
expressed in its motto: »Living better, with less,
that lasts longer«. ¬

It is understandable that graphic designers enjoy working for art-and-design sector clients as it's rather like preaching to the converted. Generally, these kind of clients don't require extensive explanations as a design solution is developed. Still it was no mean feat to take on producing a website for a company with such an enviable design pedigree as Vitsœ. What philosophy underpinned Airside's work on this project and what drives Nat and Chris' creative ambitions? ¬

Airsiding ¬ »At the beginning of a project, everyone gets around a table, thrashes out ideas and whoever comes up with the strongest, that everyone feels works, goes off and works it up. Then at stages along the way the idea gets ›Airsided‹ and by that I mean we get back together, check that the idea still works and has been developed and pushed to its fullest«, says Chris. Nat elucidates: »We have a flat creative hierarchy, which means that we don't have the standard studio model of creative director/senior designer/designer. This has its upsides and downsides, but we feel that it's mostly a good thing.« ¬

Good life ¬ »We aim for a high quality of life«, Nat says. Enjoying work has always been central to Airside's philosophy. They are averse to propagating a myth common in the design industry – that you're not a proper graphic designer unless you regularly work excessively long hours. Seeing this as largely misplaced martyrdom they encourage a studio culture that is no less obsessive, but decidedly more balanced. Airside recently moved studios to a space in north London, which includes room on their top floor for a large communal table at which they try to eat lunch together every day. The opportunity to share thoughts and discuss projects informally is part of creating a vibrant and vitalizing working environment. »If you're at work for a third of your life, it might as well be as fulfilling as it can be.« ¬

Interactive expertise ¬ »I fell into working as a graphic designer by mistake«, confesses Nat. »I took a job as an administrator in a design studio, and within three months had become their trainee designer.« After reading Psychology at Edinburgh University, where her studies included human computer interface psychology and computer programming, she gained her masters degree in Interactive Multimedia at the Royal College of Art. Alongside directing the digital projects at Airside, she works closely with everyone to maintain an overview of all projects. Chris says admiringly, »A real strength of Nat's is that she can pull apart what you have done quite ruthlessly at times. But any sense of annoyance is tempered by the fact that she wants the work to be as good as it can be, as much as you do!« ¬

Mixing media and music ¬
As half of Mercury- and Brit-nominated dance act Lemon Jelly, Airside co-founder and creative director Fred Deakin has sold over half a million records worldwide, and released three albums. Airside produces all Lemon Jelly's visual matter, but this is not the only alternative project in which they are involved. From the creation of alien god »Meegoteph«, an interactive installation that has toured music festivals across the UK, to the production and promotion of Stitches, soft toys in need of adoptive homes, Airside has always enjoyed crossing boundaries. This playful diversity is central to the studio's philosophy and growth. As Nat says, »Airside can be whatever we want it to be. We are limited only by our own resources.« ¬

Environmental enthusiasts ¬
»Everyone at Airside is on board with being an environmentally aware organization«, declares the Airside website. In real terms this includes everything from printing double-sided, replacing the water cooler with a filter tap and using recycled paper (and toilet paper), to using public transport, a green accredited taxi company and bike couriers where possible. They are proud to claim that most of them cycle and only one owns a car. Airside recently received an »outstanding« score from auditing company The Green Mark, whom they invited to help improve their environmental performance. In 2007, Nat co-founded Three Trees Don't Make A Forest, a not-for-profit social enterprise and consultancy, which aims to help the design industry produce sustainable creative work and ultimately be a catalyst for the creation of a zero-carbon design industry. ¬

Reinventing the wheel ¬
»After working in a succession of office jobs I realized that I really should do something a little worthwhile and creative with my life«, Chris divulges. »I was drawn to graphic design because I always had an interest in typography and was in awe of the work Designers Republic were doing at that time.« As a graduate of the London College of Printing and member of the International Society of Typographic Designers, Chris' passion and expertise is in typography and graphic design. Not content to stick only to what he knows, he comments, »I like trying to reinvent the wheel. Surely that's what makes us want to be designers. I hate doing the same thing the same way twice – I'm always trying to move what I do forward.« ¬

Websites have become an essential interface for business, social networking and broadcasting. For most retailers they are a pivotal part of their business strategy, allowing them to reach a potentially large global audience and diverse demographic. Vitsœ declare their business ambitions in this document, but they also spell out their desire to build relationships through the new website. As Airside summarized, the relaunched website needed: »To attract new customers and reflect the company's growing global customer base. The new ›addictive‹ site needed to become the primary outlet for information and sales of the 606 Universal Shelving System, as well as highlighting Vitsœ's free online planning service. It was also important to promote the Vitsœ ethos that values sustainable design and long-term customer relationships, while reflecting the wit and integrity of founder Niels Vitsœ.« ¬

VITSŒ

Brief for a new website

The vision for vitsoe.com

To be key to making the 606 Universal Shelving System the world's definitive shelving system.

The new vitsoe.com will not only be **alluring** (more appealing and descriptive than, say, visiting Vitsœ's shop) but it will be the **crystal-clear model** for planning and buying online a seemingly complicated product. vitsoe.com will be at the heart of Vitsœ's global ambitions and its never-ending quest for closer **customer relationships** (like visiting your favourite restaurant, being greeted by name and shown to your preferred table). Additional worldwide retail presences will support vitsoe.com, not vice versa.

The website's purpose

To dramatically simplify and shorten the visitor's journey from awareness to buying.

The most frequently heard comment from Vitsœ's new customers is: "I wish I had done this sooner". Sometimes they are meaning "15 or 20 years sooner". 20 years can be reduced to two hours. vitsoe.com must convince visitors to make the investment now. Like pensions, the sooner the better.

Website tone

Underpinned by a dry sense of humour, vitsoe.com will be engaging, fun, smart, gutsy, classic and, even, addictively usable vitsoe.com will exclaim Vitsœ's ethos — longevity, innovation, integrity, authenticity, trust, honesty, sustainability and lifelong service — and achieve this on a **multi-cultural and multi-lingual** stage. Without doubt, the website must be international in feel.

The website will be confident in its size, weight and structure. Its **navigation will be orthodox and generic.** (100 years later, the user interface for the car is still a steering wheel, two or three pedals and a gearstick.) The visitor (highly web-savvy or a total novice; design conscious or design disinterested) will always know where they are and what they can do next. As Steve Krug said, "Don't Make Me Think" (New Riders Publishing, 2006).

First impressions ¬ This project came about when Nat met Mark Adams, managing director of Vitsœ, at a party and discovered he wanted to commission a new website but wasn't sure how to go about it. She advised him on the standard commissioning process and Mark subsequently invited Airside to pitch. Jobs often come up through circumstance or chance meetings and this is a good example of how a casual conversation can pay dividends. Nat was cautious and keen to remain neutral in her advice to Mark and reflects that this honesty probably played a part in Mark's first impression of Airside and its openness and professionalism. ¬

A good brief ¬ As most designers discover, not every brief is a good brief. Frequently designers find that a key part of their task is to learn what the client may have been unable to express in writing. Vitsœ had spent considerable care and time developing a comprehensive brief. They had consulted a range of industry and interested professionals, including magazine editors, architecture critics and cultural commentators, and the resulting brief was »gospel« throughout the project process. Nat confirms: »It was the Bible«. The seven-page briefing document clearly identified key aspirations and demands and outlined the vision, purpose and desired tone of the website. It also included analysis of the service they provide and of the end-users, both existing and hoped for. Vitsœ are justifiably proud of a distinguished design heritage that includes Niels Vitsœ, Dieter Rams, Günther Kieser and Thomas Manss, and the underlying wit and humour that runs across their advertising and print. While acknowledging this history, the brief is forward looking too, seeking an »engaging and addictive« site and user experience. ¬

The brief was carefully written and structured. It included contextual quotes from industry analysts, outlined Vitsœ's perspective on the information technology environment and made clear their technical specifications. These included compliance and search engine guidelines. The site had to comply with the Disability Discrimination Act and be optimized for search engines so that it could be found easily. The brief also listed the websites that Vitsœ admired and why, and the website addresses of their chief competitors, and ended with an objective analysis of the brief itself by a freelance developer. ¬

Vitsœ do not just sell shelves, they also provide a service that Nat describes as »kind of remarkable«, at the heart of which is their sustainable ethos. From the packaging that Vitsœ take away and reuse, to the design of a modular bespoke system, they are true to their motto: »Living better, with less, that lasts longer.« Nat explains: »It's a kind of reuse and longevity model. If you buy these shelves today, in 40 years time if you need another shelf Vitsœ will be there; they'll know who you are, they'll give you great service and they'll bring the shelf to you. If you find their shelves on eBay, they'll tell you how much they are to buy new and if you're getting a good price. They'll reconfigure and refurbish them for you. It won't ever end up in landfill.« ¬

27/06 ¬ Nat met Mark at a party. ¬

22/07 ¬ Vitsœ release their brief and »What is Vitsœ?« document. ¬

These keynote slides from Airside's presentation reveal skill in distilling thorough preparatory research into simple graphic form. From their meetings with Mark, Airside were aware that they needed to »sound clever« and articulate their rationale and thinking in a clear and convincing way. Not only did the presentation address the central questions and issues extrapolated from the brief, it also gave theoretical context to Airside's approach. ¬

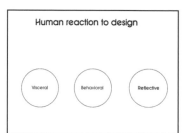

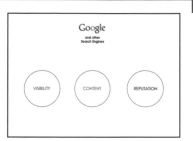

This diagram illustrates Professor Donald Norman's analysis of human reaction to design, which he breaks down into three categories: visceral – the item's appearance; behavioural – how it performs; and reflective – what it evokes in the user (»Emotional Design: Why We Love [or Hate] Everyday Things«, 2005). Airside used this structure to analyze Vitsœ's brief, telling them: »On a visceral level you've got a great base identity, but it's poorly used online. Behaviourally, your site should be beautifully intuitive. Reflective – you want people to love using the site but what do you want them to feel?« ¬

One of the key questions in the brief was whether Vitsœ's planning tool – the software that allows users to plan their own specifications for free – should be put online. »It was their 64 thousand dollar question«, says Nat. »And our response was an unequivocal, no! We said we want to make people feel love for Vitsœ; you need something to really engage people.« Airside considered the existing Vitsœ website, with its text-heavy content, to be dated in terms of user experience and proposed storytelling as a means of communicating their distinctive ethos – and the use of rich media to bring it to life.« ¬

However strong the website, it still needed to be easily found by search engines and Airside's presentation highlighted the importance of Search Engine Optimization (SEO). They used this diagram to describe the way in which the Vitsœ site should »earn the trust« of search engines. This meant ensuring visibility by using clear and readable URLs, making sure that the content contained appropriate keywords, and as search engines favour old sites over new, considering reciprocal links with established sites to boost their own ranking status. ¬

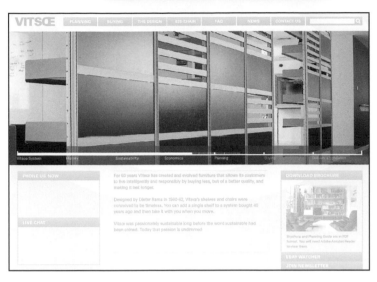

Airside wanted to convince
Vitsœ to communicate
»the Vitsœ experience«
in less than two minutes.
This slide shows a frame from
a storyboard illustrating how
they might give an overview
of all the key information
within this short time frame.
The timeline shows that Airside
divided the time into six distinct
parts: the system, history,
sustainability, economics,
planning and buying. They
proposed using a combination
of stop-motion and live action
to tell the story of the 606
Universal Shelving System.
Using rich media on the
homepage would act as a trail
to the secondary pages, which
would include more in-depth
rich media content. ¬

Pitching ¬ Pitches can take many forms and
involve a number of stages. These usually include
sending work samples and CVs before presenting
work to a client in person. A successful pitch
requires a combination of confidence, openness
and persuasiveness, and can take considerable
presentation skills, both visual and verbal.
The pitch in this case involved an initial
presentation of credentials – showing past
work that demonstrated the quality, range,
scale and appropriateness of the agency –
and a second stage pitch, which was paid
but competitive. In accepting Mark's invitation
to pitch, Airside included a caveat: »We said,
›We're happy to pitch but we want to ask you
lots of questions,‹« reveals Nat. This involved
»a lot of face-to-face« as they tried to understand
the complexities of the company and its
multifarious systems. ¬ **Investing** ¬ It was only
after winning the pitch that Airside discovered
their estimated costs were larger than Vitsœ's
budget would cover. After consideration,
Airside took the unusual step of investing
in the project. Nat explains: »We saw there was
a real business need for this website and that
it was going to increase their sales. We said,
›If you provide all our supplies and freelancers
direct, with no mark-up, and pay a third of
our fees, we'll take a percentage of your profits
for the next two years in place of the rest.‹«
This made sense on both sides and was
a model with which Mark was familiar from
the furniture world, where the designer commonly
takes a small design fee and then royalties on
the number of items sold. »We have yet to see
whether it works!,« Nat says with a smile. ¬

06/08 ¬ Pitch and keynote presentation. ¬
07/08 ¬ Heard we've got the job! ¬
23/09 ¬ Chris starts paternity leave – right at the beginning of the project! ¬

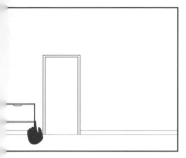
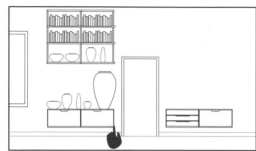
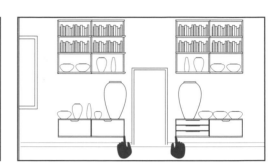

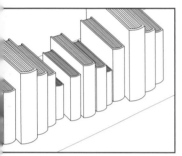
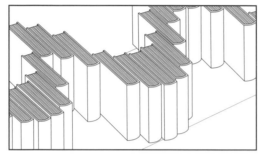

Airside convinced Vitsœ to tell the story of their 606 Universal Shelving System in a two-minute animation to feature on the website homepage. Following the pitch, which was inevitably »guesswork«, as Nat points out, the design team began defining their aims and approach for the film. For both designer and client the process of understanding one another takes time and this can make initial meetings and discussions more protracted: »You're understanding them, they're understanding where you come from: it's just that little bit of bedding-in which can be quite a slow process.« ¬

As Airside developed their first film ideas and initial storyboards they found themselves quickly bogged down in detail. »Mark is a details man«, explains Chris, and so it was hard to get him to bypass things like »this shelf is in the wrong place, or this is the wrong shelf«. Chris realized that they needed to go back to the drawing board and revive the spark he felt the film had lost. ¬

Chris met with colleagues Malika Favre and Guy Moorhouse to devise some ideas with more »emotional« content. Chris, Malika and Guy settled upon a three-act film that traced an individual's life through their ever-growing Vitsœ collection of shelving and the contents they hold. Chris explains that each act represented a stage in life – growth, nurture and reflection. Airside then had to sell this new idea to the client and Chris realized that they needed something more visually engaging than black and white sketched storyboards to do this. ¬

Airside put together these three mood boards to convey the colour and feel of each act: »In the first it's energetic and vibrant, the second is about starting to put things in order, and in the third act the palette gets more muted, and it's more reflective.« To Chris' relief, Vitsœ were convinced. »That was sort of half the battle won. Of course they had found it hard to visualize what we were saying. I think maybe we took for granted a little bit that they'd know. Once we'd got them on board, we could thrash out the details later and the film development became a much smoother process – and the website too.« ¬

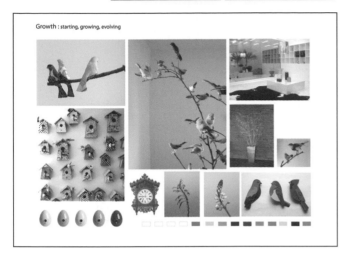

Growth : starting, growing, evolving

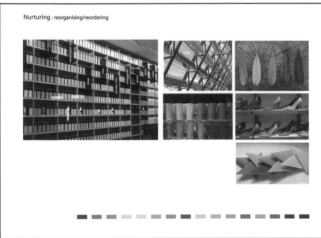

Nurturing : reorganising/reordering

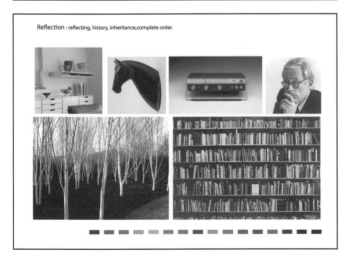

Reflection : reflecting, history, inheritance, complete order.

Rich media ¬ It was central to Airside's proposal that the Vitsœ website should be »super visual« and exploit moving image and rich media. Rich media refers to technology that can integrate audio, moving image and high-resolution graphics and is used to engage and interact with audiences on web pages. With the mass take up of broadband, an increasing number of websites are incorporating rich media. This has increased demand for animation for the web as it is well suited to digital environments. It allows for playful and memorable communication and can tell a story without words, making it universal. Not only is it possible to communicate a large amount of information relatively quickly, but moving image is also potentially more powerful than text. ¬ **Storyboards and animatics** ¬ Storyboards are an essential part of the creative process in animation, film and moving image. They allow the planning and visualization of the sequence of frames and indicate camera angles, shot choices and viewpoint and provide a framework for dialogue and timings. These are usually followed by animatics, edited series of images displayed in sequence, which give a more accurate impression of how the moving sequence will look and feel. An animatic might also include dialogue or a soundtrack. Animation is a time-consuming and expensive process and creating storyboards and animatics is an economic way of honing the narrative and visuals before starting to film or animate properly. ¬

07/10 ¬ Chris back from paternity leave: »I thought the film would be done and dusted and we'd be on to the production side of it. But we're bogged down in detail.« ¬

08/10 ¬ Creative meeting with Malika and Guy to try and get film back on track. We're really concentrating on the film, going and presenting to them every week with storyboards. ¬

15/10 ¬ We changed the way we wanted to do the back-end. We'd found this company called With Associates we want to work with. ¬

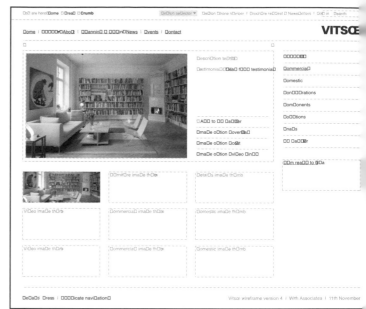

Site map columns

Home
Rich media
8 stage story
PLANNER
JOIN MAILING LIST
NEWS
LIVE CHAT
REQUEST A BROCHURE
PHONE NUMBER
FLICKR
iPHONE
EBAY Watcher
Customer quotes
Search

The Design
Rich media
Glossy slide show of
Dieter Rams, braun
products etc.
Dieter Rams
Braun
Neils Vitsoe
Good Design
Innovative
Useful
Aesthetic
Self-explanatory
Unobtrusive
Honest
Durable
Thorough
Environmentally-friendly
As little design as possible

Planning
Rich media
video of planner and
buyer planning over
phone
Call us to plan your
shelving system
Plan-it-yourself kit
**Adding, subtracting
and moving**
Rich media
show system expanding
over time.
What's the cost?
Rich media
interactive cost calculator
Walls, floors and ceilings
Shelves and cabinets info
(interactive pic x 2 of all
available items)
Rich media:
how shelves are moved,
how cabinet drawers work,
how doors work
Fixing to the wall
Wall mounted
Semi-wall mounted
Compressed

Buying
Rich media:
imelapse video of
installers arriving on site
Stockists
Installation
Collecting
Export
Change of mind
Buying second hand
Site visits
Paying

620 Chair
Rich media:
nice pics of chair and
how it makes a sofa
Design
how it works
Brochure and prices

News
slide show of exhibitions
in shop or other
recent news
Vitsoe, 606 & 620
Exhibition and displays
Press coverage
+ RSS feed

Contact us
Rich media:
slide show of inside
of wigmore st. shop
General enquiry
Keep in touch
Jobs
Press

Log in
Rich media:
aspirational pics
talks about the process
of buying

FAQ
Questions
The basics
Walls/floors/ceilings
Storage
Colours/finishes/materials
Strength
Adjusting
Dismantling
Pricing
Cleaning

Nat explains that the
information architecture had
to be resolved before any
»design with a capital D«
could begin. This site map
lays out clearly the basic
structure of the Vitsœ website.
Running along the top are
the nine section headings,
under each of which are listed
its sub-sections. Technical
descriptions are indicated
in red. ¬

□□ are here□□ome □ □rea□ □ Crumb   □e□ion se□ector ▾ | □e□ion □hone n□mber | □rpch□re re□□est □ News□etters | □o□ in | □earch

□ome | □a□□□ | □b□u□ | □□annin□ □ □□□in□News | □vents | □ontact

VITSŒ

□ma□e □□eo □□
□istor□ □ □eiter □ □oo□ □esi□n

□□□r□□□

□□□ □niversa□ □he□vin□ □□st

□□□ □hair □ro□rame

Nie□d/Vitsœ

□ieter □ams

□oo□ □esi□

□thos

What o□r c□stomers s□□

What is the □□□□

□esi□n □ □ieter □itsœ

□thos

□atest Vitsœ event

What is the □□□

□oo□ □esi□n

□estimonia□

□estimonia□

□e□a□s □ress | □□□□icate navi□ation□

Vitsœ wireframe version 4 | With Associates | 11th November

Website design ¬ While website design incorporates many specialisms, including graphic design, typography, photography, film, illustration and sound design, it also has distinct demands of its own. Designing a website involves specific considerations of format, technology and information architecture. Of primary importance is how the website functions and, crucially, how the user is able to navigate and move through it. Website navigation is both spatial and sequential and involves a range of possible paths. From the primary navigation bar or menu on the homepage, to »breadcrumb« trails, which allow the user to track their journey and location, establishing the routes and relationships between content, design and structure is essential. ¬ **Back-end** ¬ Airside began the redesign of the Vitsœ website by concentrating on back-end development. While a front-end application interacts directly with the user, back-end comprises the parts of software systems that serve the front-end. It involves the planning and programming of the information architecture of a website. Planning tools such as site maps – hierarchical lists of the sections and sub-sections of a website – and wire frames, which show basic page structure and indicate the relationship between pages, are used to test and develop the design and effective navigation of a site. Airside employed digital agency With Associates as back-end specialists for the Vitsœ site. Nat explains: »We knew they were right for the job from the beginning because Mathew, one of the partners, has a design background but he's taught himself back-end speak and he's very good with information architecture. We knew they were going to be able to bridge us and support us.« ¬

In designing the structure of the website Airside had to establish what Vitsœ wanted on the site and where it should be located. In conjunction with Mathew at With Associates, they created a wire frame of the site. »We'd never done it like this before. He did this really innovative click-through wire frame, which was absolutely brilliant. It sketched out the entire website so the client could sign it off and we could say this is what you're going to have, this is the sub-menu, this is what you will have here and so on…« ¬

These pages are from the fourth version of the wire frame. Each wire frame was user tested: »We got people in and we asked if you wanted to find the bit about the nuts and bolts where would you go, and they said, »Oh, I don't know,« or »You click that.« This allowed Airside to alter and refine the structure and design of the site accordingly. ¬

03/12 ¬ Wire frame development. ¬
   05/12 ¬ The designs are coming along nicely, I think. ¬

Design development ¬ Graphic designers tend to work closely with coders on website design projects, unless they specialize in interface design, when they may code and build the sites themselves. As senior designer, Chris brought typographic rigour to the project, while interaction designer Guy had specialist technical knowledge. Chris is refreshingly honest in admitting he doesn't fully understand the technical details of website design and that he barraged Guy with questions, »most of which he answered with ›no you can't do that‹«. Their combined skills made for a strong working team on this project. With its complex requirements, clear communication between Airside, With Associates and Vitsœ was imperative – and Guy was able to provide an important technical bridge, as Chris explains: »Although I've designed a few websites I can't talk the language and you realize that that is an important thing. You have to be able to get across what you're trying to do and Guy was able to communicate this very clearly.« ¬ **Teamwork** ¬ This project was unusual in using the full breadth of the Airside team. Nat explains: »Alex was in charge of the rich media and moving image over all, partly because of his architectural background and knowledge. A little sub-team started when we got the ethos film off the ground. Chris, Guy and Malika came up with the idea and then, through circumstance more than anything else, it was mostly Malika who ended up running with it. Guy and Chris developed the website design together and then Guy did all the iterations. I was client massaging and overseeing the information architecture, content and wording and the SEO side of things with Alex. It's the biggest job we've ever done, I think. It's very unusual to use everyone.« ¬

Inspired by the design heritage of Vitsœ, Airside wanted to keep the spirit of functionality and rationality in the website, but also to »move the overall feel on«. Designing largely in Illustrator, Chris and Guy created numerous iterations as they honed the structure and appearance of each web page. Chris and Guy each worked on individual page designs simultaneously. Although they worked separately, they found their designs often dovetailed together. »When you present to the client they tend to like some bits of this, some bits of that.« ¬

Airside wanted to use images from the Vitsœ archive to convey the aesthetic and functionality of the shelving system. These photographs were in a variety of formats so Guy explored using overlays and pop-up windows for bigger images. The mix of portrait and landscape photographs posed some problems for them – should they crop, standardize or develop a flexible system for images, which would allow for both formats to be used? ¬

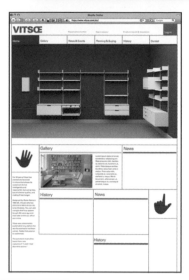

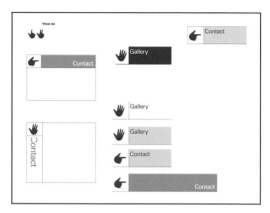

Chris confesses to loving doing layouts and tends to work »quite instinctively«. This sometimes involves sketching on paper but the scale and timeline of this project, with the film development leading straight into the website design, allowed little time for this. »It was quite intensive. We were presenting to Vitsœ every couple of days and after our experience with the storyboards, we felt we needed to show them pages, rather than sketches.« ¬

Airside is known for using strong colour and Guy was keen to explore how this might work on the Vitsœ site. While Guy went for a bold approach, shown far left, Chris explored using muted tones in a more subtle way, applying them to rules and tabs, shown above. The wire frames originally had the navigation on the right but Vitsœ asked for this to be moved to the left. Working on the gallery page over a weekend, he developed new layouts and employed tabs to clarify user location and help differentiate between navigation and information elements. ¬

Airside retained the red hand graphic from Vitsœ's design archive, but reconsidered how it should be used: »Where the hand appears now, it is there to help«, representing Vitsœ's service ethos. Chris explored how it might aid navigation and add a friendly feel to the page, but was concerned that some of his tests were starting to look rather unsophisticated as a result. ¬

08/12 ¬ The film was universally loved by the user-testing group! ¬ We finally got someone in to help with the objects. Met the first 3D animator today. ¬
10/12 ¬ Prioritizing the film and the Japan micro site and getting the back-end sorted. ¬ Vitsœ have decided they want the secondary navigation bar on the right, which seems counter-intuitive to me, but we can make it work. Edit of objects as 3D modeller starts tomorrow. Guy starts paternity leave! ¬

Airside had initially intended to make a stop-frame animation but discovered that building the shelves needed would take four Vitsœ planners two weeks. They had started test modelling various objects in 3D, planning on combining them with the stop-frame. »I was talking to the 3D guy, Tim, who asked why we weren't doing everything in 3D as it would be so much easier«, Chris reveals, prompting Airside to reassess their approach and take the plunge. ¬

When the moment came for Airside to show these renders of the Vitsœ shelving to the client he was astounded by their quality. »I'd been rashly saying I'm sure we can do it in 3D, I'm sure that 3D technology is good enough and I'd been in suspense for two weeks…«, Nat confides. She laughs as she remembers Mark's response. »›That's 3D?‹, he asked, and he literally hit my arm with excitement. For him to photograph the cabinets is a really big deal and here they were realized photorealistically in 3D. He thought it was amazing. It was a huge relief.« ¬

3D animation ¬ In 3D animation objects are built digitally, or modelled, before being rendered. Airside employed specialist 3D animators to realize their vision of creating photorealistic 3D elements in their animation. It is a highly labour-intensive process. As Chris observed: »To animate a small bird you need a modeller, a rigger, an animator and someone to texture and light it. Oh, and you may need a person to feather it too!« Once Vitsœ had signed off the idea of the three-act short animated film, Airside started looking for objects to add depth to the story. Finding appropriate objects to represent the tone and stage of life for each act promised to be a time-consuming job, so Airside commissioned a fashion stylist to research and source objects. »She came back with some interesting things that we wouldn't have thought of. It was a really interesting process. It was almost like building a set.« Malika sketched out the objects, which were then modelled by the 3D animators. 3D modelling gives the illusion of reality but the beauty is in the control it offers, as Vitsœ were quick to recognize. »Mark realized that we could change wall colour, shelf finish or lighting without the need to book a photographer, paint the wall or build the shelving system.« ¬

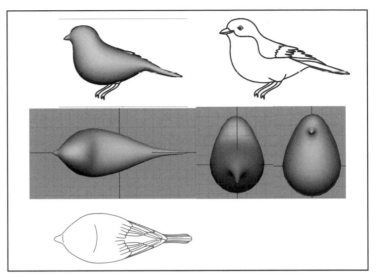

The 3D specialists Airside employed on this project came from the world of feature films. Working from Airside's sketches and reference images they modelled these 3D birds. »They took a day, maybe a day and a bit to do, which is amazingly quick. We'd never worked with anyone that good; they were so knowledgeable and just so fast, saying, ›Ok I've done it, do you want to have a look?‹« says Chris, with barely hidden wonder. ¬

11/12 ¬ Premiered the 3D rendering of the shelves to Vitsœ. ¬
15/12 ¬ The first 3D object models have been built and are looking nice. The birds are looking lovely. ¬

Audience identification ¬ As Nat admits, shelving systems are ostensibly dull. »Vitsœ said to us, ›If we're just a shelving company, we're dead‹«. Airside advised giving more prominence to the relationship Vitsœ builds with its customers, suggesting the creation of new content to bring this to life. Case studies featuring an architect, a large project for a library and fitting out a child's bedroom were all introduced. Vitsœ and Airside identified that the website needed to appeal to two kinds of people, whom they referred to as type A and type B. Type A was design conscious and typically an architect or graphic designer who knew about Dieter Rams and covet his products. Type B was their reluctant partner who equated metal modular shelving with cold office interiors rather than stylish domesticity. This analysis helped Airside refine the brief as the design, content and tone of the website and animation had to »pull in the Bs« without alienating type A. ¬

Vitsœ has a rich photographic archive, which Airside felt had been buried away on the old site. Among the seductive interior shots were images featuring people, which Airside chose to include to encourage identification with and aspiration to a lifestyle, rather than just a product. They also used rich media elements across the site to expound the Vitsœ ethos, which included explanations, archive footage and testimonials. ¬

Airside's animation traced an individual's life through their ever-growing collection of Vitsœ shelving and the objects on the shelves. Each of the three acts illustrated a stage of life. The first was about growth, which Chris describes as »finding your way, with boundless but unfocused energy«. This act finished with a cuckoo clock releasing a flock of small colourful birds into the room to signify the climax and the move to the next stage. Act two was about nurture and »putting your life in order and feathering your nest«. To reflect this, the objects became more ordered and collections started to form. The third act was about reflection: »It's about having lived a full life and being able to look back on what has gone before. Your life is represented by a tree, slowly growing through the shelving in the first two acts and transforming into a tapestry on the wall in the final act«, as a reminder of acts one and two. These acts were interspersed by three choruses, which represent Vitsœ arriving to help with the move to the next stage. ¬

The animation is entirely directed and animated by Airside, and they selected an infectious soundtrack to accompany it. »I think Vitsœ quite liked the idea of something done by Fred [Deakin]« says Nat, but instead they visited Fred's studio and spent an evening with the storyboards and the animatic of the film on screen trying a range of different music. They settled on Dee Felice Trio's 1967 jazz classic, »Nightingale«. »It was kind of set in the past like the shelves but fresh as well«, and they all liked the symmetry with the birds in the film. »Nightingale« is an instrumental piece, a consideration when designing for an international audience. With this in mind, the film has no voice-over and minimal on-screen text. ¬

17/12 ¬ We have a problem with where the page fold falls on the homepage. Removed colour from the site today while we try to get the navigation signed off. ¬

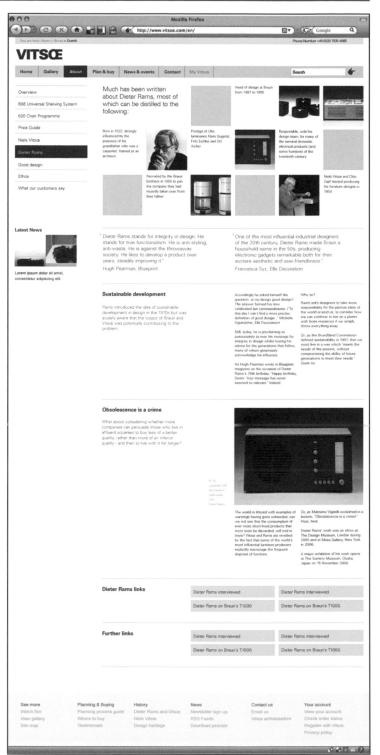

Airside's design needed to comply with the Vitsœ style guide, which determined fonts and logo usage. Vitsœ still use basic graphic elements designed by Wolfgang Schmidt in 1969–70 and continue to use his choice of font. Univers, designed by Adrian Frutiger in 1957, is an elegant and rational sans serif, with clean lines and good legibility. The Univers font family comes in a variety of weights and widths, designated by numbers rather than name, a functional and adaptable system, which has parallels with Rams' designs for Vitsœ. ¬

»This was the last page I designed personally and was when it all came together for me«, Chris recalls with satisfaction. »Everything felt very Vitsœ. It's functional and it's clear where you are. I kept the feeling of space as much as I could and also the sections as simple as I could, too«. Working first on a five-column grid, he used two columns for the title and introductory text, leaving the middle column open for picture captions if needed. The final two columns were for copy. Chris had included bulleted text at the top of the page; Nat felt this should be pushed further and suggested breaking this field with images. In response, Chris returned to an eight-column grid and introduced text and image squares, creating a more flexible and dynamic introduction to the section. ¬

Functional design ¬ A Content Management System (CMS) is simplified software which allows someone with limited technical knowledge of web coding to edit and upload web content relatively easily. Airside designed a series of CMS templates for Vitsœ to create and manage their website content. Vitsœ could choose from these and assemble them to compose pages. »We had to work out how a quote would be handled«, Chris explains, »or a section with one image and two columns of text, or video, and lay that out to show how they could be slotted together as a whole«. The original brief had specified that Open Source CMS be used for this project. Open Source software is available free for general use and is without distribution or copyright restrictions. This allows coders and designers to modify and customize the software to meet their specific requirements. As Airside explained, »Open Source is 100 per cent accessible code that is good for SEO and easy to maintain.« ¬

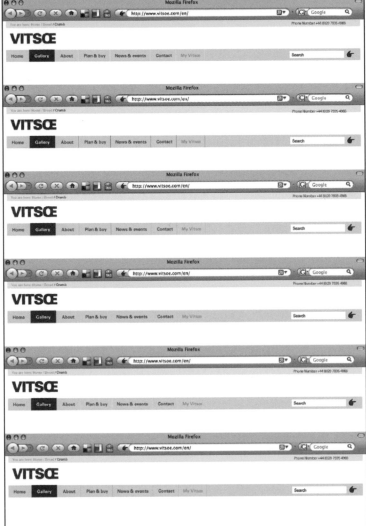

Attention to detail is an important aspect of Vitsœ's philosophy and the service they provide. These versions of the primary navigation bar show barely perceptible variations in the weight and colour of the hairline rule dividing the section headers and reveal the level of rigour and detail Vitsœ demanded in the design of their website. ¬

Nat felt that the colour was proving a distraction from some of the finer design details. She made the decision to remove the colour from the designs while they concentrated on refining the navigation and getting it signed off by the client. ¬

23/12 ¬ I have now broken a record for the number of Illustrator files I have saved. I am up to 99 or something. ¬
28/12 ¬ I think we finally have some kind of sign-off on the navigation bar. I just have to send over six more options of the buttons and we are done… ¬

Viewing ¬ The design of any website must take into consideration the technical specifications involved. This is not just about the technology the designer has at their disposal but involves thinking about who the audience is and what hardware and software they might use to view the site. In this case Airside had to ensure that their film could be small enough in file size to load and play smoothly on any web browser and be of the appropriate aspect ratio for viewing on a range of screens and appliances. ¬ **Rendering** ¬ Once the design and modelling of an animation is complete it must be rendered. Rendering is the process of converting 3D data files into individual digital frames and is a slow but essential process. The more frames per second, the smoother the animation but the larger the file size and the longer the rendering time. At Vitsœ's request the film had increased in length. This had implications for the rendering time and could have impacted on the final delivery date. Chris observed with some concern that it was taking one computer an hour to render a single frame. He calculated that if the film was 90 seconds long, at 25 frames per second (industry standard in many regions) it would take 2,250 hours to render. Even though Airside had several machines available at their »render farm«, this was still »a big ask!« ¬ **iPhone** ¬ Airside chose to design the film to a widescreen aspect ratio of 16:9 so that it would be playable on an iPhone without needing to be »letterboxed«, and effectively cropped at either side. Vitsœ's brief had been explicit about the importance of the iPhone, both as a model for mobile communication and because of the correlation between the demographic of iPhone users and Vitsœ customers. As Vitsœ proudly claim, Jonathan Ive, principal designer of many of Apple's most innovative and elegant products, openly acknowledges his debt to Vitsœ designer Dieter Rams. ¬

Currently, the majority of users view websites on a screen with a minimum resolution of 1024 pixels x 768 pixels. Airside's design was optimized to fit within these dimensions, allowing for the browser window navigation tools. Airside reduced the width of the film to 950 pixels so that it would fit comfortably within the browser window. ¬

What is immediately visible when a homepage appears in an opening browser window is important. Initially, Airside wanted the film to have maximum impact and to open full-screen. However, this meant that the »fold« of the page – where the web page stops before you have to start scrolling – would sit four-fifths of the way down the movie so some of it would have not been visible. The way to avoid this was to make the film smaller. »It felt like a disaster. The film would have to sit in a smallish area of the homepage, which was getting worryingly cluttered.« ¬

When Vitsœ first viewed the animatic of the film they felt it should be longer and match the duration of the soundtrack, which was 2 minutes 37 seconds, as opposed to the 1 minute 30 seconds they'd seen. Airside reassured them that it could be made a little longer but that it would have implications on the load times of the film. Airside looked at the options for rendering the film at different rates: »Rendering at 15 frames per second was mooted, because it seemed to be standard compression for the web. Tim, who had to render it, thought it made more sense to render at 12 frames per second and so we test rendered a small portion of the film at 25, 15 and 12 frames per second and compared results.« ¬

The render tests revealed some surprising results: »The 25-frame version was the best. The birds looked super smooth and the motion of the tree and cabinet door looked lovely.« Unsurprisingly the 12- and 15- frame versions looked a little clunkier but also had a lovely hand-made charm about them.« There was so little difference between these two that they opted to render at 12 frames per second to benefit from the smaller final file size and enable faster loading on the homepage. Airside employed »a specialist Flash bod« to compress the film and program the buffering to ensure there would be no juddering or pausing when the film played. ¬

12/01 ¬ Got the render test back today. ¬
21/01 ¬ The transition between the second and third acts is feeling a little clunky. ¬
29/01 ¬ Pitching again – just won a pitch for another piece of work. ¬
03/02 ¬ In the studio late tonight, waiting for renders as we have to have the films ready for tomorrow. ¬

Shelving system for Vitsœ by designer Dieter Rams in

http://www.vitsoe.com/

You are here: Home   Telephone +44 (0)20 742...

VITSŒ   now open!

Home | Gallery | Products | Shop | Architects | About | News | Contact | My Vitsœ

»Lots of things emerged that we hadn't expected, like having influence over the tone of the copy and seeing how the technology and their business systems integrate. There's a software tool that plans the shelves and there's a software tool that tracks customers and orders, and they're all linked. And the back of our website has to tie in with all of that. At that point you have an opportunity to streamline things, to make things more efficient behind the scenes and to save them money. It might mean spending more money on the back-end but it will save them money long term. It's gone much deeper than we ever thought it would.« ¬

Our shelving system

Designed by Dieter Rams in 1960, 606 Universal Shelving System was conceived to be timeless.

You can add a single shelf to a system bought 40 years ago and then take it with you when you move.

Learn more about our products

Visit our shop

You can buy from our starter collection from GBP 145, delivered straight to you.

Visit our shop

NY store now open

Visit our new store in NY from Monday 14 September.

Store information

Where are yo...

If your country is li... you can change yo...

United States of Ar...
Japan
Rest of Europe
Rest of World

Proof ¬ Rather than wanting to look better, Nat believes most businesses employ design because they want a return on their investment. Airside's financial investment in Vitsœ was like »putting our money where our mouth is.« Before the relaunch the average number of visitors to Vitsoe.com were roughly 180 a day. The new site had averaged over 1,000 visitors a day after six weeks with an impressive 21,000 spike on the launch date, »so it's definitely got a lot more traffic. It's absolutely brilliant to be able to say ›we believe in design‹, but to have the chance to monitor it and see if it really works is a unique opportunity«. She admits that the next few years will be interesting as they find out the »nitty gritty« about how many sales there are and what's really going on. »We've got a vested interest now – we've got a percentage of their profits!« ¬ **Lifelong relationship** ¬ Nat was enormously relieved when the site went live, on time and on budget, but admits that the intensity and scale took its toll. »We all collapsed for about two weeks afterwards; my brain was like cotton wool.« As with any project there are areas that Airside would like to have developed but the rewarding thing about this one is that »we're in this on-going relationship with Vitsœ and we're getting a chance to improve a lot of stuff, which is great.« Airside considers this unusual relationship to be »a real privilege«, says Nat. »To be trusted like that is really exciting. Being able to see things change and to have this big playground, where we can change the language and see if we can get the stats up, see if we can get the search engine findings up… When it starts working, you know you're on to something.« ¬

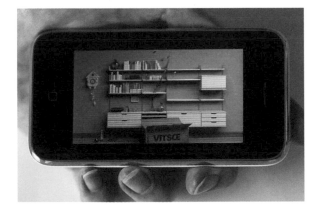

Post-launch, Nat still feels they have an important role to play encouraging greater user-centredness. »The next thing we're about to add is a little eBay watcher. We're going to really make it obvious that if you're watching Vitsœ shelving on eBay you can contact Vitsœ directly and they will tell you how much it would cost new and about their refurbishment service. At the moment people ring up and are slightly embarrassed, but we think it's a really important part of their sustainability ethos.« ¬

20/02 ¬ Over 20,000 visits on the day of the soft launch in February. ¬

As the range of projects we have followed attest, creative process in graphic design requires neither mystical muse nor exists as a one-size-fits-all formula. Shaped by diverse factors, including the brief, environment, experience, resources, individual taste and temperament, the journey from first thought to final product is different from designer to designer and from job to job. However, there are common threads running through the creative processes in the projects we have followed. Aimed primarily at those starting out, but hopefully of help to all, this section explores some of these main themes. Within them lie truths, tips and methods that may prove helpful in reflecting upon and developing your own creative process and perhaps even handling or heading off the dreaded creative block.

There is a common assumption that freedom is a desirable, if not strictly necessary, condition for the blossoming of creativity. Within graphic design, however, one might say the opposite is true. Design is a discipline defined by constraints. From a project brief, which sets parameters of time, money, function and, often, form, to the limitations of materials and restrictions of audience, every job is to some extent a tug of war between what is possible and what is not, and between the vision of the designer and the vision of the client. Graphic designers are trained, and required, to respond to a brief. Constraints can be frustrating but to be faced with a set of restrictions – be they physical or technical, enforced or self-imposed, political or ideological – demands and stimulates creative tenacity. Restrictions provide a framework, a place to start and a spur to creative ingenuity. They are for many designers a source of challenges, productivity and delight – and an essential component of the creative process. ¬

Deadlines ¬ Deadlines are an unavoidable part of graphic design. For most designers they provide a creative catalyst to bolder and more focused decision-making – to say nothing of the adrenalin rush when a courier is waiting outside – as Borries (see pages 040–041), Meirion (see pages 074–075) and Homework (see pages 052–053) know all too well. It is not always true that the longer you work at something the better it will become and deadlines can be useful, even when self-imposed. As Stefan explains (see pages 016–017), he creates his own constraints when developing initial ideas – a useful tip if you're struggling to generate ideas or get started. Working quickly increases productivity, which can be satisfying. And thinking on your feet can draw surprising things from you, which may otherwise have remained hidden. Try limiting your time and structuring it into short sessions, and reduce the opportunity for procrastination or distraction. ¬

Limited resources ¬ Graphic designers often take a perverse delight in the challenges of a brief, not just in terms of time but also in terms of budget. Bruno and the designers at Dalton Maag enjoy the mental and creative agility that juggling the two requires (see pages 112–113), as do Bond and Coyne, who find real satisfaction in the resourcefulness necessitated by a tight budget (see pages 138–139). Designers often like the aesthetics of low budget materials, in part because they are infrequently used. However, it is important to consider when it is appropriate to foreground the budget in the aesthetics and when it is not (see pages 142–143). Try limiting the materials you use and working with reduced resources as a way of prompting inventiveness. ¬

Systems and structure ¬
Designers are not just recipients of constraint, but also architects of it. Most are instinctively inclined to create order, both in their approach to a project and the visual outcome. Constraints are part of the armoury of design tools, so an often complex set of rules, systems and devices are used in order to maintain control. This is evident in Borries' systematic approach (see pages 028–029) and Meirion's pleasure in using a grid (see pages 070–071). The project management, planning and organization of both Bond and Coyne (see pages 150–151) and Airside (see pages 214–215) demonstrate how structure and strategic thinking, at every level, are integral to the success of design projects. Good organization and a clearly structured approach to the design and management of a project will help ensure your ideas are fully realized and you deliver on time and budget. ¬

Design philosophies ¬ Many designers evolve or align themselves with a design philosophy, which provides a framework of fundamental principles or values to underpin their practice. Both Emmi and Bond and Coyne take a political stance, believing that design can and should be socially responsible; this necessarily restricts the type of client, work and content they feel prepared to endorse, accept or promote (see pages 092–093 and 138–139). Experimental Jetset ally themselves with modernism (see pages 156–157) as does Borries (see pages 028–029), following the clearly expressed maxim that form follows function. Know your position and the ideas, values and principles you hold to be important as you develop your creative voice. Work out what shape you draw around yourself, and what you will and won't follow or do. ¬

Future forecasting ¬
Enforced limitations can prompt reflection on what it is that matters most in a project, and what drives it. While Frauke finds inspiration in limited budgets and materials, she also sees this relationship in starker terms. She finds the vacuum left by an absence of money is an opportunity for a project to be driven instead by passion (see pages 128–129). Limited budgets place constraints not only on how you design, but also on how much you can earn – and therefore how you live. Be honest with yourself and work out where you think you fit and the type of client, budget and lifestyle to which you aspire. ¬

To design is to create with intent: to plan and structure and purposefully develop ideas and solutions. However, despite the largely rational and systematic nature of their work, most designers would agree that risk is an essential ingredient in the creative process. If they did not dare to let go of preconceived ideas and open themselves to new ones, their creative output would be sterile, samey and predictable. Without risk, not only would they be more likely to disappoint their clients, but they would bore themselves. To be innovative and imaginative requires the creative courage to embrace failure as part of the design process, and to put aside fear – of the unknown, of rejection, of the client and ultimately, of course, of failure. As fear is a human emotion common to us all, it is true to say that all designers feel fear at some point. It is also true that the creative process – immersion in the exploration of methods and materials, researching and developing ideas – generates momentum and propels projects forward, instilling confidence and fortifying nerve. ¬

Courage ¬ While still at college, Borries not only set up a design studio with fellow students, but also aspired to get his thesis published (see pages 028–029 and 038–039). Emmi took what she felt was a big risk in applying to Fabrica (see pages 092–093) and still finds that going round and selling her badges, in the face of possible rejection, requires courage (see pages 100–101). Frauke is candid in admitting that in order to fulfil her ambition – to make less commercially focused and more experimental work – she has to be prepared to make other compromises (see pages 124–125). You too must be prepared to be bold. There is truth in the old adage »nothing ventured, nothing gained« and the advice here is to feed and fire-up your ambition and nurture your courage. ¬

Ambition ¬ Although graphic design is ultimately a humble discipline, at the service of a client or message it must project, designers are ambitious. Many are idealists and harbour the desire to make the world a better place, to help find and establish order from chaos and to design things which meet a need and serve a purpose, efficiently and elegantly. Cultivate your ambition and self-belief – they are important ingredients in the creative process as a source of motivation and drive, as our contributors have demonstrated. ¬

Chance ¬ Serendipity and happy accidents frequently play a part in the design process, but this is dependent upon a designer recognizing and exploiting these moments and mistakes. Be proactive and prolific and you'll find that you become more alert to the possibilities you produce. Some designers create the circumstances for chance and randomness to occur not only as part of their creative process, but also as part of their solution. Stefan's logo generator gives control and choice to the user (see pages 020–021) and in her DIY kit-of-parts Frauke relinquishes the application and implementation of her designs to someone else (see pages 132–133). Although these designers have created the constraints within which chance can occur, there is still risk in surrendering control in projects. However, there are rich possibilities in harnessing the unforeseen and unpredictable. Be brave, make your own luck and be open to what comes your way – even if it isn't part of the grand plan. ¬

Balance ¬ Every job involves taking a step into the unknown. Working on new things and in new ways can be daunting and designers must constantly weigh up and balance the risks involved in projects. While Frauke finds it exhilarating to have clients who push her to extremes (see pages 124–125), Stefan prefers to build from a firm foundation. When tackling a project his desired ratio between doing things he knows and things he doesn't is 50:50 (see pages 012–013). Dalton Maag and Experimental Jetset took risks in accepting projects that were based in other countries, working with other cultures and in other languages (see pages 110–111 and 160–161). While for Airside, the desire to reinvent and explore ever-broader creative practices and new technologies drives their studio ethos and is at the core of their daily practice (see pages 194–195). Taking risks is not always easy, but the more you do it the easier it becomes. Discovering your own parameters, and finding the conditions conducive to creating work and taking risks will be immensely valuable to you. ¬

Failure ¬ Each project we have followed in this book has involved the chance of failure. Design is an iterative process: one of testing and improving, in which failure plays an inescapable role. Failure helps a designer identify problems and strive for more successful or meaningful solutions. However, failure is frequently a matter of perception. Remember that what you may consider a failure, your client may not, so try to be objective in appraising your work and where failures do occur, see them as opportunities. ¬

Risk ¬ The notion of what it means to fail changes as careers develop and many designers find it becomes harder to take risks the more established they become. This is not just because clients have usually commissioned on the basis of previous work, and they want more of the same, but also because it gets harder to carve out the time to try new things. The further a designer is in their career, the greater the risks appear to be as the more there is to lose. Build taking risks into your practice and welcome failure as a part of your creative process – you are more likely to achieve results and solutions that surprise you. ¬

Ideas and solutions do not often appear fully formed in a designer's mind. At the core of the creative process is the exploration and experimentation of a range of thoughts and starting points, with the aim of discovering, crafting and honing an idea. Designers generally start visualizing their ideas in scribbles, lists, notes and drawings before developing, testing, analysing and refining solutions and outcomes. Although design is now a dominantly digital activity, this process of exploration and play occurs both on and off-screen and across a wide variety of media. Visual exploration is an analytical process, where ideas are explored, examined and experimented with, in order to establish the potential, problems, or success of the results. Visual exploration is not a substitute for an idea but coupled with and informed by research, it will help in the generation and development of ideas. ¬

Sketchbooks and notebooks ¬ Drawing, sketching and making notes are immediate and instinctive activities for most designers, and sketchbooks and notebooks are still relevant and revered repositories for gathering, examining and interpreting these activities and research. While Stefan favours a particular colour, format and binding for his sketchbooks (see pages 016–017), Borries collates his workings in a series of neatly ordered lever arch files (see pages 034–035). Experimental Jetset are less precious and make sketches and notes on loose sheets, envelopes, post-it notes or whatever is at hand (see pages 162–163). Finding a system that works for you is important, as your visual research and experiments are part of an evolving archive of ideas on which you may wish to repeatedly draw. Both Stefan and Borries also keep different sketchbooks or notebooks for different activities (see pages 016–017 and 034–035), a useful tip for organizing and collecting different types of research. ¬

Doodles and drawings ¬ The marks that designers make in their sketchbooks or notebooks and the ways in which they record their thoughts are individual and varied. For Frauke, drawing is fundamental to her thought process and provides a connection between eye, brain and hand (see pages 128–129) that enables her to generate and shape ideas. Homework usually starts by sketching ideas and associated thoughts and images as thumbnails in notebooks (see pages 056–057), before translating these drawings into digital form in Illustrator. Stefan's early visual explorations use a range of media and show playful and thorough visual thinking and analysis around his subject (see pages 016–017). Explore different methods, materials and ways of making marks and thinking visually. ¬

Be prepared ¬ Emmi carries her notebook with her at all times (see pages 096–097) and perhaps this is the most important sketchbook tip of all – ideas can arrive at unexpected moments, so always carry a pen and paper or sketchbook with you! ¬

Getting started ¬ It may be a cliché, but it is nonetheless true that it takes perspiration to create inspiration, and ideas rarely come to those that sit and wait. Working to deadlines, designers do not have the luxury of time for indulging creative block and they must generate ideas quickly and get started straight away. Bond and Coyne collect materials and visual references as cues (see pages 138–139). Homework starts by jotting down first associations before generating visual metaphors (see pages 052–053 and 056–057). Frauke, however, prefers to use lists and words as triggers, rather than rely on visual clues (see pages 128–129), while Airside found it useful to develop a conceptual framework before starting to develop visuals (see pages 198–199). Borries believes it is the problem that will dictate the solution (see pages 028–029). There is no general rule or simple methodology here, only that you will probably have to test a range of processes as you evolve your understanding and build an armoury of methods and processes that work for you. Don't wait for your Eureka moment. Make the ideas happen. ¬

Lists and layouts ¬ Drawing is not the only way of exploring and developing ideas. Borries is more of a list writer than a sketcher (see pages 034–035). However, visualizing his book in his sketched-out flatplan helped him keep his thoughts in order and see the design problems more clearly (see pages 032–033). For Meirion and his team a working flatplan is also an important initial tool in giving an overview of the content, composition and extent of each issue of »Wallpaper*« (see pages 068–069). Seeing the design problem on the page, rather than imagining it in your head, will allow you to know it more clearly. Get your thoughts and ideas down on paper early, and give yourself time to test, evaluate and evolve solutions. ¬

Testing ¬ Testing is essential in generating meaningful and successful solutions, as Meirion explains of the development of the »Wallpaper*« grids and typefaces: »until you try, you don't know if it's going to work« (see pages 070–071). Testing can take different forms – Homework collects a visual vocabulary of associated elements before beginning to design and illustrate with them, creating options from which they can select (see pages 058–059). Dalton Maag's process is highly systematic and usually focuses initially on the development of 12 characters of the alphabet (see pages 112–113), which will be drawn, evaluated and gradually refined in a process of incremental evolution. Test your ideas and designs thoroughly so that you can make judgements based upon evidence rather than guesswork. ¬

Variations ¬ Paula's extensive renderings of leaf variations (see pages 186–187) show the extremes that can be necessary to arrive at the best solution – and to demonstrate and convince your client that this is the case. This is a useful tip. Generate a broad range of options from which to edit and select. The more rigorous you are in this process, the greater the confidence you are likely to have in your eventual solution and the more persuasive in explaining your argument to your client too! Force yourself to be prolific – producing 50 or 100 ideas from a single starting point will take you beyond what is obvious and elicit unusual, unconscious and unconventional ideas and thoughts. ¬

The ability to look at things from different angles and through other people's eyes is key to the design process. Knowledge and curiosity about the world around you, including and beyond design, is essential in understanding and gauging the broader context in which your work must function and exist. Awareness of cultural trends, current climates and contemporary concerns comes from absorbing and experiencing diverse sources and situations. It is important to be open to new – and old – ways of seeing, doing, thinking and designing. For many designers this includes searching out the things that inspire them, whether famous designers, fonts, paper samples or punk rock. The challenge for a designer is to make meaningful connections between these inspirations, perspectives and their own ideas – and through this synthesis evolve their own distinctive creative voice. ¬

Looking back ¬ Despite the glittering allure of the new, the past can be a source of information and inspiration. For Borries, the history of form design was fundamental to the development and content of his project (see pages 036–037) while knowledge of the history of font design informed the choice and outcome of the »Wallpaper*« »refresh« design (see pages 072–073). Exposure to the original drawings of seminal typeface Gill Sans gave Ron at Dalton Maag (see pages 106–107) a revelatory glimpse into the beauty of typography . Homework acknowledges their debt to the rich cultural design heritage of Polish poster design, of which their work is an extension (see pages 052–053). The advice here is to use what you glean from those that have gone before as a base on which to build. It was astronomer, mathematician, physicist and philosopher Isaac Newton who commented that his ability to see further came from standing on the shoulders of giants. Use the past. Look back to help you move forward. ¬

Other hats ¬ A design brief almost always requires an audience specific solution and being able to empathize with your audience and see design problems from other viewpoints is invaluable. Bond and Coyne are exponents of design thinking where input from end-users is an integral part of the design process (see pages 138–139). Mike also enjoys playing devil's advocate and interrogating their own design proposals from the perspective of the client (see pages 138–139). Try switching perspectives in this way to prompt identification and objectivity. ¬

Beyond design ¬ Outside interests can provide alternative perspectives and drawing on diverse references makes for distinctive work. Experimental Jetset are intrigued by subcultures and passionate about the underground music scene, which they see as a mirror of design (see pages 156–157), while Frauke's African upbringing influences how she uses the natural world (see pages 124–125) for visual references and inspiration. Politics and current affairs have always been important influences for Emmi (see pages 092–093), while Paula's painting is both an extension and escape from her commercial work (see pages 178–179). Draw on diverse references – it will make for rich solutions. ¬

Feedback ¬ User feedback can make the design process more inclusive and Airside found user-testing instructive in developing a friendly and ergonomic website structure and navigation system (see pages 202–203). Where possible, test your ideas and solutions on appropriate audiences at intervals throughout the design process. Find out what others think. Weigh up criticism and don't be afraid of the judgement of others – see it as constructive. Look at the problem and the solution from various viewpoints. ¬

Be alert ¬ To the curious, inspiration can be found everywhere, not just in the extraordinary, but also in the everyday. Don't ignore things close to home or under your nose as sources of inspiration – potential projects and new ideas can be found from looking at familiar things with fresh eyes. Stay aware and alive also to the broader culture in which you live and work – read, listen, observe, participate, initiate, question and learn. ¬

Before a designer can answer a brief, solve a problem or communicate an idea, subject or message, they must understand it; this is a process invariably involving research and investigation. Research extends knowledge, providing breadth, directing focus and informing ideas and avenues for development. Good research is enquiring, insightful and useful – it will help you evolve intelligent and relevant design solutions. It will also provide a rationale for your work, helpful when pitching or convincing a client of your ideas and design choices. ¬

Understanding ¬ Good design is born of solid understanding of a brief. Meirion ensures his designers read any copy they are laying out before designing (see pages 076–077) so they are sensitive to the meaning and content of what they are handling. After some false starts, Stefan found the solution and rationale for his identity design after focused research into the building he was designing the identity for (see pages 018–019). It might seem obvious advice, but always start by ensuring you explore and fully understand a brief and the design content of a project. ¬

Knowledge ¬ Research can be focused and local, but it should also be wide-ranging and rigorous. Experimental Jetset undertake extensive contextual research and are avid readers. They draw upon their considerable theoretical, philosophical and political knowledge to inform and support their work (see pages 162–163). Airside found their theoretical research not only helpful in framing their creative thinking, but that it was also crucial in convincing their client of the relevance and appropriateness of their design proposal (see pages 198–199). Substantial and in-depth research should lead to real understanding of the content, context and issues of the subject you are working on. Good research will provide intellectual support for your ideas, inform creative thinking and will help you develop intelligent design solutions. Designers should always be learning. Know the world around you – discover something you didn't know already in every project and approach research with verve and rigour. ¬

Experience ¬ Research can take many forms and while using books, the Internet or watching films is of value, don't underestimate the importance of primary evidence and first-hand experience. Wherever possible you should search out the source of your interest and experience it: visit archives, go to places, talk with people and get involved. Experience is multi-sensory and 3D, and will provide you with opportunities for discovery and engagement not possible through second-hand accounts. Although Homework develops concepts through careful analysis – reading the play script, watching and re-watching the film – they also talked to the director when possible (see pages 052–053) to humanize and extend their knowledge before designing. Working with typographer Paul Barnes, Meirion commissioned new fonts for »Wallpaper*« in response to some woodblock type Paul uncovered in the archive at St Bride Library (see pages 070–071). Both Airside and Stefan found that it was through face-to-face discussions with the client that they were able to discover clues to unlock the issues that constituted the real brief (see pages 198–199 and 014–015). Be curious. Get out of the studio and out into the world. Feel, touch, engage and learn. ¬

Collaboration ¬ It is common for designers to involve other people in their creative process. This may be an invited expert, studio colleagues, creative partner or even the client. Although many designers choose to set up independently, most design jobs would simply not be achievable by a designer working on their own. Meirion, for example, relies heavily on his team (see pages 066–067), while Stefan enlisted the support of interactive design specialist Ralph Ammer to help him evolve and achieve his ambitious logo generator (see pages 020–021). Paula brought in Pentagram colleague Daniel Weil to form a project team with expertise across 2D and 3D design (see pages 182–183), and Bond and Coyne worked closely with 3D designer Steve Mosley on the design and construction of the exhibition stands for their project (see pages 144–145). Bruno involved experts in Arabic to advise on the project featured here (see pages 116–117 and 118–119). Collaboration is not always easy and it's important to work out the roles and relationships early. But the benefits of pooling talents and ambition almost always outweigh the pitfalls. Don't be insecure or too proud to bring in collaborators with relevant expertise on a project. Build a network of people who can advise or contribute in areas where your skills may be limited or where you lack expertise; use collaboration as a catalyst. ¬

Teamwork ¬ A more established working pattern and collaborative dynamic exists between designers who work as part of a studio. Jerzy and Joanna of Homework work separately before sharing ideas (see pages 056–057), as do Bruno and his colleagues as they each contribute to the design of a typeface (see pages 112–113). Experimental Jetset's cohesive and collegiate approach means that all aspects of their design work are only ever attributed to the group, and never to an individual (see pages 156–157). Airside operates as more of a collective – a studio of individual designers and animators who work together in different combinations depending upon the project, exploiting the possibilities of pooling and pushing ideas as a group (see pages 194–195). Work out if you see yourself as a designer who works best on your own or in a team by getting experience of working in groups. Think carefully about what kind of team player you are. ¬

There are highs and lows within any creative process. While it is undeniably exciting, challenging and rewarding, it can also involve frustration, moments of despair and be fraught with obstacles. Passion for what you do is essential. To be a designer requires a curious and unquantifiable combination of qualities, character, skills and application. It demands commitment and takes hard work and dedication – and creative process requires the same, evolving and developing through constant and continuous practice. It may be a cliché but it is nonetheless true: being creative is not a job – it's a way of life. So enjoy it. Strive, smile and keep going! ¬

Obsession and perfection ¬ Many designers have a pedantic eye for, and love of, detail, whether painstakingly colour correcting a photograph of clouds (see pages 080–081) or delighting in the beauty of typographic texture and the structural forms of individual letterforms (see pages 106–107). Bruno confesses his compulsive obsessive tendencies (see pages 106–107), but not all designers are so candid. Obsession and perfection are important traits for designers as they combine to create a determined, thorough and rigorous approach to design. Admittedly, to be an obsessive and a perfectionist can be as much of a curse as a virtue, but the advice for designers remains: cultivate your obsessive tendencies and strive for perfection. ¬

Tenacity ¬ Design is rarely straightforward and in order to succeed designers must develop creative stamina in parallel to their creative process. There are tricks and traits you can harness to achieve this. For Emmi, personal projects provide what she calls her »creative lifeline« and sustain her commercial practice (see pages 092–093). A hunger to keep evolving and pushing things underpins Meirion's work ethic but he admits that he keeps calm by eating (see pages 066–067). The designers at Dalton Maag find themselves motivated by the thought of the next job and the momentum that comes from being immersed in a project (see pages 120–121), while Borries' dry humour helps him laugh in response to the rejection and criticism design inevitably involves (see pages 042–043). Design can be high pressure and stressful. Meeting deadlines, dealing with clients, balancing books, managing production and staying creative can be intensely demanding and you will need to develop your own strategies for survival. Explore what it is that keeps you going and start developing your tenacity now! ¬

Keeping perspective ¬ Despite all the advice above, relentless perseverance is not always fruitful. Many designers find that having an activity that gets them away from their screen or desk is part of their creative process and that the perspective and proportion this provides helps stave off the inevitable moments of creative block. For Borries this involves clearing his head by walking or cycling (see pages 028–029), while Meirion's pressure valve is his weekly football, which provides not only exercise but also valuable networking opportunities (see pages 066–067). Homework finds that when creative block looms, taking a break or picking up a different tool provides the necessary respite or creative jolt (see pages 056–057). So, whether you read or run, sing or swim, remember to lift your nose from the page and look around you to refresh and revive lagging creative spirits. Before you get right back to it and keep going… ¬

Walking away ¬ Few projects run entirely smoothly and there will be occasions when you will wonder if it is all worth it. Designers mostly work to find a way of resolving differences and solving the problems that occur. However, perseverance is not always the best course of action as Experimental Jetset found in the project we have followed here (see pages 174–175). Recognizing that the obstacles of bureaucracy, communication and client had become insurmountable, they took the brave decision to walk away. Knowing if and when it is the right time to throw in the towel is extremely difficult, not least because it can feel like admitting failure. The advice here comes in the form of a caution – you are only as good as your client allows you to be. Have conviction in your ideas, compromise where appropriate but know your limits and be prepared for anything. ¬

compiled by
James West

a   b   c

animatics
An animated version of a storyboard using basic movement and cut-out characters to a soundtrack. Used to visualize how a final project might look in order to get client sign-off on a concept. ¬

ascender
The part of a lower-case letter that »ascends« above the x-height. For example, the stems of the letters »h« and »l«. ¬

back-end see CMS

baseline grid
A series of evenly-spaced, non-printing horizontal guides, usually measured in points. Each line indicates where the base of lower-case letters without ascenders or descenders sits. By setting up a baseline grid all type can be aligned to common reference points. ¬

bellyband
A thin strip, usually paper, that wraps all the way around a book or magazine to hold it together with any accompanying leaflet or promotional publication. ¬

blad
»Basic Layout and Design« or »Book Layout and Design«, a promotional tool used by publishers to give commercial book-buyers an idea of what a finished book will look like, showing the front/back cover and sample spreads. ¬

blank dummy
An unprinted sample document (for example, a book) made with the intended stock and binding. Used to give designers, publishers and clients a feel of the finished object before committing to a print run. ¬

bleed [off]
One or more sides of an image, or area of solid colour, that runs off the edge of a page. These areas are set up to extend slightly beyond the page edge to allow for inaccurate trimming. ¬

buffering
The process of storing data temporarily in computer memory. An example would be the data of a video clip online which downloads more quickly than the real playback speed and so is stored in the buffer until it's ready to be displayed on screen. ¬

calibration
The process of testing and adjusting various devices (scanners, monitors, printers, etc) to achieve consistent and reliable colour output. ¬

cmyk
The printing (usually offset lithography) of cyan, magenta, yellow and black inks, one after the other. Combining different percentages of these inks produces a wide range of colours, so cmyk printing is often referred to as »full colour«, in contrast to printing with Pantone inks, which are premixed pure colours. ¬

CMS
Content Management System. A password-protected area online set up by a web development company so that clients can make content changes to their own websites without any programming knowledge. Also referred to as the »back-end«, in contrast to the publicly viewable parts of a website which are known as the »front-end«. ¬

coders
Another name for computer programmers. Coders write computer code to perform certain functions. They might program a CMS, for example. ¬

colour balance
The relative proportion of, generally, cmyk colours in an image. These are often adjusted, or »corrected« to make the colour balance of an image as representative of the original subject photographed as possible. ¬

colour bars
A standard row of coloured squares printed along the edge of a digital proof. When produced to a recognized standard (for example FOGRA) these bars are used by printers as a colour reference when a job is on press. Colour bars are also produced on live jobs so that printers can measure ink density with a densitometer. ¬

coloured [stock]
Paper or card that has been dyed during the manufacturing process. The colour is impregnated throughout the paper, so the edges are coloured, unlike paper that has been printed in a colour. ¬

cromalin
A form of proof. True cromalin proofs are infrequently used now, but many designers and printers still (misleadingly) refer to high-quality digital proofs as »cromalins«. Before the onset of large format digital printers, a cromalin was considered to be one of the best ways to see a colour accurate (or nearly accurate) version of a print job prior to the print run. Making a cromalin involved exposing a specialist tacky paper to UV light that hardened in the areas where colour was not required. This was then covered with a powder which stuck to the tacky areas that were left. Generally used to proof cmyk, this process was repeated in each of the four colours. Cromalin proofs were relatively accurate because they used the film that would be used in making the plates for printing. However, film is nowadays mostly superseded by CtP (Computer to Plate) technology (see offset lithography). ¬

DDA
Disability Discrimination
Act, a piece of UK legislation
that »promotes civil rights
for disabled people and
protects disabled people from
discrimination« (direct.gov.uk).
There is equivalent legislation
in the USA and in many other
countries. All have implications
for graphic design practice:
from considering type
sizes and colour in print
to programming of websites,
the objective is to ensure
access for disabled users.
The Web Accessibility Initiative
developed by the World Wide
Web Consortium lists various
international policies relating
to accessibility on its website,
www.w3.org/WAI/Policy/ ¬

debossing/embossing
Stamping a metal shape called
a die into paper or card to make
a sunken or raised area. ¬

densitometer
A tool used by printers to
determine the density of ink
on a printed surface to ensure
consistency. ¬

descender
The part of a lower-case
letter that »descends« below
the baseline. For example,
the tails of the letters »g«
and »y«. ¬

die cut
A shape cut out of a substrate
(for example, paper or card)
using a sharp metal die stamped
through the material. Intricate
shapes may be better achieved
by laser cutting. ¬

digital proof
A proof produced on
a digital printer and ranging
from an inkjet printout
made in a design studio to
a colour-matched large-format
proof produced in pre-press. ¬

dot gain
The amount a dot grows
in size as it is absorbed by
the paper in printing methods
that use dots to form images
and areas of colour. Different
papers cause different
amounts of dot gain depending
on how absorbent they are.
Printers allow for this by
making adjustments to the
size of the dots that are
printed. If dot gain is not
accounted for, colours can
bleed into each other and
areas of shadow in images
can be left without detail. ¬

field see grid

finishing
Additional processes necessary
to finish a job once printed,
for example, laminating, folding,
creasing and binding. Finishing
is often handled by specialist
companies, although a printer
may have basic finishing
capabilities in-house, such
as folding and trimming.
On short runs, or for one-offs,
some finishing is done by
hand. Processes that cannot
be finished by machinery may
also be hand-finished, even
on large print runs. ¬

flatplan
A series of mini-spreads that
gives an overview of a whole
publication, with labels and
sometimes colour-coding
to show a page's intended
content. Designers sometimes
print out small copies of each
page to stick to a flatplan
mounted on the wall. Flatplans
are also useful for planning
where changes in stock can
occur economically when
printing in sections. ¬

focus group [in design]
An arranged meeting of
people, often from a particular
demographic, who are asked
for their responses to a design.
Designers and marketing experts
sometimes use these comments
to test and inform their work. ¬

foil blocking
As debossing and embossing,
but using a thin layer of coloured
or metallic foil between the
die and the paper which leaves
an area of flat colour the same
shape as the die. ¬

full bleed
An image, or an area of solid
colour, that runs off the edge
of a page on all four sides.
These areas are set up to
extend slightly beyond the page
edges to allow for inaccurate
trimming. ¬

full colour see cmyk

gatefold insert
A page that has a fold along the fore-edge to fold out, like a gate, to double its original size. ¬

glyph
A single character in a font file. This could be a letter or other character, such as a punctuation mark or symbol. ¬

grid
A series of non-printing horizontal and vertical lines that divide a page and help designers position elements within a layout. A grid usually consists of margins, columns, inter-column spaces and sometimes a baseline grid. Some designers also separate vertical space into fields. In books and magazines, the margins (the areas around the edges of the pages) are generally kept clear of text, except perhaps for page numbers, also known as folios, and information that appears on every page like a chapter name, also known as a running head or foot. Complex grids are often used in newspapers and magazines, where narrow columns are combined to form wider columns depending on the content to be displayed on the page. ¬

gsm
»Grams per square metre«, used to define the weight of paper. A 160gsm piece of paper, if one metre square, weighs 160 grams. Generally speaking, gsm can be taken as an indicator of paper thickness, but different kinds of paper can be different thicknesses even though they have the same gsm. Certain uncoated papers are quite bulky and thick, yet still relatively light. ¬

gutter
The area of a spread where two pages meet at the spine. ¬

hand-finishing see finishing

high-key photograph
An image that is brightly lit with even contrast, usually featuring a white background and few shadows. ¬

high-resolution/low-resolution
The resolution of an image-based file. Digital image data, such as scanned photographs or illustrations, are made up of tiny square units called pixels. Each pixel can only represent one colour, but the combined effect of all the pixels together on screen gives the impression of continuous tone. The more pixels an image has when it is captured (via scanner, digital camera or other method), the better that image reproduces when printed because it contains more detail. The »resolution« of an image refers to the number of pixels it has, measured in »ppi«, or pixels per inch. This number reflects the pixels along one side of an inch, so 300ppi would mean 300 x 300 (90,000) pixels in one square inch. A high-resolution (high-res) file has lots of pixels, a low-resolution (low-res) file has fewer. Although there is no agreed definition of high or low resolution, it is usual for images that are going to be used in print to be at least 300ppi, whereas a low-res file may only be 72ppi. A high-res image can be changed into a low-res file by reducing the image data in an image editing programme, but a low-res image can't be converted into a high-res file. ¬

inferior/superior figures
Small figures that are used for footnote references and scientific compounds, for example »McCarthy[1] says in his essay«. Also called subscript/superscript figures. ¬

information architecture
The way information is structured, grouped and labelled in a system, for example on a website. Effective information architecture takes into consideration the typical needs of users, as well as the requirements of the website owner, and assesses how information is accessed and navigated. ¬

interface design
The design of an on-screen environment, for example a software program or website. ¬

kerning
The process of adjusting the space between two letters. Ideally, letter-spaces should appear to be regular throughout a word, but sometimes (particularly in large display setting) spaces need to be manually adjusted to be visually even. Not to be confused with tracking. ¬

lamination
The process of sticking two surfaces together. In printing this usually refers to the application of a thin layer of transparent gloss or matt plastic on to paper after printing has been completed to provide a protective and durable coating. ¬

Latin [font]
Also known as Roman, a Latin font is comprised of characters used in the Latin alphabet. ¬

leading
Vertical space between lines of text, usually measured in points, the same unit used to measure type. Type that is set 12/15pt, for example, has 3pts leading between the lines. The term is derived from metal typesetting. Extra space between lines was literally a piece of lead placed between the rows of metal characters. ¬

ligature
Two glyphs joined together into a single character which would otherwise crash uncomfortably into one another. ¬

line break [in typesetting]
The shape and sense made as words turn from one line to the next. Some designers aim for a particular rag, for example a short line followed by a longer one, while others are keen not to split proper names and endeavour to keep definite and indefinite articles with their corresponding nouns. ¬

lower-case
Text set in lower-case, or »small«, letters. The term is derived from metal typesetting. Compositors hand set type stored in two cases, one placed above the other. The »lower case« held all the small letters, the »upper case« all the capitals. ¬

maquette
A scale model of an unfinished project (for example, a building or sculpture) that allows the object to be assessed as a physical entity rather than a plan or sketch. ¬

Modern [font]
A style of typeface with high contrast between the thin and thick strokes and vertical stress. First designed in the eighteenth century, examples include Bodoni, Didot and Modern No 20. ¬

moiré pattern
An unwanted pattern made when a set of dots or lines is reproduced by another process that also uses dots or lines. For example, if a previously printed image is scanned, the dots that make up that image can cause visual »interference« with the frequency of the dots (or pixels) of the scanner. ¬

monospaced font
A typeface where the area occupied by each character in width is the same. This does not mean that the letters themselves change in width to fill a set size, but rather that the space on either side is adjusted. These fonts can be useful in tabular matter where figures need to be visually centred above one another. ¬

non-ranging figure
Numerals with ascenders and descenders, designed more like lower-case letters. Sometimes called »non-lining figures«, »old style figures« and even »lower-case numbers«. Some typographers consider them easier to read within text than ranging figures, which are more like capitals in design. ¬

offset lithography
The most commonly used commercial printing process. As paper is supplied in large sheets or rolls, the first step in the process is the »imposition« of files to make them suitable for printing on large sheets. Once imposed, files are sent to the »RIP« or »raster image processor«. This separates the files into their component colours, most commonly cmyk, and turns the data into a series of lines, dots and solid areas to be transferred to the plates that carry the printing ink. The RIP is set to consider the kind of paper, press and inks being used and make adjustments allowing for dot gain. In Computer to Plate (CtP) technology plates are output directly. On the printing press, each metal plate is wrapped around a roller that touches a second roller covered in rubber (called a rubber blanket). During the print run, ink is applied to each metal plate which rotates and transfers the ink on to the rubber blanket, which in turn transfers the ink to the paper. Combinations of cyan, magenta, yellow and black ink in a cmyk print job can create a full-colour image. All inks are semi-transparent so that one colour printed on top of another will make a third. ¬

OpenType
The newest font format, with expert character sets and other glyphs included in a single font file. The same OpenType file can be used on both PC and Apple Macintosh computers. ¬

Pantone/PMS see special

perfect binding
A method of binding, commonly of magazines, using a strong, flexible glue that is applied to the spine before the cover is attached. The spine is roughened to aid absorption and the cover generally uses a heavier weight of stock than the text pages. PUR binding follows the same process, but uses a stronger glue and so is more durable. ¬

perforation
Small holes cut into the surface of paper, card or other material to allow for one part to be cleanly torn from the other. ¬

pictogram
A simplified representation of an idea or object, for example a basic drawing of a cloud on a TV weather map or a road sign depicting a railway crossing. ¬

plate
A sheet, usually made of metal, that carries text and images to be printed on a printing press. Plates vary in size depending on the press being used. A printer that uses B1 sized presses uses B1 sized plates and so on. ¬

pre-press
An overarching term to describe all the things that need to happen in order to prepare a job for printing, generally referring to preparing files for print after they have been designed in page layout software. This might include making high-quality scans of original materials, checking the resolution of all images (see high-resolution/ low-resolution), applying colour profiles, retouching, and setting up the imposition (see offset lithography). ¬

quarter-bound
A style of book-binding in which the front and back covers are made of board covered with paper or cloth, and a separate material (traditionally leather) covers the spine and extends on to the front and back covers, running to about a quarter of the way across. ¬

ranged-left
In which every line of type is set to align with the left side of a column (as opposed to ranged-right, centred or justified setting). The space between words and letters is uniform and not stretched or distorted. The right edge of the type is ragged, so »ranged-left« is sometimes also called »ragged right«. ¬

recycled stock
Paper or card made from recycled material. It is important to note the percentage of recycled fibres; some »recycled« papers are made from as little as 30 per cent recycled fibres and 70 per cent »virgin« fibres, whereas some are 100 per cent recycled. ¬

rendering
In 3D modelling, the process of a computer translating mathematical data that describes the various objects in a scene into an image on-screen. This rendering takes into account settings that describe lighting conditions, texture of the surfaces to be rendered and so on. The more complex and detailed the rendering, the more computer power required. So a »rough« setting might be used for on-screen rendition, and a more »final« rendering used to create a final still or moving image. ¬

repro
Short for »reprographics«. Repro is a service that forms part of the pre-press phase of a project and can be undertaken by a printer in-house or by a specialist repro company. Main tasks include making high-res scans of originals, applying colour profiles appropriate to the final stock and generally making sure all files and other parts of a job are correctly set up. ¬

retouching
The process of manipulating a photographic image after it has been taken, usually with image editing software such as Adobe Photoshop. Retouching tasks might include removing dust and specks from an image, colour correction, correcting lens distortion or adding effects. ¬

rich media
A general term describing media that contains video, audio and/or interaction on the web. ¬

SEO
Search Engine Optimization. The process of optimizing a website, either at the design stage or afterwards, to ensure it is easily readable by search engines. Google publishes a set of guidelines for webmasters that outlines what it deems important for SEO. ¬

saturation
How vivid a colour appears to be. There are complex scientific and technical explanations of saturation, but in simple terms the more vibrant a colour seems, the more saturated it is said to be. ¬

scan
A digital version of an analogue original (for example, a photographic print, transparency or illustration) captured by a scanner. Common types of scanner are flat-bed and drum (more often used in pre-press). ¬

scatter proof
A proof showing a selection of images from a book, magazine or other document all on one page, used to gauge colour accuracy against the originals. ¬

section-sewn
A set of printed pages folded, trimmed and sewn together with other similar sets of pages. The printing of most multiple-page documents requires that pages are ganged up on both sides of one large sheet of paper. Most commonly one sheet will become, once folded, an eight- or 16-page section. Many publications require more than one section to be printed. If the job is to be section-sewn, sections are placed on top of one another, in the correct running order, and then sewn together along the spine with thread. Section-sewn binding is more durable than perfect binding. ¬

setting
Also known as »typesetting«. The process of taking supplied copy and inserting it into a page layout in the font and type size agreed, in a ranged-left, ranged-right, justified or centred layout as necessary. Attention is also paid to line breaks, and orphans and widows are identified and amended. ¬

silk-screen printing
A method of printing, by hand or machine, in which ink is forced through a screen (mesh) on to a printing surface. Generally used for display materials, such as posters or signage, and also useful for printing on to thick materials as it doesn't use rollers; it is also sometimes favoured because of the intensity of colour of many opaque silk-screen inks. Silk-screen is inappropriate for reproducing fine detail or small type as the screens used are coarse. ¬

site map
A graphical representation of the structure of a website, usually drawn in a tree-style diagram that shows the relationships of the pages to each other. It can also detail areas of functionality, although doesn't necessarily show how a user navigates the site. ¬

small cap
A version of an upper-case letter, but specifically drawn by the type designer to be the same height as the x-height of the lower-case letters. Small caps are often used in postcodes or for acronyms. If there is no specific small cap version of a typeface, some design programs automatically create one by shrinking the normal capital letters in size. This is generally considered bad practice, as the line weight of these capitals becomes too thin in relation to the surrounding type. ¬

snippet [of code]
A small piece of programming code that can be reused. For example, a snippet might handle image resizing in a website's back-end and the same code may be reused on several pages. ¬

special
Also known as »spot colour« and commonly specified using the internationally recognized Pantone Matching System (PMS). A spot-colour ink is premixed and is a pure colour straight from the tin. Using specials is the only way to achieve many bright and vivid colours. In cmyk, an orange, for example, is achieved by overprinting tints of yellow and magenta. The results are dull and lifeless when compared to a Pantone ink. ¬

stock
The material that is printed on, such as paper or card. ¬

swash
A stylistic flourish at the beginning or end of a character, usually on upper-case letters. ¬

table (as in programming a font)
The instructions as to how a font should be displayed within a font file. Each table within a file controls a different aspect of the font's behaviour. For example, there is a table to provide a name for each glyph, a table to describe the shape of each glyph and so on. Different font formats have different specifications as to which tables are required, and the kind of data they should contain. ¬

tracking
The overall horizontal spacing between letters in a word or block of text. Not to be confused with kerning. ¬

type size
The size of a typeface, measured in points. The point size (for example, 9pt) is the overall height of the invisible area that a character sits inside. This includes space for the height of the ascenders and descenders. Two typefaces at 12pt may look visually different in size, because the size of the x-height relative to the ascenders and descenders can be different within the overall 12pt height. Fonts with large x-heights tend to appear to be larger than those that don't. ¬

uncoated

A paper or card that has not had a coating applied to it as part of the manufacturing process. Uncoated paper is rougher in feel and appearance than coated, with tactile qualities that some designers prefer. However, uncoated paper absorbs more ink than its coated counterparts. The resultant effects can be subtle, but can also flatten the luminosity and contrast of images. ¬

upper-case

Text set in capital letters. The term is derived from metal typesetting. Compositors hand set type stored in two cases, one placed above the other. The »lower-case« held all the small letters, the »upper-case« all the capitals. ¬

varnish

A full bleed coating applied to a printed sheet on top of the ink. A varnish provides an extra layer of protection against fingermarks. A basic »seal« does the same kind of job, but is not as hard-wearing as a laminate (see lamination). A UV varnish is a special kind of varnish that is set using UV light and offers a high gloss and even harder-wearing finish than a standard varnish. ¬

volume [paper volume]

The bulk of the paper; how thick it is rather than how heavy. ¬

web printing

A form of offset lithography that uses continuous rolls of paper for large volume printing (for example, newspapers and magazines). Smaller sheets of paper are used in sheet-fed printing. ¬

wet proof

A limited number of proof copies of a printed item made by using the real printing processes on the correct stock. This is the only way to see exactly what a print job will look like before the main run, as the combination of paper, ink and printing process all have an effect on the appearance of the finished item. Wet proofs are the most expensive proofing option. Often run on dedicated proofing presses, all the printing plates must be made prior to proofing so rectifying mistakes is costly. A cheaper and often used alternative is a digital proof, although this is a less accurate indication of the finished job. ¬

wire frame

A bare-bones version of a website or user interface, devoid of any branding or designed graphics. Used to check how the application works on a functional level and to unearth any problems that may not have been spotted from a site map alone. ¬

word break

A word split into two parts, running over two lines. The first part is succeeded by a hyphen to indicate there is more to follow. ¬

x-height

The height of a lower-case x in a typeface. ¬

While every effort has been made to trace the present copyright holders, the publishers apologize in advance for any unintentional omission or error, and will be pleased to insert the appropriate acknowledgement in any subsequent edition.

We would like to thank all of the designers and their clients featured in this book for allowing us to publish images relating to their projects.

All photographs, except those listed here, © David Shaw.

010
Arcaid/Alamy

014–018, 019 left, 022 except top right, 023, 025
design development by Sagmeister Inc

019 right –021
digital animations and rendering by Ralph Ammer www.ralphammer.de

021
top, portrait of Millimetre

022
portrait of Ludwig van Beethoven composing the Missa Solemnis by Joseph Karl Stieler, 1820, original in Beethoven-Haus, Bonn

022
middle, portrait of Nuno Azevedo by Sagmeister Inc

024
poster design Sara Westermann, art direction André Cruz and Sara Westermann

026
pro qm bookstore, Berlin, photograph © Borries Schwesinger

030
overlaid image, Waser Bürocenter Buchs

030 background, 031–035, 038–039, 040 right, 041, 042–043, 048–049 text, sketches and design Borries Schwesinger www.borries-schwesinger.de

036–037, 044–047
from Borries Schwesinger, »Formulaire Gestalten«, Verlag Hermann Schmidt Mainz 2007, English edition Borries Schwesinger, »The Form Book«, Thames & Hudson 2010

040 left,
Verlag Hermann Schmidt Mainz

050
kpzfoto/Alamy

054–055 top,
photographs © Martin Špelda, actors shown in images, left to right: Vilma Cibulková; Jirí Pecha; Boleslav Polívka; Vilma Cibulková, Boleslav Polívka, Jirí Pecha; Jaroslav Dušek, Vilma Cibulková

054–055 bottom, 056 second left and main picture, photographs and drawings © Jerzy Skakun

056 left, design © Aleš Najbrt/Studio Najbrt, photograph © Martin Špelda 2003, poster features the actor Jaroslav Dušek

058–059 background image, 060 design © Joanna Górska and Jerzy Skakun

062–063
photograph © Jerzy Skakun, »Pupendo« poster design © Joanna Górska and Jerzy Skakun

070–071
»Wallpaper*« grids designed by Meirion Pritchard

072
Plakat Narrow by Christian Schwartz, Lexicon No.2 by Bram de Does, published by The Enschedé Font Foundry

073
Big Caslon Antique by Paul Barnes

074–075, 088
paper engineering by Dan McPharlin, photography by Grant Hancock, proofs and printed magazine photographed by David Shaw

076
prop stylist Charlotte Lawton, photography by Satoshi Minakawa, printed magazine photographed by David Shaw

078–079
illustration by Nigel Robinson for »Wallpaper*« magazine, art direction by Meirion Pritchard for »Wallpaper*« magazine

081
photography by Rudei Walti, magazine proofs photographed by David Shaw

084–087
photographs © Wallpaper*

090
Galleria B, Turku, Finland, photograph by Jere Salonen

096–097, 100–103
sketches, badges and packaging by Emmi Salonen

099
photographs by Emmi Salonen

104
Kevpix/Alamy

109, 112, 114–115, 116, 118–119
design development by Dalton Maag Ltd

110–111, 120–121
Tony Howard/Transport Design Company

117
drawings by Rayan Abdullah, Markenbau

126
text © Richard de Jager

128–131, 132 left, 133
PHWOA identity concepts by Frauke Stegmann for Richard de Jager

132
right, photograph by Frauke Stegmann

134–135
fashion design by Richard de Jager, photographs by Frauke Stegmann

136
gallery space photography by Azam Farooq www.azamfarooq.com for Bond and Coyne Associates Ltd

142
left, »Frame« magazine, notes and sketches created by Bond and Coyne Associates Ltd

143
designed by Bond and Coyne Associates Ltd for War on Want

144–145
sketch by Steve Mosley, Mosley& www.mosleyand.com for Bond and Coyne Associates Ltd

146–147
designs, sketches and plans created by Bond and Coyne Associates Ltd, photography included within image by Julio Etchart www.julioetchart.com for War on Want, still photography by David Shaw

148
sketches created by Bond and Coyne Associates Ltd

149–153
gallery space photography by Azam Farooq www.azamfarooq.com for Bond and Coyne Associates Ltd, design and typeface created by Bond and Coyne Associates Ltd, photography within image by Julio Etchart www.julioetchart.com for War on Want

154
Viennaslide/Alamy

158–159
photograph © Pascal Dhennequin

162–168, 170–175
sign system, logo system, invitation, selection of badges, graphic design manual, bag, shirt, umbrella, new year card and poster system for 104, 2007, drawings, scale models, simulation/montage and graphic design by Experimental Jetset, photographed by Experimental Jetset

169
Futura typeface by Paul Renner, 1928, 104 logotype by Experimental Jetset

176
Kathy deWitt/Alamy

180
left to right, packaging © Cumberland Packing Corp, New York, Merisant Company, McNeil Nutritionals, LLC

182–191
art director Paula Scher; designers Paula Scher, Daniel Weil, Lenny Naar

196
© Vitsœ

202–203
design and development by Airside and With Associates

198–201, 204–215
design and development by Airside for Vitsœ